D0151787

*4.37*
9/19/97

# MOBILE DATA AND WIRELESS LAN TECHNOLOGIES

Rifaat A. Dayem

# MOBILE DATA
# AND WIRELESS
# LAN TECHNOLOGIES

Rifaat A. Dayem

**To join a Prentice Hall PTR Internet mailing list, point to
http://www.prehnhall.com/register**

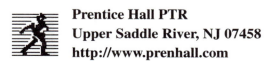

**Prentice Hall PTR
Upper Saddle River, NJ 07458
http://www.prenhall.com**

Editorial/production supervision: *Mary Sudul*
Cover design: *DesignSource*
Cover photo: *Tom Post*
Cover design director: *Jerry Votta*
Manufacturing manager: *Alexis R. Heydt*
Acquisitions editor: *Mary Franz*
Editorial assistant: *Noreen Regina*

©1997 Prentice Hall PTR
Prentice-Hall, Inc.
A Simon & Schuster Company
Upper Saddle River, New Jersey 07458

Prentice Hall books are widely used by corporations and government agencies for training, marketing, and resale.
The publisher offers discounts on this book when ordered in bulk quantities.
For more information, contact Corporate Sales Department, Phone: 800-382-3419;
Fax: 201-236-7141; E-mail: corpsales@prenhall.com
Or write: Prentice Hall PTR, Corp. Sales Dept., One Lake Street, Upper Saddle River, NJ 07458.

Product names mentioned herein are the trademarks or registered trademarks of their respective owners.

Printed in the United States of America
10   9   8   7   6   5   4   3   2   1

ISBN 0-13-839051-7

Prentice-Hall International (UK) Limited, *London*
Prentice-Hall of Australia Pty. Limited, *Sydney*
Prentice-Hall Canada Inc., *Toronto*
Prentice-Hall Hispanoamericana, S.A., *Mexico*
Prentice-Hall of India Private Limited, *New Delhi*
Prentice-Hall of Japan, Inc., *Tokyo*
Simon & Schuster Asia Pte. Ltd., *Singapore*
Editora Prentice-Hall do Brasil, Ltda., *Rio de Janeiro*

to Linda, Jennifer, Michael, Gabriel, and Leigh

# *Contents*

# *Preface*

I have had the pleasure of leading seminars on my favorite subject, Wireless Networking, in the US, Europe, and Asia over the past four years. I have greatly enjoyed meeting and interacting with all those seminar attendees who are now helping shape this exciting new industry. I began dreaming about this kind of "magically connected" world three decades ago when I started working at Bell Labs. After more than ten years there that included work on private voice and data networks and a PhD in microwave radio, I could not resist the lure of California, Stanford, and the budding Apple Computer. There I had the opportunity to start working in this exciting field and watch it unfolding. This unfolding has not been and will not be a sudden change, but rather a steady emergence of new ways of connecting with each other and with the information we crave. I am very happy to be part of this unfolding, and honored to be able to share with you the insights in this book, and in the companion book, *"PCS and Digital Cellular Technologies: Assessing Your Options."*

Many of us are beginning to depend on mobile computers and wireless modems of various form and function. Mobile Data networks and Wireless LANs empower these devices by connecting them to each other and to the information we need. In this book you will learn about:

- Successful vertical applications and emerging horizontal applications of Wireless Networking
- How Mobile Data technologies including packet radio and circuit switched data work
- The essentials of Wireless LAN technologies, both spread spectrum radio and infrared
- All about present and planned Wireless LAN products
- The fundamentals of medium access techniques including comparisons of TDMA and CSMA
- Leading standards for Wireless Networking: Mobitex, Modacom, CDPD, and 802.11
- The future promise of Hiperlan and Wireless ATM technologies

When we are in the office, our data communications needs are typically served by a LAN. Outside of the office, we usually rely on public data networks. How will our needs for mobility and wireless connectivity be met in these two environments? In the first chapter, we discuss who will be mobile and examples of vertical and horizontal applications of Wireless Networking. We present the challenges facing the industry including security, capacity, and health issues. We provide several case studies and position Wireless Networking relative to wired networks.

The second chapter is an overview of the field of Wireless Networking, starting with how we can empower mobile devices with Wireless Networking, how to define a Wireless Local Area Network and a Wireless Wide Area Network, the types of Wireless WANs, the types of Wireless LANs, and Wireless PBXs (Private Branch Exchange). To organize the evolution of services and products and the spectrum and standards activities, we present a wireless map that is based on where we spend our time. Finally, we discuss the radio spectrum, cell sizes and achievable throughput, and market forecasts.

The majority of Mobile Data traffic is carried today on analog circuit switched cellular networks. Digital cellular networks are being implemented throughout the world at a rapid pace and promise simpler access to circuit switched data. For some years, packet radio networks have provided a service that is well suited to asynchronous traffic. Emerging two-way paging networks can provide similar service at a competitive price. In the third chapter on Mobile Data Services, we address these options for carrying Mobile Data traffic and compare them; in particular we discuss the RAM/Mobitex service, the ARDIS/Modacom service, and Cellular Digital Packet Data. We also outline the capabilities of data over analog and digital cellular as well as over related cellular technologies such as DECT and PCS. Finally, we address today's paging and future two-way paging systems, and compare them with the other Mobile Data options.

The great promise of Wireless Networking is based on key underlying technologies that include packet radio, multiple access, security, and spread spectrum. In the fourth Wireless Networking Primer chapter, we discuss spread spectrum techniques, and Medium Access Control techniques that are applicable to Wireless Networks. We show how to deal with hidden nodes and go into the security requirements and options. Infrared technology is addressed for both Wireless LAN applications as well as for short point-to-point applications.

The major options for carrying mobile data in the wide area are packet radio networks, paging networks, and data over circuit switched networks, including cellular, mobile radio, cordless, and PCS. In the fifth chapter on Mobile Data technologies, we analyze the technologies behind each of these options. In particular, we focus on the architectures of the RAM/Mobitex and the ARDIS/Modacom packet radio networks. We also discuss the CDPD architecture, and a Wireless Metropolitan Area Network.

Currently, Wireless LAN products are based on spread spectrum techniques, both Frequency Hopping Spread Spectrum (FHSS) and Direct Sequence Spread Spectrum (DSSS). Several MAC alternatives are possible for handling the special requirements of Wireless LANs. Power management is critical and requires special provision in the MAC protocol for mobile applications. Interconnection with backbone networks allows roaming within a campus environment as well as in the wide area. In the sixth chapter on Wireless LAN technologies, we start with a Wireless LAN wish list. Then we go into the engineering details behind the design of a DSSS system and a FHSS system, including frequency hopping pattern selection and preambles for FHSS systems. Next, we present three alternative MACs for Wireless LANs, and discuss how power management affects the MAC formats. To finish the chapter, we go into the details of mobility within the same network as well as among different networks using Mobile IP. At the end, we discuss name and directory services and contrast the situation for Mobile Data and Wireless LANs with the situation in cellular and PCS networks.

Wireless LAN products serve office buildings and campuses and provide relatively high data rates as compared to Mobile Data networks in the wide area. A number of products are now available. How do they work? How well do they perform? How much do they cost now and what are they likely to cost in the future? In the seventh chapter on Wireless LAN products, we start with the criteria for choosing a Wireless LAN. We then describe Wireless LAN products from several manufacturers and compare them. The products fall into categories according to whether they provide mobility or whether they are aimed at the wire replacement market niche, and whether they use radio or IR (Infra Red).

At present, Wireless LANs must rely on spread spectrum technology to use the ISM bands. New spectrum allocations such as for Unlicensed PCS make possible the use of simpler radios and higher data rates. To allow communications among products from different vendors, many standards groups across the world are converging on agreed to technology choices. In the eighth chapter on wireless spectra and standards, we provide the rules for the ISM bands. We discuss Unlicensed PCS frequency allocations and the etiquette for using UPCS. Then we summarize the 802.11 standards for FHSS PHY (Physical Layer), DSSS PHY, IR PHY, and general MAC. At the end, we discuss Mobile Data standards, and finish with future Hiperlan and Wireless ATM technologies.

The final chapter presents highlights of the book, draws conclusions for the field of Mobile Data and Wireless LANs, and presents a view of future Wireless Networking in the next century and the concepts of tabs, pads, and boards.

I would like to express my deep gratitude to my loved ones for their encouragement and support with this fun but sometimes preoccupying project. And I would like to express my great appreciation to the many participants in the seminars that I have led in different parts of the world for their gracious input and feedback. I look forward to continuing to work with you all who share the dream in this stimulating world of Wireless Networking.

Rifaat A. Dayem

# 1

# *Who Will Be Mobile?*

Many of us are beginning to depend on mobile computers and wireless modems of various form and function. Mobile Data networks and Wireless LANs empower these devices by connecting them to each other and to the information we need wirelessly. When we are in the office, our data communications needs are typically served by a LAN. Outside of the office, we usually rely on public data networks. How will our needs for mobility and wireless connectivity be met in these two environments? In this first chapter, we discuss who will be mobile and examples of vertical and horizontal applications of Wireless Networking. Wireless Networking can be considered to be part of Mobile Computing as shown in Figure 1.1.

At the top layer of the Mobile Computing chart are vertical and horizontal applications. Vertical applications are those that apply to a functional part of an industry such as field sales and field service, or to a specific market segment such as banking or health care. Horizontal applications apply to many people across most market segments.

The next layer is the mobile operating systems layer. This layer provides tools for application programmers to access different mobile devices and different Wireless Networks. These tools make the job of the application programmers much easier because they do not have to be concerned with the details and complexities of the underlying networks. Further, they do not have to be concerned with how these networks or their interfaces change over time. This is a critical layer that is key to the rapid growth of Wireless Networking and the desired proliferation of compelling applications that companies can utilize to provide their customers with added value.

The next level is the devices level. These are all the mobile devices we carry with us such as notebook computers, Personal Digital Assistants (PDAs), cellular phones, Personal Communicators, and combination devices that have several functions. Combination devices are beginning to emerge. Watching the results of peoples' imagination is delightful as they produce just the right combination of features for the right market segment. Appendix A provides details of the Mobile Computing device level and the mobile operating system level.

Carrying this traffic are Wireless Networks, both wide area and local area. Wireless Networks are the main subject of this book. The area of Wireless Wide Area Networks is also called "Mobile Data." Mobile Data includes packet networks such as RAM/Mobitex and ARDIS/

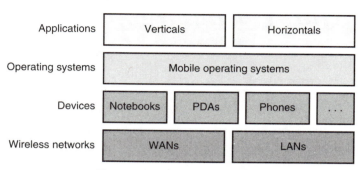

**Figure 1.1** Mobile Computing.

Modacom, paging networks, data over cellular (both analog and digital), and data over satellite channels. Wireless LANs provide much higher data rates than Mobile Data networks but are confined to an office building or campus.

In this chapter, we discuss the applications of Wireless Networking, in particular:

- Vertical and horizontal applications of Wireless Networking
- Market dynamics
- Vertical applications examples
- Challenges
- Case studies
- Applications/technology matrix
- Horizontal applications examples
- Positioning of Wireless Networking relative to wired networks

We are now focusing on the top level of the Mobile Computing chart as highlighted in Figure 1.1.

## Vertical and Horizontal Applications of Wireless Networking

The pie chart in Figure 1.2 shows that by the year 2005, almost half of the people using Mobile Computing will be performing mobile office applications.

About a quarter will be using it for personal communications. The rest will be in vertical applications such as field sales, field service, and transportation.

In the field sales application, the salesperson arrives at the customer's location armed with his/her mobile computer. He is able to perform the following functions at the customer site while

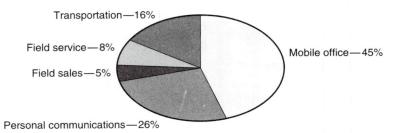

Transportation—16%

Field service—8%

Field sales—5%

Mobile office—45%

Personal communications—26%

**Figure 1.2**   Mobile Computing applications market segments by 2005.

he is connected to servers back at his home office, or to any database he needs to perform his job:

- Sales quotation
- Inventory check
- Order entry
- Credit authorization
- Invoicing

The field service engineer could be traveling through his territory in a company van, or flying around the country to his accounts. The functions that are possible with this vertical application are:

- Obtaining a maintenance history of the item requiring service
- Performing complex diagnostics that require access to databases and applications at other locations
- Checking parts inventory if required
- Updating the maintenance database after the service is done
- Invoicing for the job
- Real time dispatching of the field engineer

Perhaps the oldest Wireless Networking applications area is transportation. Wireless Networking has been used in this area for many years to communicate with fleets of trucks, fleets of taxis, fleets of parcel delivery vans, and so on. The different kinds of transportation applications are endless. The functions performed include:

- Automatically locating the vehicle
- Dispatching the vehicle to the next job
- Routing the vehicle if required
- Capturing data from the vehicle

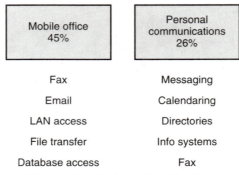

**Figure 1.3** Horizontal applications.

Horizontal applications, which are predicted to account for the majority of the market in a few years, are illustrated in Figure 1.3.

These horizontal applications are essentially what we would be doing if we were connected to a wire in the wall. With wireless, we are able to perform them wherever we are as long as we are in range of the backbone networks that contain the information we need. An interesting point to keep in mind is that when we carry the mobile devices with us, we are likely to use them for business as well as for personal use, so in designing them we have to keep in mind that a person may, for example, choose to have single calendar that contains both his business appointments as well as his personal appointments. He may choose to have single or multiple directories, one for his business associates, and one for his family and friends.

## Market Dynamics

In this section, we discuss the dynamics of the market with regard to readiness for volume shipments as well as with regard to vertical and horizontal applications. We believe that the Wireless Networking market is on the brink of a new phase, as shown in Figure 1.4. It is completing the phase of the early adopters and is ready for large growth.

To achieve this we will need large suppliers who provide the volume required and a spectrum of full services.

Figure 1.5 shows the market dynamics for vertical and horizontal applications. Initial revenue potential is higher in vertical markets. Payback of the investment in Mobile Computing is easy to quantify for vertical applications where the increase in productivity is directly identifiable.

Horizontal applications require prices to drop significantly. The payback is not as easy to quantify, but the volume of users is much larger.

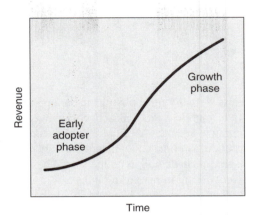

**Figure 1.4**   Phases of the Wireless Networking market.

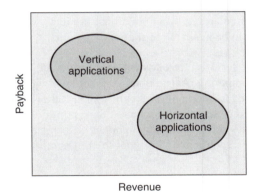

**Figure 1.5**   Vertical and horizontal market dynamics.

# Vertical Market Examples

The applications of Wireless Networking are increasing every day.
In this section, we present the following sample applications:

- Airlines
- Police
- Emergency

- Hospitals
- Maintenance
- Retail stores
- Stock exchanges

Today, the use of Wireless Networking is obvious in the operation of airports. We see airport personnel with various forms of mobile radio handsets communicating with each other and with the head office. We are beginning to see the use of these portable devices in assisting passengers in the check-in process. While standing in line, an attendant may ask you if you have any baggage to check in. If you don't, he or she can check you in on the spot. These are the very tip of the iceberg of the potential of Wireless Networking in the airline industry. In the future, we should be able to use smart cards for automatic check-in, and our baggage should be animated with smart cards that would route it to its correct destination.

The insurance example depicted in Figure 1.6 is a classical field sales application. The salesperson can use a mobile computer to provide accurate quotes and obtain approval from the underwriters in real time.

In the future, we will provide an application that can use artificial intelligence and be connected to the home office to determine what additional products would benefit this customer. An interactive presentation would be available to show the customer the products and their benefits to his or her specific situation.

Police and emergency services are classical applications of Wireless Networking and after ripe potential for Mobile Computing. As we obtain greater bandwidth, we can provide more complete information on suspects, including their pictures, or sketches of them, their last known locations, whether they are armed or not, and information that is up-to-the-minute.

In the case of emergency services such as ambulances, depicted in Figure 1.7, the availability of greater bandwidth enables emergency personnel to communicate more accurate and complete

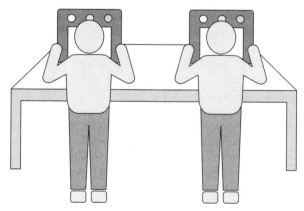

**Figure 1.6**   Field sales.

**Figure 1.7**   Emergency services.

information about the status of the patient, and obtain more detailed instructions for the start of treatment on the way to the hospital.

In the ambulance, emergency personnel can check in the patient, and start the diagnostics and treatment process with the help of an emergency room doctor who is in the hospital and connected in real time with the ambulance. Multimedia transfers can relay the patient's vital signs and even pictures of the injury to the attending physician.

At the hospital, Wireless Networking can provide more accurate and up-to-date information to doctors and nurses.

Nurses and doctors can:

- Access patient records
- Use diagnostic databases
- Preview surgery to patient
- Order medication

Another health care example that can benefit from Wireless Networking is the mobile roving doctor. This idea is being experimented with in Europe. At night and on weekends, doctors ride in vans that are dispatched to patients who need care. When the doctor is dispatched to the next patient, that patient's record is downloaded to the vehicle. After the doctor attends to the patient, he enters his report directly into the database back at the home office or hospital, and indicates that he is now free for the next call.

For a fleet of vehicles, time wasted in the shop is a critical cost factor. Today, when the operator detects a problem with the vehicle, she must schedule time in the shop to perform diagnostics

**Figure 1.8**   Health care vertical application.

and repair. In the future, sensors and smart applications in the vehicles can continuously monitor vehicle performance, perform diagnostics, and when needed contact the nearest repair center wirelessly to schedule a service appointment.

For fixed machines, maintenance engineers today perform their duty using handheld Mobile Computing devices. They essentially tour their territory to check the machines they are assigned to maintain. In the future, the fixed equipment can have sensors that call the maintenance engineer when service is required.

Application of Wireless Networking in the retail industry is illustrated by the following example. You enter your favorite department store. The shopping cart has a video display. As you walk through the store, specials in that area of the store are flashed before you. If you are looking for a specific item, you can ask the device and it shows you where it is and how to get there.

During peak shopping seasons, the store may want to add checkout counters or have special counters outdoors. Mobile Computing allows this addition with ease and without having to bother with special wiring.

In larger stores, sales personnel are already using Mobile Computing to help customers spend their money more efficiently!

Sales personnel are able to provide up-to-date information on products, make the order, and perform transactions on the spot (see Figure 1.9). Walmart Stores are using more than 19,000 portable computers, 1800 base stations, 60 wireless repeaters, and more than 16,000 portable printers.

A new chain of super stores called the Incredible Universe is also equipping their personnel with wireless terminals. The Incredible Universe is a combination of an electronics store, a computer store, an appliance store, an office products store, a record shop, a photography shop, and a home improvement store. It also has restaurants and day care! The whole family goes there for the afternoon and leaves with filled trunks and filled credit card balances. Salespeople in the Incredible Universe use Wireless Networking to:

**Figure 1.9**   Retail store customized service.

- Check inventory
- Order equipment to be ready at checkout
- Determine equipment requirements

The stock exchanges are perhaps the most exciting applications of Mobile Computing.

Without question, time can be saved and greater accuracy can be achieved on the stock exchange trading floor. Deals are made and broken in seconds. With Wireless Networking, traders can do trades wherever they are, rather than having to run to hard wired terminals.

A very interesting application of Wireless Networking is the casinos application. If you examine how a casino operates, you would discover that the gaming tables are arranged in circles or ovals. Looking closely, you would notice that each circle or oval of tables is run by a supervisor, who is responsible for the profitability of the group of tables. He is called the pit boss, where the "pit" is the group of tables he supervises. A good pit boss gets to know the high rollers who frequent the casino. He gets to know their likes and dislikes, the kind of drinks they like, the kind of games they like, and their credit limit. Casinos lend hundreds of millions of dollars annually to their high rollers. Most of these loans are on paper and are prone to error.

Suppose the pit boss were equipped with a mobile computer, preferably an unobtrusive PDA that is wirelessly connected to various databases. On this PDA, the pit boss would be able to access the server containing all the specific information about his high rollers, including all their likes and

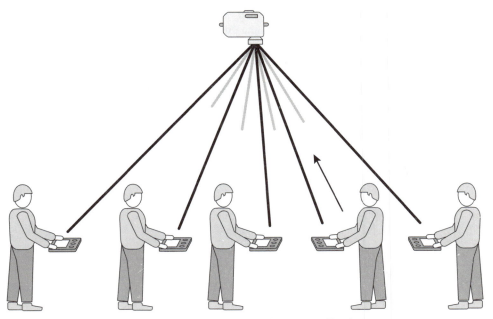

**Figure 1.10**    The stock exchange application.

dislikes as well as how much money they owe the casino. Such an application has been experimented with and forms of it are being developed.

Hotel check-in can be a frustrating experience, especially in peak times when one arrives at the hotel after a long, tiring journey only to have to wait in another line. The check-in could take place at an earlier point in the journey, for example in the courtesy bus from the airport. With Wireless Networking that set up is possible.

Taxicabs have been using Wireless Networking for a long time. They have used voice until relatively recently, when data terminals were introduced throughout the world in taxis. However, voice is still retained in most cases for the time being. The data terminal allows the taxi to be dispatched to the next customer accurately and securely. A problem with voice dispatching is that a rogue cab can intercept the voice dispatch and beat the authorized cab to the waiting customer.

Data terminals are not yet used exclusively because they do not have all the features required to help the driver operate the cab. For example, if a cab driver is lost or does not know the location of a specific point, she can ask the dispatcher. At this time, the terminals in cabs do not have this capability. Whether voice will disappear from cabs in the future is hard to tell. Putting a public cellular phone in the cab is an interesting possibility. The customer can then make a public cellular phone call in the cab. The cost of the call could be automatically added to the fare.

Rental car agencies are one of the most advanced users of Wireless Networking to date. In some airports, the process is very streamlined. When the customer arrives at the airport and has a special preferred status, he boards the rental car bus and gives the driver his rental car card. The driver takes him to an express counter, where the contract is ready, and his rental car is nearby. One more step may be eliminated. The bus driver could take the customer directly to his car, and the contract could be electronic. Upon return, the customer drives the rental car into the rental car lot, a person greets him there with a wireless terminal, checks him in, and prints out a receipt on the spot. This procedure is done today, but the terminals and portable printers the rental car employees have to carry are a bit heavy and cumbersome.

Truck exchange yards and train exchange yards are classical users of Wireless Networking. We can think of these yards as a giant packet switch where truck tractors or train cars are switched from one train or one truck to another. Each car or truck has certain goods in it that are destined to a particular place. The address of the container is like the header of a packet in a packet switch. The yard is analogous to a Packet Assembly/Disassembly function. Wireless Networking plays a critical role in this classical transportation application.

As we can see, Wireless Networking applications abound, and new ones are developing every day. Wireless Networking is the kind of technology we do not know exactly how to use until we have it. Probably 50% of the applications we will have in five years we have not yet envisioned.

# Challenges

The following are excerpts from interviews with MIS managers of major firms who are contemplating using Wireless Networking. These challenges are real, but solutions to them are at hand. The fact that the challenges are highlighted at this time is good because adequate attention is focused on them early. The major challenges that face Wireless Networking occur in the following areas:

- Security
- Bandwidth
- Software applications
- Safety

## Security

Lehman Brothers is a brokerage house with tens of millions of trades per day. They estimate that using Wireless Networking can reduce the trade execution time from 90 seconds on the average to less than 10 seconds on the average, a huge improvement. Why do they not use Wireless Networking? The major concern is security, as depicted in Figure 1.11.

Can they be sure that an intruder will not be able to enter a bogus transaction and transfer millions of shares of stock to an unauthorized account?

The security issue can be thought of in three areas:

- User authentication for network access
- Data privacy
- Privacy of the location of the user

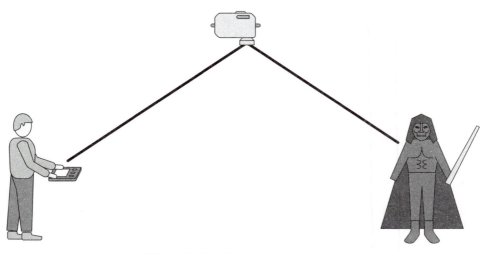

**Figure 1.11**    Concern over security.

First is the authentication issue. Authentication insures that the right people do get on the network, and unauthorized people do not. Currently, cellular fraud is a huge expense to the industry and a great inconvenience to the users. The second issue is the privacy of the data, which is obtained by encryption of the data or the voice. Encryption can use private keys or public keys. Third, due to the cellular nature of Wireless Networking, the user can be located roughly, because the network knows from which cell the call originates. The famous car chase in the O.J. Simpson case was started by locating the suspect through a trace of his cellular call. The police were able to trace the call to the specific cell and find him there. This technique is similar to call tracing in the wired telephone network today. The information is known in the network but is kept private except from government agencies such as the police.

Security of Wireless Networks is a visible issue. Because it is so visible, much attention is focused on it and solutions are provided. For this reason, wireless networks are likely to be more secure than wired networks in the end.

## Bandwidth

Another concern of Lehman Brothers is whether Wireless Networking has sufficient bandwidth to handle their application. Why would concern exist over bandwidth in a stock trading application, since each transaction is a very small amount of data? Figure 1.12 suggests the reason.

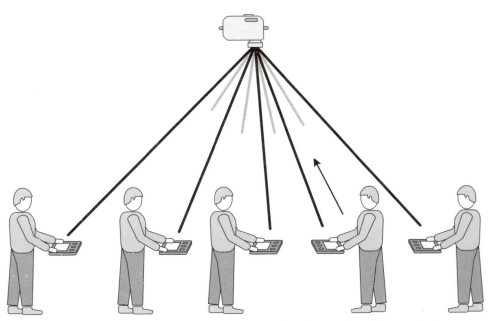

**Figure 1.12**    Concern over sufficient bandwidth in the stock trading application.

**Figure 1.13**   The hardware and software state for Wireless Networking.

In the stock market when something important happens, everyone wants to access the network literally at the same time. Even though each transaction is a very small amount of data, the system has to be able to handle almost all the terminals at the same time. Moreover, the access mechanism has to be extremely fair, and the first users requesting service must be the first served. We discuss the implications on the MAC layer from this simple requirement in chapter 4.

Citibank would like to use Wireless Networking but feels that at this time, even though hardware is coming along, the right application software is still in the embryonic stage (see Figure 1.13).

Many people from other industries would agree that software applications are probably the one biggest reason why Wireless Networking data implementations have lagged behind voice implementations.

Avon has a huge number of salespeople. They would benefit tremendously from Wireless Networking, but Avon is concerned about the safety of the salespeople and the possible health problem that may be associated with the radiation emanating from the Wireless Networking devices. But Wireless Networking has been with us for many years. We *do* have safety standards in place, and few cases have been highlighted in the past regarding the safety of these devices. So what is new that is causing added concern?

First, many more Wireless Networking devices exist today than did ten years ago, and in another ten years the number will be many fold more. Second, we are holding the devices closer to our bodies, and in particular, closer to our heads, as shown in Figure 1.14.

**Figure 1.14**   Safety concern over Wireless Networking.

613666

The modulation is digital and some people think that digital modulation can cause more damage to biological tissues than analog modulation can. The power levels of today's devices are lower than the ones that were used in the past. In the future, the power levels will be even lower. For example, today's cellular phones radiate in the range of 1 watt. Future PCS phones will radiate an average on the order of 10 milliwatts.

With the added concern about the safety of Wireless Networking, more research is being done. Fortunately, the issues are being brought into the public eye so that organizations are funding the required research. Some of the current organizations and standards for safety in the Wireless Networking field are:

- IEEE SCC 28
  - Standards Coordinations Committee 28
- IEEE COMAR
  - Scientific Advisory Board
- EPA
  - Environmental Protection Agency
- FDA
  - Food and Drug Administration

# Case Studies

In this section, we briefly discuss the following case studies:

- ADP (Automatic Data Processing)
- British Airways
- HP in the UK
- South Dakota University
- Integrated Device Technology
- Revenue Canada

Automatic Data Processing maintains an auto repair parts database. The database includes all the parts of many automobiles, where to obtain them, how much they cost, and how much labor is involved in replacing the parts. The database is used to provide estimates of repairs after an accident. Due to the high cost of auto repair, the database also includes where to obtain used parts from junkyards and how much they cost. As one can imagine, the used car parts inventory is a very volatile database. When a customer goes into the shop to obtain an estimate for repair, the estimator inspects the car using a mobile computer that is connected to the database by a Mobile Data radio. The estimator is able to pull up a diagram of the car and model. He simply points to the parts that need replacing. After he is finished, he has obtained an accurate estimate using not only new parts but possible used parts as well.

British Airways uses Wireless Networking extensively at both Heathrow Airport, which is probably the busiest airport in the world, and Gatwick Airport, closer to town. Currently, British Airways uses a Private Mobile Radio system to carry out its operations. It is now considering using a Public Access Mobile Radio system. The functions the system would perform started out traditionally with the myriad of walkie talkies that abound in airports. Now, more and more data terminals are used. Passengers with no baggage to check in are checked in as they wait in the queue. Final aircraft checkout is done by mobile engineers equipped with handheld wireless devices before handing aircraft over to the pilot. In the future, cabin staff can use handheld devices to access customer databases and serve frequent flyers with special attention. Currently, approximately 1500 users of Wireless Networking exist at Heathrow Airport, and 500 Wireless Networking users exist at Gatwick Airport. The number of communications is about 9000 over a 10-hour peak period.

Hewlett Packard in the United Kingdom uses Wireless Networking for service engineering. The service engineers are routed to their calls via wireless dispatch. They use the wireless devices to access customer data when they are on the customer site. They service the machines that need repair and enter the service completion information in the remote database while on the customer site.

South Dakota University has a server and network in the basement of one of the campus buildings. The offices that need access to the server and the network are on the first and higher floors. However, the floors and walls are filled with asbestos. To avoid the hazard of working with asbestos, South Dakota University elected a Wireless Local Area Network solution to provide the needed connectivity without having to run new wiring in the walls or floors.

Integrated Device Technology, a chip maker in Silicon Valley, had a simple requirement to provide the receptionist with access to a database containing the directory of the company. The reception area has high ceilings and a marble floor. To avoid a costly installation of wire, Integrated Device Technology used a Wireless LAN solution to provide the needed connectivity. In the future, they need to provide access to salespeople who come to the home office from time to time. At present, the salespeople have to queue up at wired terminals to perform their functions. In the future, they will be equipped with wireless access so that if they are in the vicinity of the access point, they can access the information they need.

Revenue Canada is a tax collection agency that has hundreds of branch offices that are geographically dispersed. In order to avoid having to send networking technicians to the remote sites to set up the networks there, Revenue Canada came up with an innovative solution. They bought the personal computers at the headquarters site, ordered wireless LAN devices for them, and set them up at the home office. They then put the computers back in the boxes and shipped them out to the remote offices. At the remote offices, nontechnical staff could take the computers out of the boxes, plug them in for power, and they were LAN ready. Since the LAN was wireless, it did not require any special connections or debugging by a network technician. Revenue Canada has hundreds of remote offices scattered throughout Canada, so this setup represented a significant savings over having to send network technicians to each site to set up a wired LAN. This kind of company topology is typical of many companies that have one or more headquarters locations and many more branch locations.

## Application/Technology Matrix

In this section, we present an application/technology matrix that shows the technology that best fits certain applications. The matrix appears in Figure 1.15.

The applications are shown for the private sector and for the public sector. In the private sector, we have applications such as service engineering, order entry, vehicle routing, and incident control. The technologies include cellular, paging, mobile data, and Wireless LANs. The number of stars indicates the degree of applicability of the technology to the applications.

The applications in the public network sector include facsimile transmission, text messaging, and various information services including news services, and vertical information services such as market data or financial data. Again, the number of stars indicates the degree of applicability of the technology to the application.

| Sector | Application | Technology | | | |
|---|---|---|---|---|---|
| | | Cellular | Paging | Mobile Data | WLANs |
| Private (corporate) | Service engineering | * * | * | * * | * |
| | Order entry | * * | 0 | * * | * |
| | Vehicle routing | * * | 0 | * * | * * * |
| | Incident control | * * | 0 | * * | * * * |
| Public network services | Facsimile | * * * | 0 | * | 0 |
| | Tax messaging | * * | * * * | * * * | * * * |
| | Info services<br>• News<br>• Market<br>• Financial | *<br>*<br>* | * *<br>* *<br>* * | *<br>*<br>* | 0<br>0<br>0 |
| | Location tracking | * | 0 | 0 | 0 |
| | Traffic alerts | * | * * * | * * | 0 |

**Figure 1.15** Application/Technology matrix.

# Horizontal Applications Examples

In this section, we first discuss near term horizontal applications, and then the broader horizontal applications that will account for the majority of Wireless Networking revenues in the future.

Examples of near term horizontal applications abound. One example is any sort of dynamic work environment such as a temporary work site, a trade show, or a conference. Another application is difficult-to-wire areas such as many old buildings in established office complexes. Another application is new employees who need immediate service. One way to serve new employees immediately while the wiring is installed for their new location is to provide them with a wireless terminal.

Examples of broad-based horizontal applications that will be found everywhere include essentially all the functions we do today, but that we are forced to be connected to the wall to do them. For example let us consider a meeting that uses Wireless Networking as depicted in Figure 1.16.

This meeting could be in the office, or it could be a group of individuals from different companies attending a meeting in a hotel or a business center. All the activities that require paper or transparencies or slides can be done without hard copies wirelessly, including passing private notes. In addition, if people are unable to physically attend the meeting, they can still attend it electronically. And if a person needs to attend another meeting, he can attend it electronically at the same time he is attending this meeting.

Eventually, we will be able to do most of the functions we do today without having to be tethered to a wire, as illustrated in Figure 1.17.

Another pervasive horizontal application is the wireless traveler. No longer having to depend on the big computer at work, a person can do useful work in the countless hours spent in airports, airplanes, hotel rooms, and so forth. If connectivity to the home office or to any other service is needed, it is only a wireless modem away.

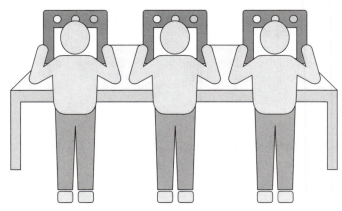

**Figure 1.16**  Wireless meeting.

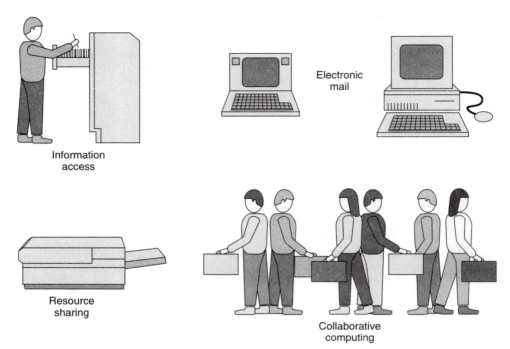

**Figure 1.17**   Horizontal office applications.

An area that has huge potential for the consumer market is interactive TV. The wireless portion of this application is a sophisticated remote control that controls a TV set top box that is more like a simple personal computer. With the new remote control, we can navigate through hundreds of cable channels, order movies on demand, participate in interactive games, order merchandise, obtain educational programs, or obtain just about any kind of information that other people are willing to publish on the Internet.

Interactive TV also has the potential of transforming politics as we know it. The power of the electronic town meetings is not yet tapped. Politicians will be able to put referendums to the people in real time and obtain the answers instantaneously.

## Positioning of Wireless Networking Relative to Wired Networks

With the plethora of applications for Wireless Networking that we have today and are sure to see in the future, what will happen to wired networks? Will Wireless Networks replace wired networks altogether? To answer this question, let us look at the bandwidth available to wired net-

| | Today | Future |
|---|---|---|
| Mobile Data | 10 Kbps | 100 Kbps |
| Wireless LANs | 1 Mbps | 10 Mbps |

**Figure 1.18**   Wireless data capabilities.

| | Today | Future |
|---|---|---|
| Wired Data | 100 Kbps | >1 Kbps |
| Wired LANs | 10 Mbps | >100 Mbps |

**Figure 1.19**   Wired data capabilities.

works and to Wireless Networks today and in the future. Figure 1.18 and 1.19 show some estimates.

Wired networks always have an edge over Wireless Networks in the amount of bandwidth they can offer. Wireless Networks are great for most needs, but we will always want the much larger bandwidth of wired networks for future high bandwidth multimedia applications. So the position of Wireless Networks relative to wired networks can be summarized as follows:

Not a replacement to wired networks
. . . but an extension to wired networks.

# Summary

In summary, in this chapter we focused on the application layer of the Mobile Computing chart. We started by discussing vertical and horizontal applications in general, showing that the dynamics of the market indicate that vertical applications have the greatest potential for early profits and are more easily justified by their users, whereas horizontal applications garner the majority of the revenues in the future but must be priced much lower to appeal to the mass market, both professional and consumer. We presented several vertical market examples, including airlines, police, emergency, hospitals, maintenance, retail stores, and stock exchanges. These are but a small sample of what promises to be an expansive industry with applications five years from now that we have not imagined today.

Next, we addressed the major challenges facing the Wireless Networking industry, namely security, bandwidth, software applications, and safety. We discussed these concerns via results of specific interviews with prospective users of Wireless Networking. Then we provided several early case studies of users of the technology. The case studies illustrated applications for Mobile Data services and for Wireless LAN products.

Next, we presented an applications/technology matrix showing the private sector applications and the public sector applications and which of the Wireless Networking technologies applied best. Next, we discussed horizontal applications, starting with early horizontal applications, followed by what will be pervasive horizontal applications that we will all use. Finally, we discussed the position of Wireless Networking relative to wired networks and argued that Wireless Networking is a great adjunct to wired networks that will serve the majority of our needs, but with regard to high bandwidth multimedia applications, the wired network remains king.

# 2 *Wireless Networking*

In this chapter, we turn our attention to the Wireless Networks that give mobile computers their connectivity—the Wireless LANs and Wireless WANs in the networking layer of the Mobile Computing chart shown in Figure 2.1.

In particular, we discuss:

- Why wireless connectivity?
- Definitions of Wireless LANs and Wireless WANs
- Types of Wireless WANs
- Wireless LANs and Wireless PBXs
- A wireless map
- The radio spectrum
- Cell Size and Achievable Throughput
- Market forecasts

## Why Wireless Connectivity?

The more wireless connectivity the mobile device has, the simpler it can be, as depicted in Figure 2.2.

With more connectivity, the mobile can have faster access to resources on the Internet, and resources at the office, at home, or elsewhere. Its cost, size, and power consumption can be held low while still having great utility. This trend is not only for mobile computers but for all computers. With increased access to the Internet, we are looking to reduce the cost and complexity of the PC in favor of having greater bandwidth to the information and services we require, and also to applications that can be downloaded from the Internet.

First, we discuss Wireless Wide Area Networks, and then Wireless Local Area Networks.

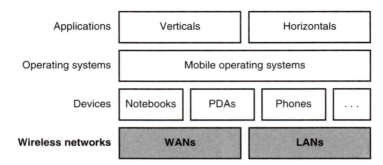

**Figure 2.1**  Focus on the network layer of the Mobile Computing map.

**Figure 2.2**  Why wireless connectivity?

# Definitions of Wireless LANs and Wireless WANs

To start, let us define what is a Wireless Local Area Network, and what is a Wireless Wide Area Network. The difference in the definitions of a Wireless LAN and a Wireless WAN is somewhat arbitrary. A distinction is suggested in Figure 2.3.

A Wireless LAN carries high-speed traffic in excess of 1 Mbps. It usually utilizes a random access technique such as CSMA, so it does not support real time voice traffic. Experiments have put real time voice on a random access LAN, but on the whole it has not provided satisfactory service. The voice traffic prefers an isochronous network that can guarantee the bandwidth, not one where the access times vary over a large range and can cause packets to get lost or arrive out of order.

The coverage area of a Wireless LAN is usually on the order of 50 meters in indoor environments. With this kind of cell size, the network supports only pedestrian speeds and not much more. The reason for this slow speed is not some sort of Doppler shift problem. It is simply that if a user moves very quickly through cells that are 50 meters in radius, the network is not able to keep track of her quickly enough because she changes cells too rapidly.

On the other hand, a Wireless WAN supports low- to medium-speed data from 10 Kbps up to ISDN rates of 50 Kbps or more in the future. WANs are the realm of real time voice. The

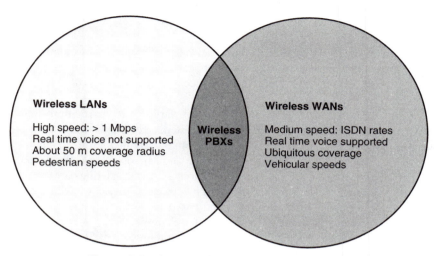

**Figure 2.3**   Wireless LANs and Wireless WANs.

switching technology used there is mostly circuit switching that dedicates a channel to a user as long as the call lasts. This is the ultimate in guaranteed bandwidth and isochronous service. A Wireless WAN is expected to provide ubiquitous coverage. A user expects that wherever he is, he has access to the Wireless WAN. Wireless LANs, on the other hand, do not have this expectation. They are expected to provide islands of coverage within a building or a campus. Finally, Wireless WANs support high-speed mobility. The cells in a Wireless WAN are sufficiently large that the user can be moving with vehicular speeds without traversing different cells at a great rate.

## Types of Wireless WANs

Many forms of wireless WANs exist, including:

- Cellular
- Paging
- Packet radio
- Satellite
- Cordless
- PCS

Cellular is now in the stage of migrating from analog to digital. Digital cellular offers greater capacity than analog cellular as well as better handling of data and encryption. Paging is inexpensive, and pagers are small and can operate on a single AA battery or AAA battery for over a month.

Mobile radio has been available for some time. Existing examples of mobile radio networks include taxicab companies and trucking dispatch networks. New examples of mobile radio include packet radio networks such as the RAM/Mobitex network and the ARDIS/Modacom network, which are designed for data exclusively.

Satellite networks are most applicable over very large areas, particularly remote regions where radio is uneconomical. Geostationary satellite systems exist, as well as Low Earth Orbiting satellite systems of different configurations, ranging from 66 satellites for the Iridium system from Motorola, to the new proposed system from Qualcomm and Microsoft that intends to use over 800 satellites. In addition to offering normal communications services, satellites are useful for providing positioning services for finding the location of objects. Such services have been used in aviation and marine applications for a long time. Land-based applications include locating the positions of truck fleets, police, and emergency vehicles, for example.

Cordless telephony such as DECT, and Personal Communications Systems are similar to cellular services but have much smaller cells and hence simpler handsets that require less power. Cordless telephony is intended to serve public areas such as shopping malls and airports, as well as residences. It is not intended for rural areas or roadways.

Figure 2.4 shows the type of wireless WAN that is best suited to each kind of traffic.

Cellular is intended primarily for voice but can handle voice grade data as well. Paging is primarily for alert traffic. Pocket radio handles voice traffic, and the new pocket radio systems such as RAM/Mobitex are designed for data. Satellite systems provide voice and data as well as positioning services. They are more expensive, hence the fewer stars. They have been providing positioning services for a long time, particularly to ships and aircraft. Cordless and Personal Communications Systems are intended for voice and data. Personal Communications Systems provide better grade of voice service and higher data rates.

| | Voice | Data | Alert | Positioning |
|---|---|---|---|---|
| Cellular | *** | ** | | |
| Paging | | ** | **** | |
| Packet radio | | **** | | |
| Satellite | ** | ** | | *** |
| Cordless | *** | * | | |
| PCS | **** | ** | | |

**Figure 2.4**   Traffic types and the Wireless WANs that best apply.

# Wireless LANs and Wireless PBXs

Several types of Wireless LANs are available:

- ISM LANs
- Infrared LANs
- "Unlicensed PCS" LANs

Wireless LANs provide the opportunity for users to build their own wireless networks to fit their own specific needs. Once built and an administration system in place, the user does not have to pay air time for using the network. ISM, the Industry Scientific and Medical band, is available now for building Wireless LANs. To use it we have to spread the spectrum in order not to interfere with incumbent users of the spectrum.

Infrared is not regulated, and a few products use this technology but not as many as the ones that use radio. Radio can penetrate walls; infrared cannot. Future Unlicensed PCS LANs use dedicated new bandwidth for Wireless LANs and do not have to use complex spread spectrum technology. Wireless PBXs also use the Unlicensed PCS bands.

The topology of a sample Wireless LAN is illustrated in Figure 2.5.

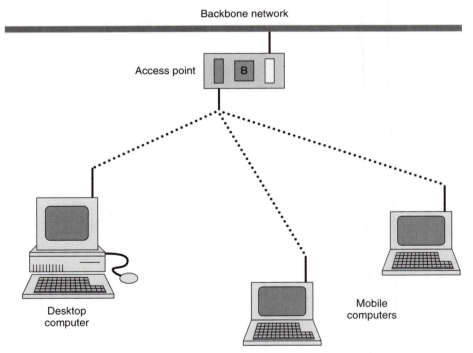

**Figure 2.5**   The topology of a Wireless LAN.

Desktop computers as well as mobile computers can have Wireless LAN adapters. An access point has the same wireless radio as well as the backbone wired LAN adapter, such as an Ethernet card. In addition, the access point contains bridging software for providing connectivity and filtering of the traffic between the wireless sub net and the backbone network.

Wireless PBXs share the Unlicensed PCS spectrum with Wireless LANs. They coexist with Wireless LANs the same way wired PBXs and wired LANs coexist today. The topology of a Wireless PBX appears in Figure 2.6.

The PBX and wired phone are shown in the left of the figure. In the right part of the figure are the portable terminals gaining access to the PBX via radio base stations. The base stations are positioned in the office campus to cover all the areas where the users are likely to be. They connect

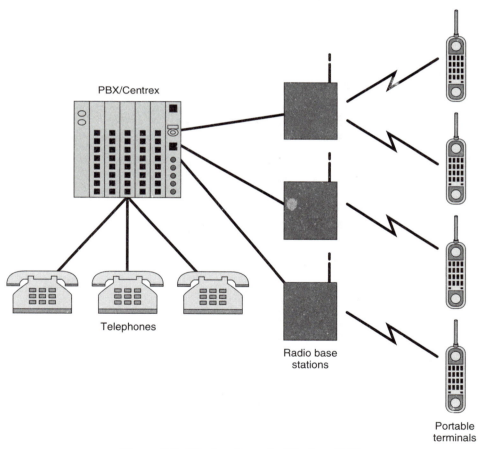

**Figure 2.6**  The topology of a Wireless PBX.

to new wireless cards in the PBX. Early Wireless PBXs have these circuits in separate standalone modules that connect to the PBX. Future PBXs such as the one shown in Figure 2.6 have the wireless capability integrated into the PBX.

# A Wireless Map

A great many activities are going on all over the world in the Wireless Networking field. In this section, we present a map to help understand the relationships among the activities; the map is based on where we spend our time. On this simple taxonomy we overlay the spectrum and standards activities worldwide, and the evolution of wireless products and services. We then discuss a vision that is very simple to state, but after seeing the complexity of the present situation, is not so easy to achieve.

The areas where we could be spending our time are shown in Figure 2.7. As illustrated, we could be in the office, in our home, at a public area such as a shopping mall or a downtown area, or somewhere in between—for example in our car, on a plane, or perhaps on vacation.

These possibilities are organized in the simple picture in Figure 2.8.

Most offices today are served by both a Local Area Network and a PBX. Local Area Networks were introduced in the 1970s to serve the needs of bursty traffic of very short duration. PBXs made an attempt at serving this kind of traffic but were not completely successful with the switching technology available at the time. PBXs use circuit switches and provide connection oriented services that are aimed at voice traffic. A circuit switch of that era takes about one second to set up a connection. The message length for bursty traffic is about 50 milliseconds on the average. So using a circuit switch that takes one second is not economical to set up a connection for transmitting a message that lasts only 50 milliseconds. In addition, the response time is unacceptable. For these reasons, most offices installed a LAN to handle the bursty traffic, and a PBX for voice. The PBX is used for data as well, usually the data that is destined to locations outside the office campus. The PBX has thus served as the gateway to the Wide Area Network.

Twenty-five years later, we now have the technology that allows a single switching fabric to meet the needs of bursty traffic as well as the needs of voice and other isochronous traffic that requires guaranteed bandwidth. This technology is Asynchronous Transfer Mode, or ATM. We are seeing LAN manufacturers use this technology to build high-speed LANs. And we are seeing PBX manufacturers use this technology to build future high-performance PBXs. With ATM we will finally be able to have a single hub in the office to serve our data, voice, and other multimedia needs. Moreover, this hub will use the same technology as that used for Wide Area Networks, making the integration between the local area and the wide area seamless.

Will we see this same integration take place around ATM technology for Wireless Networks? Unfortunately, the answer to this question is: Not in the near future. Wireless ATM is in its infancy at this time. Much research is being done on the subject; however, the first set of standards for Wireless LANs will not be based on ATM, but rather on traditional LAN technologies.

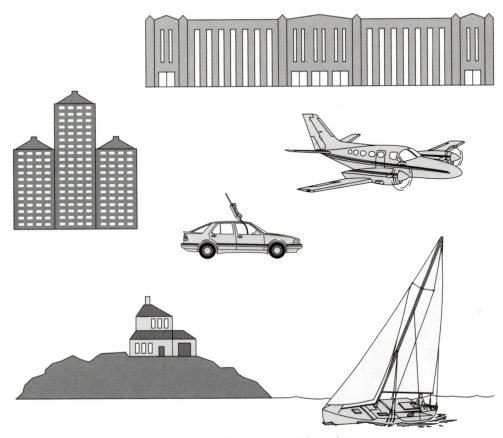

**Figure 2.7**   Where we spend our time.

In the second part of Figure 2.8, we include both residential and public areas, because, as we will see, both these applications are served by the same technology. When we are on the move, we can be communicating voice or data, and those are the categories into which the third part of the figure is divided.

The evolution of services and the spectrum and standards activities based on this simple taxonomy appear in Figure 2.9.

| Office | | Residential, Public areas | Mobile | |
|---|---|---|---|---|
| LAN | PBX | | Voice | Data |

**Figure 2.8**   A taxonomy of where we spend our time.

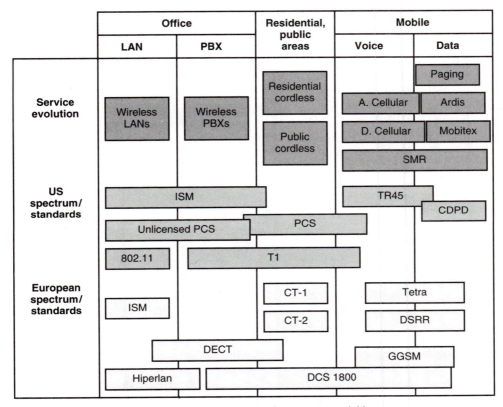

**Figure 2.9**  Standards and spectrum activities.

Today, we have Wireless LAN products from several manufacturers. We also are beginning to see Wireless PBXs from several telephony manufacturers. We can expect to see just about all PBXs having wireless capabilities in the not-too-distant future.

For residential and public areas, today we have a huge installed base of cordless phones, particularly in the US and in Japan. These phones are built to meet simple regulatory rules from the regulatory agencies in these countries, but do not meet any kind of interoperability standard. Cordless phones do not need to interoperate at this time since often a user does not need to obtain the base station from one vendor and the handset from another vendor. The regulatory rules *do* aim at making the sets coexist without mutual interference. However, the end result is not always satisfactory today. We often can hear our neighbors on our cordless phones. Nevertheless, we buy these devices and use them willingly because we like the freedom of not being tied to a cord in the wall. These cordless phones are the future roots of PCS. Their popularity shows that when the price and service are right, PCS will spread without bound. And this vision of PCS is indeed long-term. It will essentially replace telephony.

Next, we have the mobile area. Here, analog cellular services provide voice services and some circuit switched data services. Digital cellular provides voice and more data services. Paging provides mobile data service for alert traffic. Packet switched networks such as those from Motorola and Ericsson provide mobile data for bursty data traffic. The Motorola packet switched networks have different names in different parts of the world. In the US the network is called Ardis, in Europe it is called Modacom, and in parts of Asia it has different names such as Datatac. The Ericsson network is called Mobitex in most parts of the world. These two networks are competing for the customers whose applications have bursty traffic. They are both racing to build networks. At the same time, two-way paging is beginning to be introduced by companies such as SkyTel and Mtel. The packet switched networks from Motorola and Ericsson will have to prove their price/performance advantage over the two-way paging networks.

Specialized Mobile Radio is perhaps the oldest kind of service shown on the chart. SMR services are the roots of Wireless Networking. They serve police departments, fire departments, ambulance drivers, taxicab companies, trucking fleets, airport operations staff, security services, and so on. All the walkie talkies and the one-way dispatch units we see in truck fleets and cab fleets are based on SMR licenses.

Next, we discuss the spectrum and standards activities in the US, Europe, and other parts of the world. Wireless LANs today have had to use the Industrial, Scientific, and Medical bands. To use the ISM bands, the products are forced to use complicated spread spectrum technology as required by Part 15 of the FCC rules. Spread spectrum is needed in order not to interfere with the primary users of this band. Several ISM bands are available. The most popular band that is available in many parts of the world including the US, Europe, and parts of Asia is the 2.4 GHz ISM band. This is where most Wireless LAN manufacturers are aiming their initial products. The hope is that in the near future a band dedicated to this kind of traffic will be made available in most parts of the world. The first step has been taken in the US with the provision of an Unlicensed PCS band for asynchronous traffic. This 10 MHz band has been allocated by the FCC, but many implementation issues still remain before this band can be effectively used by the Wireless LAN industry.

A few manufacturers are using the ISM bands for other purposes. For example, Spectrix builds a wireless PBX that uses the ISM bands. Also, Metricom uses the ISM bands to provide what is essentially a wireless Metropolitan Area Network. Other uses of the ISM band abound. For example, some cordless phones use the lower ISM band. These cordless phones provide much greater range, almost a mile, at about four or five times the price of an average cordless phone that barely covers a large house. The other half of the Unlicensed PCS band is aimed at isochronous traffic, which requires guaranteed bandwidth such as voice and other multimedia traffic, including video. Wireless PBX manufacturers are paving the way for effective use of this 10 MHz much more quickly than the Wireless LAN industry is able to do with the 10 MHz earmarked for asynchronous traffic.

The bulk of the spectrum for PCS is licensed and will be used for services aimed at the residential and the public area markets. In addition, PCS may possibly find its way into business systems, and some manufacturers are considering using PCS spectra to provide large-scale mobility as is provided by cellular services.

The standards body that is responsible for Wireless LAN standards is IEEE 802.11. IEEE 802.11 products are likely to be provided throughout the world. PCS standards are developed by the T1 committee, as well as the TR 45 committee. The T1 committee is a huge organization consisting of more than 1500 companies that are involved in all facets of communications equipment and services. Although its aim is the residential and public area markets, it has impact on the business market as well as the mobile market. The TR 45 committee is involved primarily in developing cellular standards, and now it is involved in developing PCS standards as well. The TR 45 committee issued the IS 54 digital cellular TDMA standard, the later version of the digital cellular standard IS 136, the IS 95 digital CDMA standard, and the IS 41 interconnection standard. TR 45 and T1 work together closely on projects, such as PCS, where they both have great interest.

Cellular Digital Packet Data (CDPD) is a standard that was developed by an industry consortium comprised of IBM, six of the seven RBOCs, and other major organizations. The aim of CDPD is to provide a packet data service for bursty traffic that is derived from the existing circuit switched cellular services. It leverages the tremendous installed base of cellular base stations and switching equipment to provide a packet service. In essence, this packet service provides additional revenues from the same infrastructure that is being used for voice traffic with relatively small additional investment.

Whereas the US and Japan lead the market for cordless phones in the home, Europe and Asia lead the market in telepoint services, which are cordless services in public areas. They can be thought of as wireless pay phones. They are one way outgoing and are provided in islands of high density coverage. The standard used for these services at this time is CT-2. Initial telepoint services include Rabbit in the UK and Bibop in France. They seem to be declining in popularity. Their purpose seems to have been to serve as a learning tool more than anything else. Even their names do not sound like they should be taken seriously. Their market position was not clear relative to GSM, and their penetration was too little to warrant further construction of the networks. In parts of Asia they enjoyed greater popularity, especially when combined with paging. However, even there they are beginning to wane as they are replaced with GSM and other more mature PCS services.

Digital European Cordless Telephone (DECT) was proposed by Ericsson as a wireless PBX standard. It is a mature standard that is implemented in chip sets by several manufacturers in Europe and in the US. DECT has a good chance of becoming a worldwide standard for wireless PBXs. In addition, DECT can be applied in residences as a small cordless key set providing several handsets that are served by a single base station. DECT can also be used as a telepoint service replacing present CT-2 implementations, if the market justifies it.

In the mobile data area two standards have been developed by the European Telecommunications Standards Institute—Digital Short Range Radio and Tetra. DSRR is aimed at Private Mobile Radio, and Tetra is aimed at Public Access Mobile Radio. Not much activity is occurring with DSRR, but Tetra is being considered in all parts of the world. One of the keys to the success of the Tetra standard is how well it can meet the needs of closed user groups with stringent peak traffic requirements, such as police departments, especially in time of emergency.

Finally, and most importantly, is the GSM 900/DCS 1800 standard. The new name for GSM is Global System Mobile, and it seems to be living up to its name. It is the cellular digital standard with the widest acceptance throughout the world. However, it will not remain unchallenged as other digital cellular standards such as TDMA and CDMA reach maturity. GSM 900 provides larger cell applications than does DCS 1800. The higher power levels and the lower frequency of operation of GSM allow it to cover wider areas more easily than the lower power levels and higher frequency of operation of DCS 1800.

In this book, we focus on the middle three columns of Figure 2.9. These are the areas that are served by telephony companies and cellular carriers. They provide wireless PBXs for on-site private system applications. They provide residential cordless systems for home use, and public cordless systems for use in shopping malls, downtown areas, and other high density areas. They provide cellular services for ubiquitous coverage wherever users are likely to be, including roadways and rural areas.

Figure 2.10 shows Wireless Networking products and services relative to the taxonomy of where we spend our time.

Wireless LAN products are available from several vendors—some large, some very small. The large vendors include ATT, IBM, and Motorola. The small ones include Proxim, Xircom, and Spectrix. The Wireless LAN market is still in the startup mode compared to the cellular market. A small company has difficulty remaining viable in such a slowly developing market. However, eventually this market doubtless will develop as the price/performance formula becomes attractive.

The wireless PBX business is served by all the telephony manufacturers. A small sampling appears in Figure 2.10. The same companies serve the residential and public areas market; cellular carriers serve the mobile voice market; and paging and packet radio companies serve the mobile data market.

| Office | | Residential, public areas | Mobile | |
|--------|--------|------|-------|------|
| LAN | PBX | | Voice | Data |
| Lucent | | CT-X | ATT | Paging |
| IBM | ATT | | | |
| Proxim | NorTel | | RBOCs | Ad. paging |
| Xircom | Ericsson | Ericsson | | ARDIS |
| Motorola | SpectraLink | | GTE, . . . | |
| Windata | | NorTel | | Mobitex |
| Photonics | | | | |
| Spectrix | | Hutchinson | McCaw | CDPD |

**Figure 2.10**  Products and services.

Now that we have seen all the Wireless Networking activities taking place around the world, we can discuss what the vision might be. Simply stated, one view is that Wireless Networking should be:

- Available everywhere
- Invisible to the user

This vision is very simple to state but is not so easy to achieve today, because many different options do not interoperate well. When we are at work, we have a wireless PBX and a wireless LAN that use different infrastructures. When we are at home we have a cordless phone. In the car, we have cellular service. In the plane we have an air phone. Can we get to the point where we can access all the networks we need with a single device without having to think about it (see Figure 2.11)?

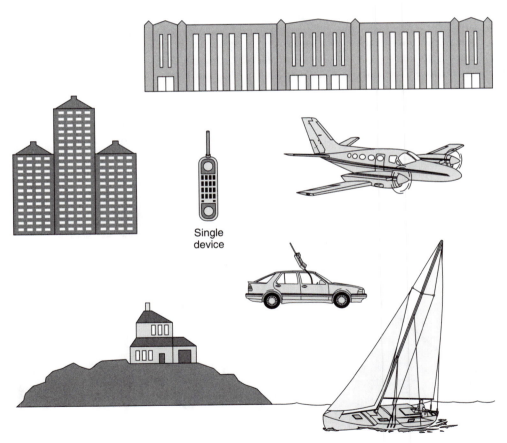

Single
device

**Figure 2.11**   The vision.

Can we use the same light, long-battery-life device to access the wireless PBX at the office and the system we have at home? Can we use that same device when we are in the car traveling in sparsely populated areas and access large cell systems by connecting to our higher-power car-based system? Can the plane have a base station that allows this same device to access air-to-ground circuits instead of using yet another distinct system for communicating from planes, and having to turn off our own systems for fear of interfering with the plane's navigation systems? Will we be able to carry these devices from one part of the country to another and have good coverage and seamless provision of the services for which we signed up? Can we take our phones with us around the world? Will we have to subscribe to expensive satellite services to achieve worldwide roaming?

## The Radio Spectrum

Most of the Wireless Networking services are crowded around 1 GHz, as Figure 2.12 shows.

Figure 2.12 shows the frequency ranges for Extremely Low Frequencies, Very Low Frequencies, Medium Frequencies, High Frequencies, Very High Frequencies, Ultra High Frequen-

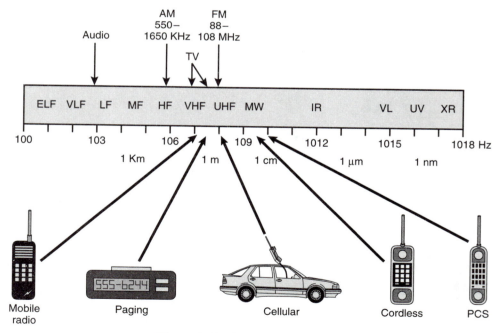

**Figure 2.12**   The radio spectrum.

cies, the microwave region, the infrared region, the visible light region, the ultraviolet region, and finally X-rays. The audio frequencies that we hear range from 20 Hz to 20 KHz. AM radio stations are in the 1 MHz range. FM radio and TV are in the 100 MHz range. Paging systems fall in the 50 to 500 MHz range. Mobile radio and cellular systems use the band just below 1 GHz. Cordless and PCS systems use the bands around 2 GHz. The Infrared region is huge. It has its applications in the Wireless LAN areas and in short-range, point-to-point communications, including remote control systems.

Why are so many services crowded around 1 GHz, and why are future high density services moving to the 2 GHz bands? One reason is simply the availability of spectrum. The spectrum around 1 GHz is becoming full. To obtain greater bandwidth, we must move up in the frequency band. As we move up, the amount of bandwidth increases exponentially. The challenge is to build equipment that can operate at the higher frequencies and achieve acceptable range with reasonable power. Silicon integrated circuits as of a few years ago could only handle frequencies up to 1 GHz. Higher frequency systems were forced to use Gallium Arsenide, which was more expensive at the time. Now Silicon can achieve greater speeds, and GaAs is becoming cost effective.

## Cell Size and Achievable Throughput

Figure 2.13 is another very useful map of wireless services. This time the service types are plotted on a matrix of achievable data rate versus cell size.

The cell sizes vary from tens of meters to thousands of kilometers. A break occurs in the horizontal axis between the tens of kilometers range and the thousands of kilometers range. In the upper left-hand corner we have Wireless LANs. They provide data rates in the range of 1 Mbps.

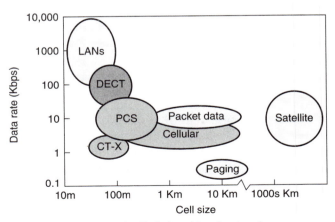

**Figure 2.13**   Relationship of networks.

Their cell sizes are usually in the range of 50 meters indoors. This figure is a nominal range that includes propagation through the walls inside a building.

On the other extreme are satellite services. The cell sizes can be thousands of kilometers and cover continents. The data rate that is usually provided is in the 10 Kbps range.

On the lower extreme are simple one-way paging systems. They provide very low data rates below 1 Kbps. The range of a paging base station can be quite large, tens of kilometers. This makes implementing a paging network relatively fast compared to a cellular network. For example, to install a paging network that covers most of the population of a small Asian country like Vietnam, a total investment on the order of $100 million and a time frame of about one year would be required.

The frequency allocation for a paging network is extremely small relative to the allocation required for a cellular, PCS, satellite, or Wireless LAN service. This bandwidth is used very efficiently to provide the service. Since the required bandwidth is so small, it is often allocated at a low frequency band that is much lower than the bands used by higher data rate services. The low frequency means that the cell sizes can be large while keeping the power relatively low. Advanced and two-way paging networks would move paging up and to the left, towards packet data on the chart, because they provide higher data rates, which require greater bandwidth. This size of allocation is not available at low frequency bands, so it is provided at higher frequencies. The higher frequencies require greater power to achieve the same range as the lower frequencies. In addition, the higher data rate in itself requires higher power to transmit.

Packet data networks have cells that can be tens of kilometers in size. Their data rates are on the order of 10 to 20 Kbps. This data rate is shared among the customers contending for the use of the channel. The sharing mechanism is usually a random access scheme typical of a Local Area Network. The total bandwidth allocated to a packet radio network is relatively small compared to the bandwidth allocated to a cellular service, a PCS service, a satellite service, or a LAN service. It is not as small as a one-way paging service, but it is not much more than the equivalent of one single voice channel in a cellular network. This bandwidth is then shared by all the data users who are typically sending transaction type traffic. The traffic is sent through the network on a store and forward basis. Depending on the application, extremely fast response time may not be needed. For example, for electronic mail, a response time of a few minutes may be acceptable. For an interactive session, a response time of less than one second would be required. Users of packet networks are charged a flat monthly charge plus a charge per packet.

In the middle of the chart, we have cellular, cordless (CT-X), and PCS services. The cell sizes for cellular can range from a few hundred meters, to tens of kilometers. The small cell sizes are for denser downtown areas, and the larger are for more sparse densities. The data rates are on the order of 10 Kbps. Cordless systems have cell sizes around 100 meters. Many of them serve indoor or very dense urban areas. The data rates of CT-X systems, which include CT-2 and CT-3, are on the same order as cellular. The definitions of CT-0 and CT-1 for cordless telephony in the home do not include digital data at this time. PCS promises to provide greater data throughput than cellular. DECT provides very high data rates for a service that is not LAN based. It provides on the order of 1/2 Mbps, coming close to what a Wireless LAN can provide.

The services are clustered along a curve that begins at the upper left-hand corner of the matrix and descends to the lower right-hand corner. No services exist in the upper right-hand corner or the lower left-hand corner. In the upper right-hand corner, the data rate is high and the cell size is large. This situation is very difficult to realize because as the cell size increases, more and more people are likely to be in the cell. If each of them is demanding a large data rate, the service would have to provide a huge aggregate data rate.

At the lower left-hand corner, the data rate is low and the cell size is low. When the data rate is low, the cell size can easily be large, for example with paging, so we do not see many services in this corner. This fact does not mean that some niche services may not now exist, or some such services may not materialize in the future. One example would be an extremely low cost, very localized service that needs very little bandwidth.

Most of the services are grouped along a curve that implies that the higher the data rate, the smaller the cell size must be. The reason is that the smaller the cell size, the more frequently the bandwidth can be reused, and the smaller the cell size, the less power must be transmitted.

In this book, we focus on the Wireless LAN area and the Mobile Data area. First, we begin with some market forecasts for these areas.

## Market Forecasts

The focus of this section is not on the *exact* magnitude of market sizes, but rather on the *relative* sizes. First, discussing the typical life cycle of a product or service is instructive (see Figure 2.14).

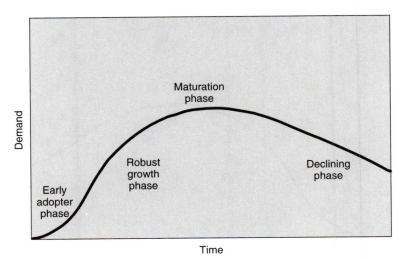

**Figure 2.14**   The life cycle of a product or service.

This life cycle is very familiar. What is interesting is to apply it to the products under consideration here, namely Mobile Data and Wireless LANs. Since most of the Mobile Data is carried today on analog cellular and digital cellular, putting these services on the chart in Figure 2.15 is also interesting.

As the shape in Figure 2.15 implies, analog cellular is in the maturation stage whereas digital cellular is definitely in the robust growth phase.

These remarks apply to the whole field of analog cellular and digital cellular, over which the predominant form of traffic today is voice. Digital cellular was in the early adopter phase for several years; now it is in the robust growth phase in many parts of the world. Service providers are racing to put systems in place. Users are signing up for the service and are beginning to truly depend on it. Digital cellular will serve as the launching pad for future value-added systems.

What about Mobile Data and Wireless LANs? In general, Mobile Data can be thought of as being in the early adopter phase. Wireless LANs are perhaps in the very early adopter phase. To discuss Mobile Data fully, we need to discuss the different kinds of Mobile Data, including:

- Data over analog cellular
- Data over digital cellular
- Packet radio networks
- Two-way paging networks

With this refined definition, we can propose that data over analog cellular is in the early adopter stage, and that it is also the most mature of the four kinds of Mobile Data. Next would be packet radio networks, followed by data over digital cellular and two-way paging networks. These ideas are depicted in Figure 2.16.

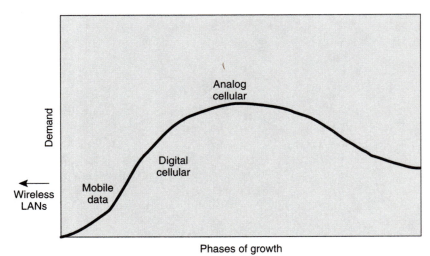

**Figure 2.15**   The phases of growth of cellular and related services.

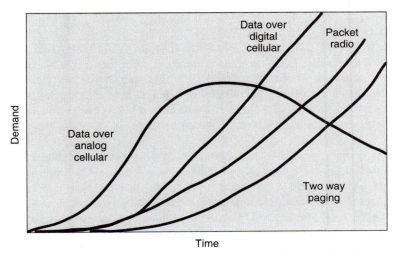

**Figure 2.16**   The growth patterns of Mobile Data services.

Mobile Data over analog cellular is beginning to move beyond the early adopter stage. Cellular modems have capitalized on the advanced technology and low cost of wired modems, now achieving 14.4 Kbps in PCMCIA form factor and costing little more than an equivalent wired modem. Packet radio networks have been offered for some time and they are growing. Mobile Data over digital cellular is likely to overtake packet radio networks in terms of traffic carried. Two-way paging networks are just beginning to be implemented. How they fare relative to packet radio remains to be seen, and depends on how they are priced and how much capacity they offer.

## Summary

In this chapter we provided an introduction to Wireless Networking. We began by showing the potential of Wireless Networking for simplifying mobile devices while making them more powerful. This trend applies not only to mobile devices but to PCs in general as they achieve greater connectivity to the Internet. We defined Wireless LANs as high-throughput, small cell size, low-speed mobility networks that serve asynchronous data traffic well in localized areas, but are not well suited to isochronous traffic such as voice and video. We defined Wireless WANs as medium-throughput, large cell size, high-speed mobility networks that serve voice very well and are available wherever users are likely to be located.

We discussed the various kinds of Wireless WANs and their applicability to different kinds of user traffic. In particular, we argued that cellular carries voice well and data fairly well. Paging serves alert traffic very well. Packet data networks serve data very well. Satellite networks serve voice and data well at an expense, and provide positioning services very well. PCS serves voice very well and data well.

We discussed the different kinds of Wireless LANs, including ISM Wireless LANs, infrared Wireless LANs, and Wireless LANs in future Unlicensed PCS bands. We put these services into perspective by presenting several wireless maps. The first map showed the evolution of products and services as well as the standards and spectra for Wireless Networking activities throughout the world, including not just Wireless LANs and Mobile Data services, but also cellular and PCS. We presented a map of data rates and cell sizes that compared the services and analyzed their present relationship.

We proposed some qualitative market forecasts for the field of Mobile Data and Wireless LANs. The whole field is in the early stages of development. Some major questions still exist that can alter the shape of the market in the next few years. The current view is that the development of the services occurs in the following rough order: Mobile Data over analog cellular, packet radio networks, Wireless LANs, Mobile Data over digital cellular, and two-way paging.

# 3 *Mobile Data Services*

The majority of Mobile Data traffic is carried today on analog circuit switched cellular networks. Digital cellular networks are being implemented throughout the world at a rapid pace and promise simpler access to circuit switched data. Packet radio networks have provided a service that is well suited to asynchronous traffic for some years. Emerging two-way paging networks can provide similar service at a competitive price. In this chapter, we address these options for carrying Mobile Data traffic and compare them; in particular we discuss:

- The RAM/Mobitex Mobile Data service
- The ARDIS/Modacom Mobile Data service
- Cellular Digital Packet Data
- Data over analog and digital cellular
- Competing Mobile Data services
- Paging and two-way paging
- Comparison of paging and cellular

## The RAM/Mobitex Mobile Data Service

The RAM/Mobitex Mobile Data service is owned jointly by Bell South and RAM in the US. The Mobitex protocol was developed by Ericsson. RAM/Mobitex provides 8 Kbps in the US and 9.6 Kbps in other parts of the world. In the US the data rate is being upgraded to 19.2 Kbps to match the data rate of CDPD. Some of the early applications of RAM/Mobitex and who is using them include:

- Point of sale where dial-up is not available: MasterCard
- Inventory control of rental cars: National Car Rental

- Train exchange yards: Conrail
- Passenger check-in: British Airways
- Field service: GE consumer service
- Public safety: Chicago Parking Authority
- Insurance claims
- Transportation
- Electronic mail

The point-of-sale application for MasterCard allows stores to have cash registers in any place they please without having to worry about wiring the register. National Car Rental employees use handheld units to update their inventory of cars in the rental car parking lots by driving through the lots and inputting the data into their portable units. An interesting note is that the early applications of RAM/Mobitex are primarily vertical at this time. The only truly horizontal application is the last one, electronic mail.

Mobitex networks are being installed all over the world, including in the following countries:

- Australia
- Canada
- Finland
- France
- Netherlands
- Norway
- Sweden
- United Kingdom
- United States

Installation plans are in place for Mobitex networks in the rest of Europe, in Latin America, and the Pacific Rim.

Figure 3.1 depicts what you need to use the RAM/Mobitex network.

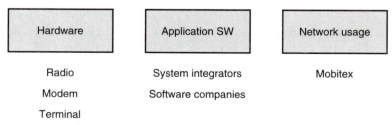

| Hardware | Application SW | Network usage |
|---|---|---|
| Radio | System integrators | Mobitex |
| Modem | Software companies | |
| Terminal | | |

**Figure 3.1**   What you need to use the RAM/Mobitex network.

The radio and the modem are combined into one unit called the Mobidem that is made by Ericsson and others. The initial Mobidem had the following specifications:

- Portable wireless modem and radio
- Connectible to RS-232 serial port
- 8 Kbps migrating to 19.2 Kbps
- 1 pound
- $3.3 \times 2.68 \times 7.87$ in
- Max transmit power: 2 w
- > 10 hours per battery charge
- Support for nationwide roaming

The 2 watt transmit power allows fairly good penetration into buildings, better than that achieved by most cellular networks and cellular phones. This Mobidem is now available in the PCMCIA form factor. It has its own 9 volt battery that is attached to the PCMCIA card. On the outside of the battery enclosure is a short telescoping antenna.

The terminal can be anything that has an RS-232 connection. A notebook computer or a PDA are typical. The end user application resides on this terminal and is typically communicating with some host. For example, the application could an electronic mail package that is communicating with an electronic mail gateway such as the one provided by RadioMail. The RadioMail gateway provides access to most electronic mail services such as:

- Worldwide TCP/IP Internet
- LAN mail systems such as cc:Mail
- ATTMail
- MCI Mail
- CompuServe

In vertical applications and other horizontal applications that are provided by the user's company, the host is resident on the company's premises. It is connected to the RAM/Mobitex network by private lines that are leased by the user's company from the telephone company or other private line service provider. The client part of the application is installed in the user's terminal. The client part of the application communicates with the server part of the application over the RAM/Mobitex network.

The last part of what is needed to use the RAM/Mobitex network is the air time. RAM/Mobitex charges a flat monthly fee plus a per packet fee. Typical fees are discussed shortly.

The way the RAM/Mobitex network operates is as follows. The Mobidem automatically registers with the nearest base station. The network is a store and forward network. The Mobidem scans the network for incoming messages. It alerts the user's terminal of incoming messages. If the terminal is not available, the Mobidem stores the messages. If the Mobidem is not available, the network stores the message.

The subscription types for the hosts include:

- CCITT X.25
- ISO/HDLC
- SNA 3270
- Mobitex asynchronous communications

Many other host interfaces are available through third parties. The subscription types for the mobile terminal are:

- Continuous linkage to a particular terminal
- Personal subscription that is linked to a person, not a terminal, in which case the user logs in via name and password
- Group subscriptions that can consist of mobile and fixed users

The pricing in the US has three plans that appear in Figure 3.2.

The flat monthly charges range from about $25 for the consumer plan to about $135 for the power user plan with unlimited traffic per month. The slopes of the fees reflect a charge per packet of about $ 0.25. The break points occur at about 100 Kilobytes and about 400 Kilobytes. One page of text has about 400 words. Each word has an average of perhaps 4 characters, so one page has 1600 characters or bytes. Therefore, 100 Kilobytes is about 62 pages. If the working month has 20 days, 100 Kilobytes equates to roughly 3 pages of traffic per day. Discerning how long an average electronic mail message is can be difficult. If it is in the range of one-half a page, then 100 Kilobytes is 6 messages per day. The next break point at 400 Kilobytes would be 24 messages per day.

Users of electronic mail and Wireless Networking are likely to have filters on their electronic mail so it is not all delivered to their mobile terminal. For example, they could set up the filter to deliver only messages that are addressed to them directly, and not the messages on which they are just copied. They could make the filter more restrictive, for example to deliver only those mes-

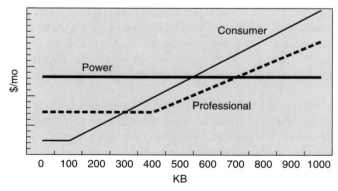

**Figure 3.2**  RAM/Mobitex network pricing structure.

sages that are addressed just to them, or only those messages addressed to them from certain senders. The possibilities are many and depend on individual requirements.

Many Mobitex partners include companies who are other manufacturers, such as:

- IBM
- HP
- Motorola
- Intel
- Fujitsu
- Ericsson
- AT&T

Developer and System Integrator partners include:

- DEC
- Lotus
- Novell
- WordPerfect

RAM/Mobitex has a heritage of openness that is likely to enhance their ability to interface to a variety of equipment and services.

## The ARDIS/Modacom Mobile Data Service

The ARDIS/Modacom Mobile Data service has installed networks in:

- US
- Germany
- UK
- Hong Kong

Efforts are underway to install ARDIS/Modacom in many other parts of the world. RAM/ Mobitex and ARDIS/Modacom are racing to provide service in as many places as possible so that they can attract customers.

ARDIS/Modacom was the IBM Field Engineer network starting in 1983. Since IBM's field engineering network essentially spanned the country, IBM and Motorola, who was providing the network for IBM, decided to offer the service to the public. It was first put in public service in the US in April 1990. The ARDIS/Modacom network provides 4800 bps in the US, migrating to 19.2

Kbps like the RAM/Mobitex network, to match CDPD. In other parts of the world, the ARDIS/Modacom network provides 9.6 Kbps.

The applications as stated by ARDIS/Modacom are as follows:

- Field technicians can access
  - Dispatch information
  - Diagnostic information
  - Service history
  - Parts availability
- Messenger service couriers can
  - Receive and dispatch messages while making deliveries
  - Notify customer that delivery was made
- Salespeople can
  - Obtain latest product specifications
  - Provide accurate price quote
  - Check product availability
  - Make the order

Additional applications include:

- Fleet management
- Insurance and financial services
- Real time data applications
- Point of Sale (POS)
- Telemetry
- Electronic mail

The advantage of the ARDIS/Modacom network and the RAM/Mobitex network for handling data, as compared with carrying data over circuit switched cellular, is greater efficiency for asynchronous traffic. The average message length for asynchronous traffic is short compared with the time that setting up a circuit in a cellular network takes. In addition, both the RAM/Mobitex network and the ARDIS/Modacom network are designed to offer better coverage inside buildings. Both these advantages can change, however, if cellular carriers decide to offer special billing for short messages, and if they design their networks to have better coverage indoors, as they are likely to do as the networks mature. Offering reduced rates for short calls is not necessarily a good long-term solution since it does not reflect the true cost to the network of carrying short messages.

The radio and modem combination for the ARDIS/Modacom network is built by Motorola and is called the InfoTAC. Its specifications are summarized by:

- Connects through RS-232 port
- Receives, stores, and responds to messages
- Canned responses can be programmed
- 10 KB buffer
- 3 watts transmit power
- 6.8 × 3.3 × 3.3 inches
- 18 ounces
- 4 × 20 line backlit LCD display
- 8 hour battery life
- Compatible with
  - ARDIS/Modacom network
  - RAM/Mobitex network

The first ARDIS/Modacom network was installed in the US. The second network was installed in Germany. The events that led up to the German network are interesting. Two studies were carried out, one to determine the overall potential of mobile data, and the other to determine whether a specific market existed for major companies. The bottom line of the results of the studies was that a need exists for high-quality mobile data transmission, and that the market potential is large enough to justify implementation of a dedicated Mobile Data network.

The German PTT, Telecom, issued an RFP for a Mobile Data network in 1991. Two proposals were received, one from Motorola and the other from Ericsson Mobitex. The Motorola system was selected. A field trial was conducted from March 1992 to October 1992. Service began in 1993. About a year later a RAM/Mobitex network began installation as well.

# Cellular Digital Packet Data

In this section, we discuss what CDPD is and what we envision its applications to be. CDPD, or Cellular Digital Packet Data, is an industry standard that was developed by a consortium of companies that included:

- IBM
- 6 of the 7 RBOCs
  - Ameritech Mobile Communications
  - Bell Atlantic Mobile Systems
  - NYNEX Mobile Communications

- PacTel Cellular
- Southwestern Bell Mobile Systems
- US West New Vector Group
- McCaw Cellular Communications
- Contel Cellular
- GTE Mobile Communications

The one RBOC that is not part of the consortium is, of course, Bell South, which is part owner of the RAM/Mobitex network. The purpose of the consortium is to develop a common industry specification for CDPD systems. It is to be an open architecture that allows any underlying data transport network, multiple equipment vendors, multiple network, and cellular operators. Commercial developments of CDPD systems will be done by the network operators that comprise the consortium.

Four CDPD Application categories exist. The first is transaction applications, which usually involve one request and one yes or no answer. The second category is interactive applications, which typically have multiple message exchanges. The third is broadcast applications, which are broadcast to a whole cell or the whole country. The fourth is multicast applications, which are broadcast to a specific user group.

Transaction applications include:

- Credit card authorization/transaction
- Package pickup, delivery, and tracking
- Fleet management
- Point of sale
- Inventory control
- Emergency services
- M-ES/vehicle theft recovery
- Display of calling party name or number
- Notice of voice mail
- Electronic mail
- Information retrieval services
- Telemetry

Telemetry services have a number of examples such as:

- Location service
- Vehicle statistics
  - Mileage

- Speed
- Engine status
- Burglar or fire alarm reporting
- Vending machine status
- Weather statistics
- Traffic statistics
- Field measurements

Information retrieval services include:

- Weather report for a particular place
- Traffic report for a specific area
- Directory assistance: White pages
- Local service assistance: Yellow pages
- Location and direction information
- Restaurant reservation service

Interactive applications use remote access to hosts via direct network connection or via a PAD (Packet Assembly/Disassembly). Broadcast services can provide:

- News
- Sports
- Weather
- Advertising

Multicast services can be a subscription to an information service to obtain:

- Market information
- Business news
- News related to a specific area
- Classifieds for a particular area
- Recreational information

Multicast services can also be a subscription to a private bulletin board to obtain:

- Service bulletins
- Company functions
- Product information
- Fraud warnings

For the law enforcement application, the information could include suspicious character information, license plate numbers of stolen vehicles, and a list of missing persons.


## Data Over Analog and Digital Cellular

Data over analog cellular can today provide up to 14.4 Kbps without compression at a price that is slightly higher than data over the wired analog network. The modems are available in PCMCIA form factor, and some provide access to both the wired network and the analog cellular network. Data over digital cellular actually provides less throughput at this time. The reason for this fact is that data over digital cellular is based on one equivalent voice circuit. An equivalent voice circuit in digital cellular provides 9.6 Kbps. In the future, the standards will allow the combination of more than one voice equivalent channel to provide higher throughputs. For GSM this service can provide in the neighborhood of 100 Kbps, since the carriers of GSM are 200 KHz in bandwidth and have a raw bit rate of 270 Kbps. For Digital TDMA, the rate is likely to be limited to about 30 Kbps or so since the carrier spacing is only 30 KHz as based on AMPS.

UPS in the US chose to use cellular for their fleet of trucks. The decision was tough. The traffic is transaction-based and so theoretically would better fit on a packet network such as RAM/Mobitex or ARDIS/Modacom. However, neither of these networks provided adequate coverage at the time for a service such as UPS, which serves many small municipalities. The cellular carriers provide UPS with special short message billing. As discussed earlier, this does not reflect the actual cost of carrying the short messages. We would not be surprised if at a later time, the cellular carriers want to switch UPS to a packet based network so they can use the cellular capacity more efficiently to serve voice traffic. The switch over could be smooth since the same companies provide cellular as well as CDPD, but could involve a significant upgrade of equipment in all the trucks.

GSM, as well as the newer IS 136 digital TDMA standard, provides a service called Short Message Service. An SMS is limited to about 100 characters or so. It can be replied to, so it can be thought of as two-way paging, or acknowledged paging. SMSs are derived from the signaling structure of the service. The first applications of SMS were to notify cellular users of having a voice message or a fax (the cellular operators typically provide their users with voice mail when they are not reachable). When a voice message is deposited for a user, the system sends the user an SMS to notify him or her of the event. Some cellular operators also store faxes for their users and send them an SMS to let them know a fax is waiting for them. They can retrieve the fax either via the cellular network to their own terminal, or have it delivered to a wired terminal, for example at the hotel fax machine.

A variation exists to SMS called SMS cell broadcast. These messages have a maximum length less than the point-to-point SMS discussed above. SMS cell broadcast can be sent to all phones in a geographical area. The applications of this kind of service are, for example, warnings of traffic delays or accidents, or any other condition that affects a contiguous geographical area.

# Competing Mobile Data Services

Figure 3.3 compares RAM/Mobitex, ARDIS/Modacom, CDPD, and data over cellular.

The first item in Figure 3.3 is coverage. As was noted above, this issue is one of the first questions asked by prospective customers such as UPS. Without the coverage, usually no further discussion occurs. Therefore, the network providers are racing to put in the networks throughout the world. The first to have the coverage is the first to gain market share and begin to achieve profitability. As we can see, RAM/Mobitex has taken over 800 base stations to cover more than 100 metropolitan areas. ARDIS/Modacom has taken over 1800 base stations to cover more than 400 metropolitan areas. ARDIS/Modacom has been building the network for a longer time than RAM/Mobitex since they started out as the IBM field engineering network at an earlier time.

CDPD hopes to provide coverage in over 700 metropolitan areas by equipping over 9000 existing cellular base stations with special CDPD hardware and software. CDPD leverages the cost of the installed base of the cellular network.

The building penetration of the RAM/Mobitex network and the ARDIS/Modacom network is quite good because of their relatively high transmitted power. CDPD has less in-building penetration that is about the same as the in-building penetration of cellular services. The data rates are comparable for the ARDIS/Modacom and RAM/Mobitex networks, and the CDPD network. These rates are shared among the users who have access to the packet channel. The data rate for data over cellular is on a single user basis, so it is effectively quite a bit higher.

| | RAM | ARDIS | CDPD | Data over cellular |
|---|---|---|---|---|
| Metropolitan areas | 100+ | 400+ | 700+ | 700+ |
| Base stations | 800+ | 1300+ | 9000+ | 9000+ |
| In building penetration | yes | more | some | some |
| Power (watts) | 2 | 3 | 0.6–1.2 | 0.6–3 |
| Performance (Kbps) | 8 >>19.2 | 4.8 >> 19.2 | 19.2 | 14.4 |

**Figure 3.3**   Comparison of Mobile Data services.

## Paging and Two-Way Paging

The very first paging systems were used for reaching doctors and nurses without distressing patients in the 1950s. Before paging was available, public address systems were used, with the resulting noisy and hectic environment. The aim of paging is to solve the need to reach a person anywhere, anytime. A pager is low cost, small, lightweight, and can be unobtrusively worn. It relies on the wired network to complete the return communication.

The architecture of a paging network appears in Figure 3.4.

The trigger of the page is usually someone dialing the pager number. The trigger can also be activated by an operator, or it can be activated automatically by a machine. The trigger arrives at the central controller, which broadcasts the page to local controllers. Most paging networks broadcast the page to all local controllers since the network has no knowledge of where the user may be. The cell sizes of paging networks are quite large, allowing coverage of large areas with relative ease. For this reason, paging is very popular in Asian countries where little telecommunications infrastructure exists.

The architecture of an on-site paging system is illustrated in Figure 3.5.

Cell sites are located throughout the campus to be served. They are controlled by a paging controller that is tied to the PBX. A messaging application is typically provided to run on a PC.

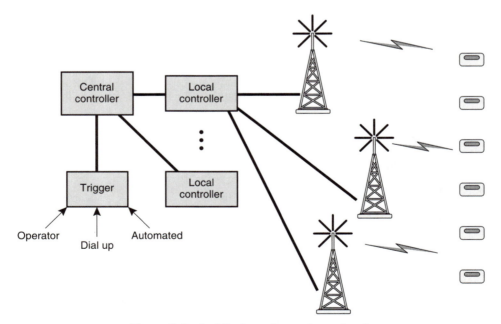

**Figure 3.4** Architecture of a paging network.

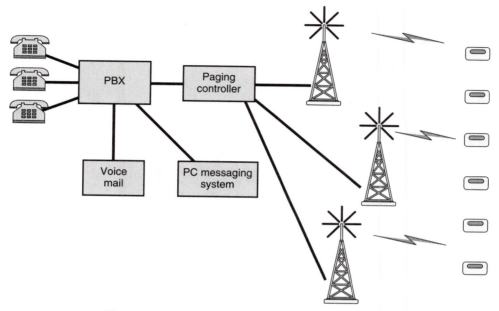

**Figure 3.5**   Architecture of an on-site paging system.

The paging system is usually tied to the voice mail system so that it can alert users that they have voice mail waiting.

In the US, paging began over 30 years ago. Today well over 10 million paging users are in the US. Today's users send mostly just a phone number to call. Some users send brief text messages and short electronic mail. Simple paging has survived because it is reliable and cost effective, and because a pager can run on a single battery for a month or more.

Advanced paging has been available for a number of years. It is still one-way receive, like simple paging, but the data rate is higher, being on the order of 2400 bps instead of about 200 bps for simple paging. The Motorola EMBARC service is an example. The EMBARC network uses land line connections to hosts. It uses satellite transmission to connect the base station to the central controller, as illustrated in Figure 3.6.

It is still one-way broadcast to the users. The advanced pagers are about the same size as the simple pagers but they are significantly more expensive. The advanced pagers are also available in PCMCIA form factor for use as receivers in notebook computers and PDAs. Sample NewsStream services are:

- USA TODAY daily updates on
  - Technology
  - Investing

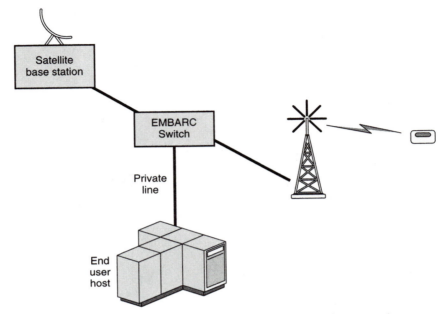

**Figure 3.6**   The Motorola EMBARC advanced paging network.

- Sports
- Health
- Real estate
- Business
- News and weather
- Updates from company's offices

Beyond advanced paging, we have the new two-way paging network from companies such as SkyTel and Mtel. Two kinds of emerging two-way paging networks exist:

- Two-way asymmetrical paging networks
- Two-way symmetrical paging networks

The two-way asymmetrical paging networks use a protocol that is developed by Motorola. They are closer to today's simple one-way paging systems than the two-way symmetrical networks. These latter networks use a protocol that is developed by AT&T and resembles packet radio networks. Both the asymmetrical and symmetrical paging services use the new narrow band PCS allocation that is located in the 900 MHz band and is 50 MHz wide. This bandwidth is huge compared with that allocated to simple paging, but is still minuscule compared to the allocations for cellular and PCS.

The asymmetrical paging networks have two separate networks—one for outgoing traffic and one for incoming traffic, as you see in Figure 3.7.

The idea behind this asymmetrical structure is to keep the two-way pager as simple as possible by making the incoming network receivers more dense than the outgoing transmitters. The traffic that can be sent from this asymmetrical pager is less than the traffic it can receive. Many applications are sure to fall into this kind of pattern in which the user makes a simple query but receives a much longer response.

The symmetrical approach is very much like a packet radio network. In fact, compared to a packet network, the allocations for narrow band PCS are about the same, if not slightly more, so we can expect competitive services.

One more kind of new paging service is being built using the narrow band PCS allocations. This service is based on voice mail; the idea is to receive the actual voice mail at the pager. The pager is not text-based but is audio-based. The user can not only know when he has a voice message, he can listen to it. The success of such a service remains to be seen. Voice is a very natural medium for people. The question is whether transmitting the voice can be done efficiently over a relatively narrow band network.

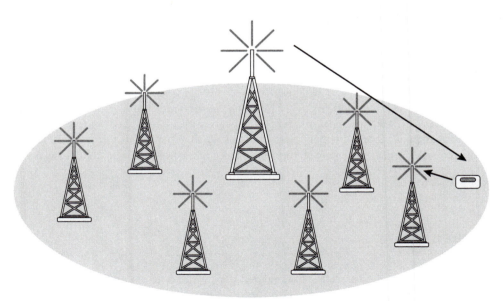

**Figure 3.7**  Asymmetrical two-way paging network.

|  | **Paging** | **Cellular** |
|---|---|---|
| Connection | Receive only | Two-way |
| Proof of receipt | Not guaranteed | Self evident |
| Message type | Alert | Voice/data |
| Size | Pocket | Handheld |
| Battery life | 3 months | 1 day |
| Battery type | Low cost disposable | Rechargeable, high cost |
| Service reliability | High | Medium |
| Relative cost | Low | High |
| Spectral efficiency | Very high | Low |

**Figure 3.8**   Comparison of paging to cellular.

## Comparison of Paging to Cellular

Figure 3.8 compares paging to cellular.

Paging and cellular are two very different services. Paging is much less expensive, more ubiquitous, and with limited applications. Its strengths are also its weaknesses. Paging never caught on in Europe. It is priced relatively high for the service it provides. GSM came out with SMS from the start. Therefore many more cellular phones than pagers exist in Europe. In the US, paging is very popular, even with teenagers, and is likely to remain so. It meets a different market niche than cellular. It can also become very powerful when combined with a PDA because of its simplicity.

## Summary

In this Chapter we discussed and compared packet radio networks such as RAM/Mobitex and ARDIS/Modacom with CDPD, data over cellular, and paging. The two packet radio services are quite similar in structure and services provided. They are presently installing networks throughout the world to achieve coverage that is satisfactory for their initial customers. CDPD leverages the investment in current cellular services by deriving a packet service from the same frequency spectrum and much of the same equipment. The CDPD standard is complete, and the consortium members are busy installing networks to span the US. Whether a CDPD service emerges in other parts of the world depends on how quickly GSM can provide a packet service like CDPD. If it is slow in providing the service, CDPD may indeed emerge in countries that have implemented GSM.

The majority of Mobile Data traffic today is carried over analog cellular. Analog cellular modems provide over 14.4 Kbps uncompressed with slightly more expense than a wired modem. Ironically, data over digital cellular is lagging behind data over analog cellular because it is provided on the basis of an equivalent voice channel. It is typically limited to about 9.6 Kbps. This speed can be increased in the future by combining equivalent voice channels. This is being considered in GSM and other digital cellular standards and could yield from 30 Kbps to over 100 Kbps.

Paging is flourishing in the US and in Asia. Its low cost, excellent coverage, and long battery life make it attractive for a significant market segment. It is not very popular in Europe because its cost is kept high and because GSM had the SMS feature from the start. Two-way paging networks use the Unlicensed PCS bands that come in 50 KHz allocations. This allocation can provide a service on par with packet radio networks.

Asymmetrical two-way paging networks exist that are similar to simple one-way paging with a higher density incoming network that allows the two-way pagers to remain simple. Also, symmetrical two-way paging networks exist that look very much like packet radio networks. Finally, some providers are using the narrow band PCS allocations to build voice messaging paging networks that deliver the voice messages themselves to the pager.

# 4 Wireless Networking Technology Primer

The great promise of Wireless Networking is based on key underlying technologies that include packet radio, multiple access, security, and spread spectrum. In this chapter, we discuss:

- Microwave and infrared wireless media
- FHSS and DSSS spread spectrum technology
- Media Access Control (MAC) techniques
- Hidden nodes in Wireless Networking
- Ordered MAC techniques and Wireless Networks
- Deterministic MACs
- Comparison of MAC techniques for Wireless Networks
- Security alternatives
- Infrared technology

## Microwave and Infrared Wireless Media

Most Wireless Networking traffic is carried in the microwave frequency bands; some is carried in the infrared band. Infrared is playing an increasing role in short-range wireless communications. Most microwave bands are licensed. Some are unlicensed. Some are unlicensed and require spread spectrum technology. This categorization is shown in Figure 4.1.

The services that use licensed microwave bands are cellular, paging, Specialized Mobile Radio, and Personal Communications Services. Network operators obtain the licenses from the regulatory agency of the country they are operating in and have exclusive use of that license in a particular area of the country for a duration of time, on the order of 10 years. During those 10 years

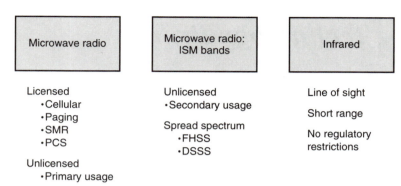

**Figure 4.1** Wireless media.

they are required to use the license and serve the population of that part of the country. They cannot have the license and not use it. Bandwidth is regarded as a resource that can yield services that the public wants and needs, and the holder of a license is required to provide services on the band for which they hold licenses.

A new type of band allocation exists that is unlicensed but primary. First, let us discuss the Industrial, Scientific, and Medical bands. These bands have a number of uses. Some equipment in the medical, scientific, and industrial fields does radiate without the intent of communicating. Their radiation occurs in these bands. An example is microwave ovens, which radiate in the 2.4 GHz band. Also, point-to-point microwave operators hold licenses in these bands. They are the primary users of the bands. Some time ago, some innovative manufacturers suggested to the FCC that they could make use of these bands without disturbing the primary users of the licenses. They proposed using a technology that arose in defense systems to spread the spectrum of their signals to such an extent that they don't interfer with the primary user. The FCC agreed and hence Part 15 of the ruling. Part 15 specifies secondary users can use the band if the spectrum is spread in such a way that it will not interfere with the primary user. No license is required, just type approval to insure that the equipment meets the spreading rules.

Two spreading schemes are available, Frequency Hopping Spread Spectrum and Direct Sequence Spread Spectrum. Both these methods are fairly complex. They require the manufacturer to develop equipment that is more expensive, and that has less performance than equipment that could have primary use of the band. That situation presently applies for the Part 15 products. Almost all present Wireless LAN products use the ISM bands.

A number of years ago, Apple Computer took the initiative to propose a new band where Wireless LANs could be primary users. This was the start of the effort to obtain the unlicensed primary use bands. Apple petitioned the FCC for 40 or more MHz of spectrum for Wireless LANs. The FCC was in the process of defining the bands that are now allocated to PCS. The bands requested for Wireless LANs became known as the Data PCS bands. This was actually a misnomer since PCS itself provides both voice and data services. After some time, the FCC determined that Wireless LANs are a private system that is installed on a customer's premises like PBXs. Thus the

FCC requested that Apple and the other computer manufacturers who had joined the Apple effort by that time to confer with the PBX manufacturers and determine what their joint needs are.

The group, which was called Winforum, expanded from just computer companies to computer companies *and* PBX manufacturers, which are of course telephony manufacturers. This combination was a difficult one. Some euphoria existed at the start but that soon turned to mistrust, and general lack of communication and understanding. After some time, the group essentially split the request into two bands, one called the Asynchronous for Wireless LANs and one called the Isochronous band for Wireless PBXs. The bands then changed names from Data PCS to User PCS, to reflect their private use nature, and finally to Unlicensed PCS.

Why do we want unlicensed bands for Wireless LANs and Wireless PBXs? In the case of Wireless LANs, the issue is one of frequency coordination. If a notebook computer user roams from one Wireless LAN in one part of the country to another, the equipment would have to know what frequency is allocated to it in that part of the country. This coordination is manageable for public cellular systems that are provided by a network operator, but becomes a much more difficult task for a Wireless LAN user.

The great disadvantage of an unlicensed band is, of course, the chance that the band will turn into a garbage band where users overstep each other and no one can operate successfully. To insure that problem does not become the case, as it has for example in citizen's band radio, Winforum developed an industry "etiquette" that users of the band have to use. The word "etiquette" implies politeness, but this etiquette is required. A user cannot use the Unlicensed PCS bands unless they conform to the etiquette; it is checked through type approval.

Infrared transmission is not regulated, at least not yet. The reason it is not regulated is that it is very short-range, and one user will not likely interfere with another. The realm of the FCC and other regulators is to protect users from interfering with one another. Therefore, IR is very attractive since manufacturers and users do not have to be concerned with regulations and also do not have to be concerned with having to comply with different regulations in different parts of the world. One product can meet customers' needs worldwide.

A few Wireless LAN products utilize IR. We expect that by far the largest application of IR will be the very short-range point-to-point applications between notebook computers and PDAs using the newly developed Infra Red Data Association (IRDA) standard. We expect every notebook computer and PDA in the near future will have an IRDA port for short point-to-point communications with other notebooks, other PDAs, desktop computers, and a variety of shared resources.

Those media are the primary wireless media that are the basis for the products and services we discuss in the coming chapters. Now let us look at the environments to which each of the media can be applied. Figure 4.2 illustrates the possibilities.

Within a person's office, IR is perfect. It provides the needed range, and at the same time is more secure due to its limited capability to go beyond the walls of the office. The user can apply IR to communicate among the machines she has in her office, such as her notebook computer and her desktop computer, or with one or a few colleagues who may be meeting with her in her office.

Next is a conference room with dimensions on the order of 100'. In this case, IR can be used as well, although IR Wireless LANs have a range that is generally less than 100'. If the room is

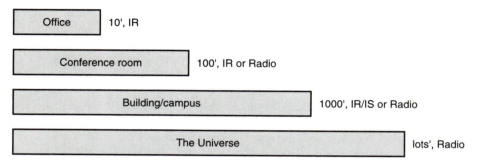

**Figure 4.2** Radio and infrared applications.

less than 30' in diameter, a one access point IR Wireless LAN system would suffice. If it is any larger, more than one access point would be needed. Some Wireless LAN products offer ad hoc networking, which requires no access point as long as all the users in the ad hoc network are within range of each other. The IRDA point-to-point IR capability mentioned above does not provide Wireless LAN connectivity. It is strictly a point-to-point service at this time. Radio can of course be used in a conference room as well as in a person's office, or in any of the other situations.

Next we have a whole building or campus. In this case, IR can be used only if a dense infrastructure of access points is installed. IR access points would have to be installed in every room with walls around it, in open spaces every 30' or so, and also down the halls about every 30' or so. This frequency may seem daunting; however, if the access points are economical enough, it can be cost effective. Finally, outdoors IR is of no use during the day due to the large amount of heat generated by the sun. Radio is required there.

The next idea that is useful in way of background to this area is the concept of a Basic Service Area and an Extended Service Area, illustrated in Figure 4.3.

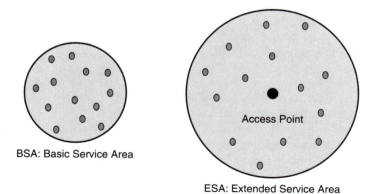

**Figure 4.3** Basic Service Area and Extended Service Area.

Within a BSA, everyone can communicate with everyone else directly. As a result, an ad hoc network can take place in a BSA; no access point is needed. An ESA is served by an Access Point. Users within an ESA can communicate directly with each other, or if they are out of range of direct communications, they have to communicate through the Access Point. If the range of the radio or IR system is x meters, then the *diameter* of a BSA is x meters, whereas the *radius* of an ESA is x meters. So the area of an ESA is roughly four times as large as a BSA using the same radio or IR system. It is not exactly twice as large because the Access Point may be elevated, thus slightly decreasing the size of the served area at floor level.

Most systems use Access Points. Having Access Points not only increases the range of the system, but also provides connectivity to the backbone network where most of the information and services reside. The APs are then connected together and to backbone networks via whatever network technology the user has—for example, Ethernet as you see in Figure 4.4.

The types of backbone networks that may require connection include:

- Wired LANs, including standard LANs and de facto standard LANS, such as
  - Ethernet
  - Token Ring
  - Novell networks
  - TCP/IP networks
  - Microsoft networks
- Wired Wide Area Networks, present and future
  - Telephony networks
  - High bandwidth WANs, and Metropolitan Area Networks

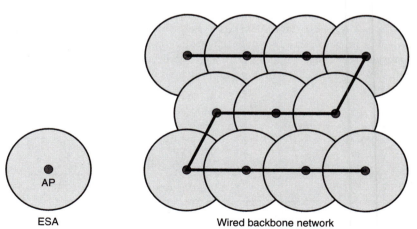

**Figure 4.4** ESA and backbone network.

- Cellular networks, and Personal Communications Services networks
- Satellite networks

# FHSS and DSSS Spread Spectrum Technology

Next let us discuss spread spectrum technology that we have to use in the ISM bands. The two major methods of spread spectrum technology are Frequency Hopping Spread Spectrum and Direct Sequence Spread Spectrum. These techniques reside at the physical layer. Figure 4.5 shows the first three layers of the ISO protocol stack.

The first layer is the physical or "PHY" layer. The second layer is the Data Link layer. It has two sub-layers, the Medium Access Control sub-layer and the Logical Link Control sub-layer. The third layer is the network layer. The upper four layers are the Transport layer, which is responsible for reliable transmission of data, so among other functions it handles ACKs and NACKs. The fifth layer is the Session layer, the sixth is the Presentation layer, and the seventh is the Application layer.

The responsibility of the Physical later is to transmit bits over the medium. Here the capacity of the channel is determined. Given a certain number of MHz, the physical layer, through choice of modulation technique, determines how many Mbps can be sent over that bandwidth.

Most systems modulate the information onto a carrier centered in the spectrum allocation. Alternatively, they divide the allocation into smaller channels in frequency and modulate a carrier in the center of each of those channels. In a few cases, the most notable of which is infrared, the information is sent at base band. This process involves putting the information directly onto the infrared energy of the medium. The information then turns the infrared energy on and off rapidly in response to the information bit stream.

Most Wireless LANs use the ISM bands as secondary users. They must use a spread spectrum technique in order not to interfere with the primary user who holds the license for that band. If in fact the primary user can show that someone is interfering with his license, he can ask the regulator to stop the interferer. FHSS is illustrated in Figure 4.6.

| Layer 3 | Network | Internet protocols |
|---------|---------|--------------------|
| Layer 2 | Data Link | Logical Link Control (LLC) |
| | | Medium Access Control (MAC) |
| Layer 1 | Physical | Physical (PHY) |

**Figure 4.5**  Protocol layers.

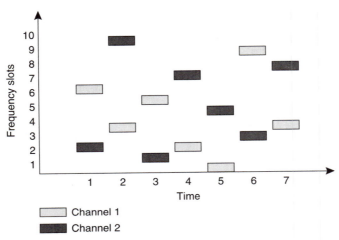

**Figure 4.6**    Frequency Hopping Spread Spectrum.

In order not to interfere with the primary user, the FHSS system must hop its whole information signal over the band of frequencies of the ISM band in use. As an example, Figure 4.6 supposes that ten frequency slots exist in the band. The system sends the information signal in frequency slot 6 for the first time slot, then frequency slot 3 for the second time slot, then frequency slot 5 for the third time slot, and so on. A user wishing to receive this channel number 1 must tune its receiver to frequency slot 6 for the first time slot, and frequency slot 3 for the second time slot, and frequency slot 5 for the third time slot, and so on.

Channel 2 is distinguished from channel 1 by having a different frequency hopping pattern. Channel 2 uses frequency slot 2 then frequency slot 9, then frequency slot 1, and so on. The receiver of channel 2 must hop his receiver according to this pattern. So each channel is a different frequency hopping pattern. It is not a different *frequency* as in Frequency Division Multiplexing; it is a different *frequency hopping pattern.* If it were FDM, then each channel would simply stay on one frequency slot for the duration of the transmission.

The typical bandwidth of the information signal is 1 MHz, and the typical length of the time slots is 0.1 seconds. How does FHSS help to not interfere with the primary user? To answer this question, drawing Figure 4.6 more or less to scale is helpful. We will take the 2.4 GHz ISM as an example since it is the one that is available worldwide. The real situation appears in Figure 4.7, where about 15 channels, each representing a different frequency hopping pattern, are placed in the space of 80 MHz, and the time slots are 0.1 seconds long. This bandwidth is available at 2.4 GHz.

The space does seem rather full. It would in fact be at most 15/80 or 12.5% full, and the maximum power allowed is 1 watt. The primary user usually has a much greater power limit, so the level of interference should not be noticeable to the primary user.

What would happen if the primary user were transmitting in his band? This scenario is represented in Figure 4.8.

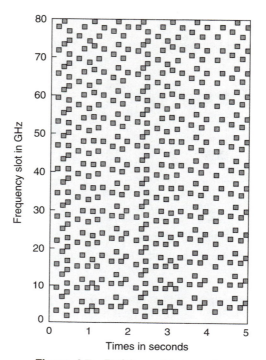

**Figure 4.7**   FHSS roughly to scale.

In this case, the FHSS frequency slots that encounter the primary user will lose those packets. How much degradation does that loss cause? For every primary user about 1/80 or 1.25% of the throughput. For the example shown, the throughput would be degraded by about 2.5% due to the two primary users transmitting.

Direct Sequence Spread Spectrum operates quite differently as illustrated in Figure 4.9.

The input data stream, which is running at 1 Mbps, is multiplied by a chip stream running 11 times faster at 11 Mcps. A chip is a zero or a one, just like a bit. And just like a "bit," the word "chip" is not an acronym. It is called a chip to distinguish it from a bit. Many more chips exist than do bits. In fact, exactly 11 times more chips exist than do bits. When the bit stream is thus multiplied, its frequency spectrum becomes spread out as shown. It occupies about 11 times as much bandwidth, and its spectral energy is about 11 times lower. It is so low that it does not interfere with the primary user. Of course, as more and more DSSS systems occupy the band, the overall noise level rises. This rise causes the DSSS systems to degrade in performance, and the interference to the primary user to increase a bit. The increased interference to the DSSS users is expected to become a problem long before the primary user notices any interference.

At the receiver, the input chip stream is multiplied by the same coded chip stream that was used at the transmitter. The two codes are synchronised. The result is that the original bit stream is

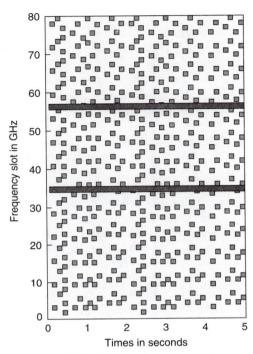

**Figure 4.8**   FHSS with two primary users transmitting.

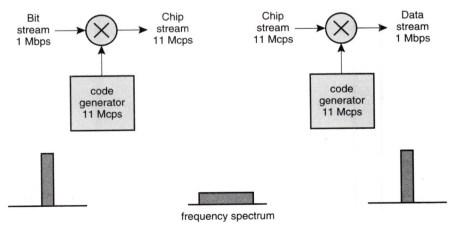

**Figure 4.9**   Direct Sequence Spread Spectrum.

correlated. Any interference on the air, when it goes through the correlator, becomes spread out, as you see in Figure 4.10.

The amount of the interference energy is reduced by the spreading factor. This condition anti-jamming effect makes this technology useful for defense applications. The DSSS continues to operate at its stated throughput. As more and more interference is introduced in the channel, the noise level increases until even though it is spread out by the correlator, it still becomes too much for the DSSS system to operate. At that point, the DSSS system stops working and the throughput declines to zero.

The degradation of the FHSS and DSSS in the presence of interference is thus quite different. FHSS degrades gradually, and DSSS degrades rather drastically. Figure 4.11 illustrates this fact.

The steps of degradation in the FHSS case are about 1.25% of the total throughput. The steps of degradation in the DSSS are not 100%, but rather 50% because in most cases, the DSSS system is designed so that it uses about one-third to one-half of the band so it can allow for interference to occur without losing the whole system. This difference is another major one between FHSS and DSSS. FHSS can provide on the order of 10 to 15 channels, each with a different frequency hopping pattern. DSSS usually can only provide two or three channels separated by frequency in the band.

One advantage to DSSS is that the instantaneous data rate can be larger than in FHSS. With FHSS, the maximum bandwidth of the signal is specified to be 1 MHz at the 2.4 GHz band, so the data rate is limited to realistically 1 or 2 Mbps. With DSSS, the rule is to spread by at least a factor of 11. Theoretically then, a possibility is to use the whole 80 MHz band and provide a data rate on the order of 6 or 7 Mbps. This would mean that the circuitry would have to run at a very high rate of 66 or 77 Mbps in order to generate the chip stream necessary to support the 6 or 7 Mbps bit rate. This high rate would be very expensive and we do not see such systems in the industry at this time.

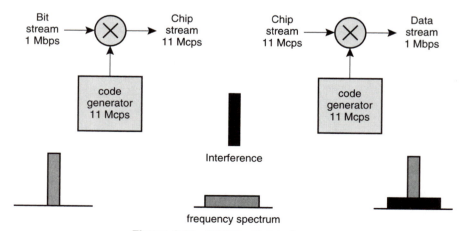

**Figure 4.10**  DSSS with interference.

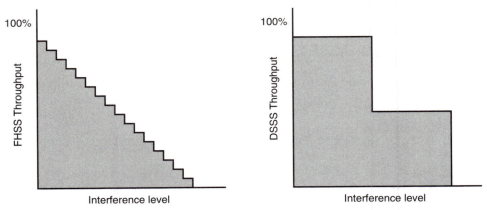

**Figure 4.11**   FHSS and DSSS throughput in the presence of interference.

To summarize the comparison between FHSS and DSSS, we have:

- FHSS
  - Can have up to 10 or 15 channels
  - Each channel can provide 1 or 2 Mbps
  - Degrades in steps of 1.25% in the presence of interference
- DSSS
  - Can have up to two or three channels
  - Each channel can provide 1 or 2 Mbps
  - Degrades in steps of perhaps 50% in the presence of interference

# Medium Access Control

Now let us discuss the alternatives and how they compare for the MAC layer of Figure 4.5. First, the responsibility of the MAC sub-layer is to define how a user obtains a channel when he needs one. The sub-layer right above the MAC, the Logical Link Control sub-layer, is where the framing takes place. In constructing the frame, the LLC inserts certain fields in the frame such as the source address and the destination address at the head end of the frame, and error handling bits at the end of the frame.

The alternatives for the MAC layer are organized in Figure 4.12 according to whether they are random, ordered, deterministic, or some combination.

ALOHA and CSMA are examples of random access MACs.

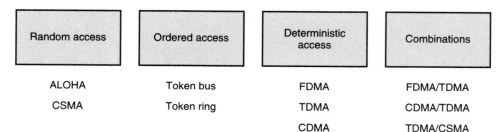

**Figure 4.12** Medium Access Control alternatives.

At this point, let us briefly discuss packet radio, its prime applications, and its origin.

Packet radio is a set of systems that is best suited for data transmission because of its packet nature. In particular, it is best suited for the bursty type of data transmission that we find in many wired LANs, Wireless LANs, and Mobile Data systems. The first well-known packet radio system was implemented in the University of Hawaii. The system was used to connect the campuses of the University of Hawaii on each of the islands. The system is relatively narrow band, and is in the lower region of the microwave band. The access protocol for the University of Hawaii system was a very simple system called ALOHA. ALOHA is not an acronym; it simply means Hello and Goodbye in Hawaiian. Many modern packet radio systems employ a very similar access mechanism—for example, the Motorola network, which is known as ARDIS in the US and as Modacom in other parts of the world, and Mobitex, the Ericsson packet radio network. As Appendix C shows, the maximum throughput of slotted ALOHA is about 36% of the data rate of the channel. It is very simple, but it is not very efficient.

The various random access MAC techniques are:

- ALOHA
  - Asynchronous ALOHA
  - Slotted ALOHA
- CSMA
  - CSMA/CA: Collision Avoidance
  - CSMA/CD: Collision Detection
  - Nonpersistent
  - P-persistent

These techniques and their performance are detailed in Appendix C. The most common scheme that is used in Wireless LANs is CSMA/CA. Figure 4.13 shows the performance curve of CSMA as compared with pure ALOHA and slotted ALOHA.

CSMA peaks at about 60%. Still, when the traffic becomes heavy, it degrades badly. Ways of dealing with that situation exist, including using p-persistence. Other ways, discussed shortly, are combining CSMA with TDMA.

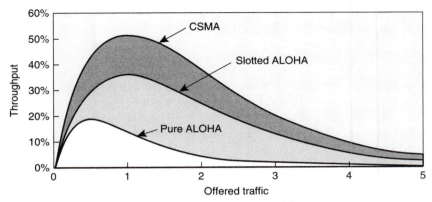

**Figure 4.13** Performance of CSMA.

The degradation in performance results not only in reduced overall throughput, but also in rapidly increased delay time as Figure 4.14 shows.

To avoid this catastrophic drop in performance, most network administrators plan their networks to operate well below this knee in the response time curve. Typical points of operation are at about 30% of the data rate. So, for Ethernet with a data rate of 10 Mbps, the planned operating point is at about 3 Mbps. For a 1 Mbps Wireless LAN, the planned operating point is also usually in the neighborhood of 30% of the data rate, or about 300 Kbps.

Carrier sense in a wired network means listening to the medium, which is the network cable. In a Wireless LAN defining the cable is not so straightforward. Is it everyone in the Basic Service Area? Or is it everyone in the Extended Service Area? Or is it some other set of nodes? This situation gives rise to the problem of hidden nodes.

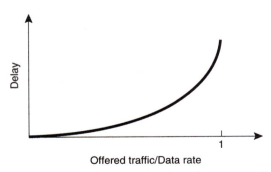

**Figure 4.14** Delay performance of random access MACs.

## Hidden Nodes in Wireless Networks

Figure 4.15 depicts the situation.

Imagine three nodes more or less in a line—nodes A, B, and C. Node A wants to send a packet to node B. It listens for carrier, hears nothing, and transmits. As Figure 4.15 shows, B is within its area of coverage. Meanwhile, node C, which is within range of node B but outside of range from node A, also wants to send a packet to node B, so it also transmits at about the same time. The two packets collide at node B. This collision is the hidden node problem in Wireless Networks. In effect, nodes A and C are hidden from each other and yet they can cause collision at an intermediate node such as node B.

We could do nothing about hidden nodes. The result would be degraded performance, and frequent retransmissions due to collisions such as the one described. Most Wireless LAN vendors and the 802.11 standard use the following method for dealing with hidden nodes. Figure 2.16 illustrates the process.

When node A wants to send a packet to node B, it first sends a Request To Send packet indicating when and how much data it would like to send. Node B sends back a Clear To Send packet with the amount of data and the time of transmission back to node A. What makes the technique work is that now node C can hear the CTS packet sent by node B. It and other nodes use the following modified algorithm for accessing the network (it is essentially CSMA/CA modified to work in the presence of hidden nodes):

- Check to see if a carrier is present
- If no carrier is present, check the table of CTSs to see if anyone that you cannot hear is transmitting at this point in time
- If no carrier is present and the table indicates that the medium is free of transmitting hidden nodes, then transmit.

The RTS/CTS algorithm does add overhead to the network as well as delay. It is chosen by most designers because it makes the overall performance better than ignoring hidden nodes and relying on retransmissions.

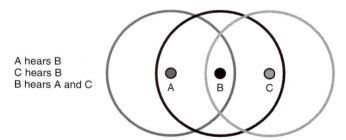

A hears B
C hears B
B hears A and C

**Figure 4.15**   Hidden nodes in Wireless Networks.

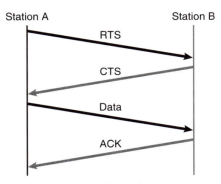

**Figure 4.16** RTS/CTS/ACK protocol.

This protocol was actually invented at Apple Computer and is used in the AppleTalk protocol stack. AppleTalk uses CSMA/CA. In contrast, Ethernet uses CSMA/CD, or Collision Detection. CSMA/CD offers second-order improvement over CSMA in the following way.

- If the channel is free, transmit and continue to listen for collisions
- If a collision is detected, stop transmitting the present packet since it will be destroyed anyway
- Wait a random time, and repeat

Is CSMA/CD possible in a Wireless Network? It requires that the node transmit and receive at the same time so it can detect whether its own transmission is colliding with another node's transmission. In a CSMA network, nodes transmit and receive on the same frequency band. No up link and down link frequency bands exist like we have in cellular—not usually. Receiving at the same time as transmitting would be fatal to the receiver. Thus, CSMA/CD is not usually used in Wireless Networks, and we forego the second-order improvement.

## Ordered MAC Techniques and Wireless Networks

I want to say a quick word about ordered techniques such as Token Bus and Token Ring and whether they can be applied to Wireless Networks. As mentioned above, Token Bus and Token Ring are examples of ordered MAC protocols. They are called ordered protocols because they are not random, and yet they are not controlled by a central control point that allocates channels.

In a Token Bus, the nodes are arranged in a logical bus. Each station is aware of its two nearest neighbors. The station with the token transmits if it has something to transmit. Afterwords, it passes the token to the next node in the logical bus. A Token Bus is passive—the nodes do not regenerate the signal. For this reason, the maximum length of a Token Bus is limited to about 1 kilometer.

Can a Token Bus be applied to a Wireless Network? It would require that the nodes have a logical order. What would happen if a node leaves the vicinity of the bus? The logical order would be broken, and the bus would cease to function unless some reordering algorithm is developed. For this reason, Token Buses are not usually considered for Wireless Networks.

In a Token Ring, the nodes are also ordered, except their logical order is their physical order on the Token Ring cable. The station with the token transmits if it has a packet to transmit. Otherwise, it passes the token to the next node on the ring. Each node does regenerate the signal, unlike Token Bus, which is passive. For this reason, Token Rings can be longer than Token Buses. The ring is susceptible to single node failure. Therefore, Token Ring systems have two counter-rotating rings. If the ring fails in one direction, the other direction becomes the backup network.

Can we use Token Ring networks for Wireless Networks? The same problem that arose with Token Buses arises for Token Rings as well. Because the nodes are moving, they often leave the vicinity of the ring and break its order.

## Deterministic MACs for Wireless Networks

In a deterministic MAC, when a node needs channel capacity, it must request a channel from a control point. This procedure of course, will slow down the lightning fast access times of random access techniques. We consider deterministic techniques for two reasons:

- To improve the throughput and response time when traffic is heavy
- To offer isochronous traffic the guaranteed bandwidth it requires

FDMA, TDMA, and CDMA are examples of deterministic techniques. The one that fits in most easily with CSMA is TDMA. In fact, the method that is suggested is CSMA/TDMA. It would work as follows:

- A frame is introduced into the system
- The frame is divided into a random access part and a reserved part
- A control point monitors the channel
- When the traffic is light, it is left to be mostly random
- When the traffic is heavy and the throughput is in danger of declining, or if a node requires isochronous bandwidth, the control point allocates bandwidth deterministically

CSMA/TDMA approaches CSMA performance under light traffic, so it has very fast access time. It approaches TDMA performance when the traffic becomes heavy, so its throughput can rise to close to 100% of the data rate. It does, however, require additional complexity and a control point. The performance is depicted in Figure 4.17.

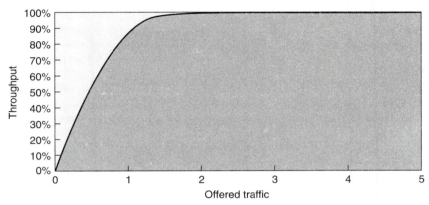

**Figure 4.17**    Performance of CSMA/TDMA.

# Comparison of MAC Techniques for Wireless Networks

We have discussed four kinds of MAC techniques for Wireless Networks: Random access MACs, ordered MACs, deterministic MACs, and combinations. The ordered techniques are not used for Wireless Networks. The other three are compared below:

- Random protocols: CSMA
  - Under light load: Fast response time
  - Under heavy load: Throughput declines
  - Simple to implement
- Deterministic protocols: FDMA, TDMA, CDMA
  - Able to provide guaranteed bandwidth
  - Larger average delay
  - Smaller delay variance
- Mixture: CSMA/TDMA
  - Under light load: Fast response time
  - Under heavy load: Throughput approaches TDMA
  - Higher overhead

Most Wireless LANs implement a random protocol, specifically CSMA/CA with some modifications to deal with hidden nodes. Most Mobile Data networks also use a random protocol, usually one that is simpler, namely slotted ALOHA. Some new entrants to the market are using the mixed CSMA/TDMA idea.

## Security Alternatives

The vulnerability of Wireless Networks to intrusion is obvious and is such a concern that a great deal of attention is paid to security in Wireless Networks. For this reason, Wireless Networks will most likely end up being more secure than wired networks. In wired networks, we have a false sense of security because the information is running on a wire that is physically within a building or campus. At the same time, gaining physical access to the medium is often easy as well as using a device such as a network sniffer and having access to every packet on the network. Moreover, physical cables radiate, and that radiation can be picked up with sensitive receivers. With Wireless Networks the vulnerability is so apparent, that security is addressed thoroughly and dealt with through positive means that protect the Wireless Networks well.

Four different kinds of security issues exist:

- Authentification of users before they gain access to the network
- Privacy of the information
- Privacy of the location of the user
- Digital signature

Privacy of the location of the user is not one that is usually dealt with in Wireless Data Networks. It is dealt with in cellular and Personal Communications Services networks. In Wireless Data Networks, it has not been an issue as yet because the cell sizes of Mobile Data networks are quite large, sometimes encompassing a small city. With Wireless LANs, the network is private in an office building or campus, and privacy of the location of the employees has not surfaced as an issue.

Authentification, privacy of the information, and digital signature can use one of two alternatives for security:

- Symmetric keys
- An example is Data Encryption Standard (DES)
- Asymmetric keys, or public keys
- An example is Rivest/Shamir/Adelman (RSA)

DES was developed by IBM for the National Bureau of Standards. RSA was invented by the people that constitute its acronym. It was patented by MIT in 1978.

The symmetric key uses a key to encrypt the data and its inverse to decrypt it, as follows:

- Clear signal        $s(t)$
- Encrypted signal $c(t) = K [ s(t) ]$
- Decrypted signal $s(t) = K^{-1} [ c(t) ]$
- Symmetric key    $K[ \ldots ]$.

This encryption is depicted in Figure 4.18.

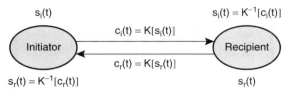

**Figure 4.18**   Symmetric key operation.

The initiator encrypts her signal with the symmetric key K. The recipient decrypts it with the inverse of the key. The recipient uses the same key to send information back to the initiator, and the initiator uses the inverse of the same key to decrypt it. One issue with symmetric keys is where the two users obtain the key—the problem of key distribution. This problem becomes more complex if users need to change the key often to increase the level of security.

The asymmetric or public key scheme is quite different and simplifies the problem of key distribution. It is depicted in Figure 4.19.

When a user initially obtains his Wireless Network adaptor, he is issued a pair of keys—a private key and a public key. The private key he keeps secret; the public key is known by anyone who needs to send him a message. For example, it would be available on servers. When the initiator wants to send a packet to the recipient, he encrypts it with the public key of the recipient. He obtains the public key of the recipient from a server as mentioned. The only way to decrypt this message is by using its asymmetric other half, which is the private key of the recipient. Decrypting the message with any other private key would result in noise.

When the recipient sends a message back to the initiator, she encrypts it with the public key of the initiator. The only way to decrypt that message is to use the private key of the initiator.

Digital signature uses the public key and private key pair in reverse to convince someone that the initiator is who he says he is. This procedure occurs as Figure 4.20 shows.

As an example, suppose that John would like to order some merchandise from an Internet store. He sends the order, signed by his name encrypted in his private key. The only way to make sense out of his signature is to decrypt it with his public key. The merchant does so and is convinced that it must have been John, because he is the only one who knows his private key. Digital

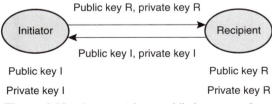

**Figure 4.19**   Asymmetric or public key operation.

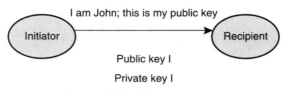

**Figure 4.20**   Digital signature.

signatures have far-reaching implications. Internet commerce with Wireless Networks as the on ramp are just the beginning.

Public keys are very secure. They are based on the difficulty of factoring the product of two very large prime numbers. Advances have occurred in factoring and testing of primality. These advances have barely dented the strength of the algorithms. However, public keys are complex and require processing power and time, both of which are not plentiful resources in a portable device powered by batteries. Furthermore, public keys are so strong that some governments do not allow them because having them listen in and perform national security functions becomes too difficult. For both these reasons, a combination of the public key scheme and the symmetric key scheme is often used. This combined method appears in Figure 4.21.

To start the conversation, the initiator picks a symmetric key and encrypts it with the recipient's public key. The recipient decrypts the symmetric key with his private key and stores it. The initiator then encrypts the message with the symmetric key. The recipient uses the same symmetric key to answer the initiator.

This combination key method has several advantages. It uses the strong public key method to protect the symmetric key, and hence has a good way of key distribution. The symmetric key can be changed as frequently as desired. It uses the symmetric key to encrypt the information, so it does not tax the processors in the limited portable devices. It is very secure, but not so extremely secure that governments would disallow it. Many vendors and standards use this combination scheme to provide security.

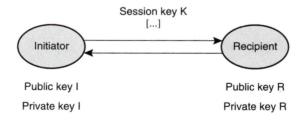

Session key encrypted using public/private keys
Messages encrypted in session key

**Figure 4.21**   Combination keys.

The evaluation of the three methods is summarized below:

- Public keys are
  - More secure
  - More complex
- Symmetric keys are
  - Simpler
  - Need to be distributed for each session
- Combination keys
  - Can use a public key to distribute a symmetric key
  - Message encrypted in symmetric key
  - Faster processing

The questions to ask when acquiring a security method are:

- What method is used?
- Are the algorithms standard?
- How are the keys distributed?
- Can they be used internationally?

Products on the market include a product by Digital Equipment Corporation called DESNC. It is a DES product for Ethernet LANs. It is a four port unit that isolates a LAN segment and makes it secure. Another product is from Semaphor. This product divides the LAN into sub nets that are encrypted. It uses RSA for key distribution, and DES to encrypt the information. A product from Cylink protects inter-LAN communications and LAN-to-WAN connections. It also uses RSA for key distribution, and DES to encrypt the data.

NetWare 4.0 also uses this combination scheme. When a new user ID is created, a private and a public key pair is generated for the user. The user's private key is stored encrypted by the user's password and used to create symmetric keys to encrypt data.


# Infrared Technology

In this section, we discuss infrared sources, the channel model for infrared transmission, and base band modulation schemes over infrared channels. The two main sources of infrared are Light Emitting Diodes (LEDs) and laser diodes. The two are compared below:

- Laser diodes
  - Sub nanosecond switching times
  - Good power efficiency
  - Expensive
  - Require complex drivers
  - Perceived hazard
- LEDs
  - Inexpensive
  - Sub microsecond switching times
  - Low power efficiency

This comparison continues in Figure 4.22 when the duty cycle is below 1%, and in Figure 4.23 for a higher duty cycle (>50%).

Figure 4.24 shows specific diodes and their operating parameters.

LEDs are evolving to become more and more effective. They are available in heat sinkable packages so they can operate at higher duty cycles and last longer. They are becoming available with faster switching times so they can support higher data rates. They are also becoming available in higher radiant flux levels so they provide greater range.

A typical IR transmitter block diagram appears in Figure 4.25.

The data bits are encoded. Line coding shapes the spectrum and eases the synchronization function. Error coding increases performance and reduces power needs. Then it is modulated. The most popular methods of modulation at base band for IR transmission is On Off Keying, and Pulse Position Modulation. We show examples of these shortly. Figure 4.26 shows the corresponding IR receiver.

| Duty Cycle <1% | LED | Laser diode |
|---|---|---|
| Optical output power | 300 mw | 3 w |
| Electrical input power | 3.8 w | 10 w |
| Rise/fall time | 10 ns | 0.5 ns |
| Efficiency | 0.08 | 0.3 |
| Cost | 0.7 | 2500 |
| Cost/w | $2.33/w | $833/w |

**Figure 4.22**   LEDs and laser diodes with low duty cycle.

| Duty Cycle >50% | LED | Laser diode |
|---|---|---|
| Optical output power | 45 mw | 3 w |
| Electrical input power | 0.27 w | 10.7 w |
| Rise/fall time | 10 ns | 0.5 ns |
| Efficiency | 0.167 | 0.28 |
| Cost | 0.7 | 2500 |
| Cost/w | $15.56/w | $833/w |

**Figure 4.23**   LEDs and laser diodes with high duty cycle.

| Manufacturer | Siemens | Stanley | Hamamatsu | Hitachi |
|---|---|---|---|---|
| Part number | SFH 34V2 | DN 304 | L 3989 | HE 8812 SG |
| Forward current (ma) | 100 | 50 | 50 | 50 |
| Voltage (v) | 1.5 | 1.55 | 1.45 | 1.5 |
| Max rev current (ua) | 1 | 100 | 20 | 100 |
| Junction C (pF) | 120 | 65 | 100 | 30 |
| Radiant flux (mw) | 11 | 15 | 8 | 14 |
| Center wavelength (nm) | 830 | 850 | 830 | 870 |
| Half bandwidth (nm) | 36 | 40 | 40 | 30 |
| Half intensity angle (deg) | 9 | 35 | 80 | 57 |
| Response time (ns) | 20 | 10 | 10 | 10 |
| DC efficiency | 0.073 | 0.193 | 0.11 | 0.187 |

**Figure 4.24**   LED operating parameters.

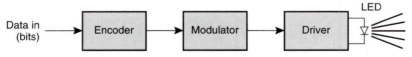

**Figure 4.25**   IR transmitter block diagram.

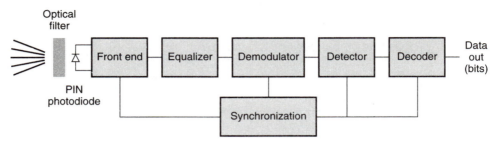

**Figure 4.26**  IR receiver block diagram.

The received IR energy is first filtered by an optical filter that passes the wavelengths of the diode, but not the other wavelengths incident on the receiver. Then a PIN photo diode turns the IR energy into electrical energy in the front end. Next come the equalizer, demodulator, detector, and decoder.

IR systems have to contend with a different channel model from radio. The sources of interference for IR systems are sunlight and artificial lights. Incandescent lights generate heat and are thus a source of IR energy. Fluorescent lamps have harmonics that can interfere with IR systems as well. Multipath affects IR systems in the same way it does radio systems. Its potential for causing Inter Symbol Interference depends on the room dimensions and can limit the maximum data rates to somewhere in the neighborhood of 1 to 2 Mbps.

The two most commonly used modulation schemes for IR systems are On Off Keying (OOK), and Pulse Position Modulation (PPM). Figure 4.27 depicts an OOK base band modulation scheme.

The Non Return to Zero bit stream is shown at the top of Figure 4.27. OOK Manchester sends a pulse of IR energy in the first half of the bit period for a one, and a pulse in the second half of the bit period for a zero. Manchester encoding is used in Ethernet and is easy to implement. It provides easy clock recovery because one transition occurs in every bit period. It has minimum DC component, and thus it has little power component at low frequencies, and we can use high pass filters for interference rejection. However, its baud rate is double the information bit rate. This is in essence requires 4.5 more dB in power.

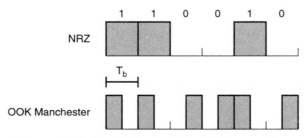

**Figure 4.27**  On Off Keying Manchester encoding.

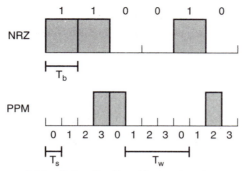

**Figure 4.28** Pulse Position Modulation (2 bit word).

Figure 4.28 illustrates pulse Position Modulation.

The example shown in Figure 4.28 is for a 2 bit word. This means that words of 2 bits each are first put together, and a single pulse is sent to represent each word. A coding step is required, and the coding used in Figure 4.28 appears in Figure 4.29.

The first word in Figure 4.28 is a "11", so the pulse is sent in the third position. The second word is a "00", so the pulse is sent in the zeroth position. The next word is a "10", so the pulse is sent in the second position.

PPM uses a single pulse for each two bits, so it has low average power. Its synchronization is more complex because it has very few transitions, and it requires both slot and symbol synchronization. The PPM IR transmitter is depicted in Figure 4.30.

The data passes through the encoder, the PPM modulator, and the LED driver.

The corresponding PPM IR receiver appears in Figure 4.31.

An optical filter reduces the effect of shot noise and other optical interference. A PIN photodiode turns the IR energy into electrical energy in the front end. Next comes a matched filter to the transmitted signal and finally the detector, which yields the information bits.

The two base band modulation schemes are compared below:

| Word | Pulse position |
|------|----------------|
| "00" | 0 |
| "01" | 1 |
| "10" | 2 |
| "11" | 3 |

**Figure 4.29** Word code for the PPM example.

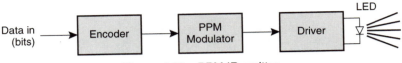

**Figure 4.30**   PPM IR emitter.

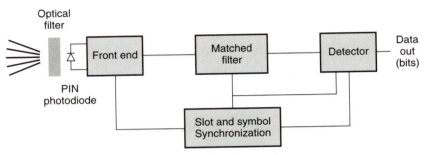

**Figure 4.31**   PPM IR receiver.

- OOK Manchester
  - Good spectral shape
  - Easy synchronization
  - Simple implementation
  - Poor receiver sensitivity
- PPM
  - Improved receiver sensitivity
  - Lower average optical power
  - Increased complexity

## Summary

In this chapter, we presented a series of topics that are the basis for Wireless Networking technologies to be discussed in later chapters. We started with spread spectrum techniques. We described FHSS and DSSS and compared them in detail. Apparently, FHSS is superior, given today's processing speeds. We discussed MAC alternatives including slotted ALOHA, CSMA/CA, and possible combinations with TDMA. Slotted ALOHA is most often found in Mobile Data networks. CSMA/CA is usually found in Wireless LANs, and a beginning is underway to use combined

CSMA/TDMA in some of the newer products to improve the throughput under heavy load and to have the opportunity of providing asynchronous service as well as isochronous service. We discussed the problem of hidden nodes in Wireless Networks and ways of dealing with them by use of the RTS/CTS/ACK protocol.

We discussed security alternatives for Wireless Networks, including public keys and symmetric keys, and showed how a combination key scheme satisfies most requirements. Finally, we reviewed infrared technology, both the sources of IR, and the most popular base band modulation schemes, namely OOK and PPM.

# 5 *Mobile Data Technologies*

The major options for carrying mobile data in the wide area are packet radio networks, paging networks, and data over circuit switched networks including cellular, mobile radio, cordless, and PCS. In this chapter, we analyze the technologies behind each of these options. In particular, we focus on:

- RAM/Mobitex network technologies
- Motorola ARDIS/Modacom network technologies
- Cellular Digital Packet Data network technologies
- A Wireless Metropolitan Area Network
- Data over cellular and related services
- Comparison of packet radio networks to data over cellular and paging
- Cell size classification

As Figure 5.1 points out, we now discuss the Mobile Data area in the networking level of the Mobile Computing diagram. And in Figure 5.2, we now address the packet data area.

Mobile Data networks have an aggregate data rate on the order of 10 to 20 Kbps. Their cell sizes can be quite large, up to tens of Kilometers. In many cases, a small city can be covered with one or a few base stations. As the demand rises, more frequencies can be used, and ultimately more cell sites can be constructed.

## The RAM/Mobitex Network Technologies

RAM/Mobitex is offered by Ericsson in most parts of the world. In the US, it is jointly owned by RAM and Bell South. Figure 5.3 illustrates network configuration.

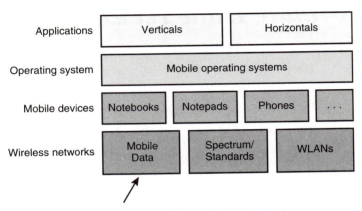

**Figure 5.1**   Mobile Computing technologies.

The Network Control Center is the heart of the network. This is where most of the network intelligence resides. It is connected through a three-level exchange network to the base stations that cover the areas of service of the network. The user's equipment comprises the end user host, the Mobidem, and the user's mobile computer. The host is connected to the network exchanges via private leased lines that are paid for by the user. At the mobile end, the user has her computing device, which is connected to the Mobidem. The Mobidem is the packet radio and packet radio modem. It talks to the base station using the Mobitex set of protocols.

The user buys the Mobidem and buys air time on the RAM/Mobitex network for a flat fee plus a charge per packet over a set monthly limit. Three plans are available, depending on how much data the user transmits. Typical monthly bills are in the range of $100. The application running on the host could be a sales support application that has its server part running in the host, and

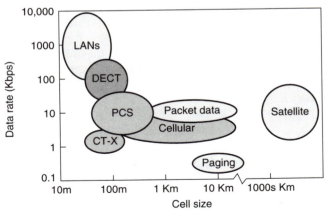

**Figure 5.2**   Relationship of services.

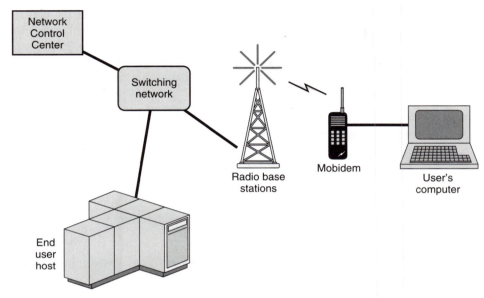

**Figure 5.3**   RAM/Mobitex network configuration.

the client part running on the mobile computers. It could be an electronic mail package. It could be a field service package.

As an example of network parameters, the RAM/Mobitex network in the US is described by:

- Transmit frequency: 896-902 GHz = 6 GHz
- Receive frequency: 935-941 GHz = 6 GHz
- 10-30 channel pairs in each metropolitan area
- Channel spacing: 12.5 KHz

The RAM/Mobitex protocol was developed by Ericsson and is open. It is available to users and value-added developers to use and enhance. As a result, RAM/Mobitex has the largest number of value-added capabilities of the packet network options.

The air interface of Mobitex is described by:

- ROSI: RadiO SIgnaling
- 0.3 GMSK: Gaussian Minimum Shift Keying with BT = 0.3
- Block interleaving
- 16 bit CRC for error detection
- Reduced Hamming code for error correction
- Selective Automatic Repeat Request

GMSK is a form of FSK with a Gaussian shaped spectrum that fits within the license spectrum shape. Block interleaving scrambles the blocks of data. This action prevents runs of errors from occurring even though the channel may impair blocks contiguous in time. Interleaving also helps error correcting codes correct errors better. In addition, CRC is performed as well as ARQ. The air interface provides a robust transmission mechanism that yields good error performance.

The terminal interface is given by:

- MASC: RAM/Mobitex ASynchronous Communications
- Handles data between the terminal and the Mobidem
- Provides control and status monitoring of the Mobidem

The network layer is:

- MPAK
- Max packet size of 512 bytes of information, plus header
- 24 bit addressing for the Mobitex number

The transport layer protocol is called MTP/1. It facilitates session based applications. Figure 5.4 shows the RAM/Mobitex packet.

The sender and receiver addresses are 24 bits each. An optional distribution list exists for multicast messages, as well as a 24 bit time stamp. The maximum throughput of the packet is 512 bytes. This equates to approximately 100 words, or about one quarter of a page of text. Many electronic mail messages are about a paragraph long, so a typical short electronic mail message could fit in one Mobitex packet.

The channel access mechanism for Mobitex is reservation slotted ALOHA. The base station transmits synchronization pulses and the number of free channels. The mobile terminal transmits during free slots. Collisions are detected by the lack of an ACK. Orders to change frequency are transmitted by the base station if required.

| Sender 3 bytes | Receiver 3 bytes | Flags 1 byte | Packet type 1 byte |
|---|---|---|---|
| Optional distribution list 22 bytes | | | |
| Time stamp 3 bytes | | | |
| Information Up to 512 bytes | | | |

**Figure 5.4**   The RAM/Mobitex packet.

The Mobitex protocol layers are depicted along with the network architecture in Figure 5.5.

The mobile computer application interfaces at layers 4-7 via the MTP/1 transport layer protocol. It communicates through the MPAK network layer and the MASC data link layer, and finally through an RS-232 physical layer that connects to the Mobidem. The Mobidem speaks MASC to the mobile computer, and ROSI over GMSK to the base station. The base station speaks ROSI over GMSK to the Mobidem, and HDLC over X.21, a circuit switched protocol to the switching hierarchy. The switches then connect to the end user host over an X.25 packet network connection.

The gateway services available on RAM/Mobitex are provided both by RAM/Mobitex directly and by third parties. A partial list appears below:

- Mobigate to hosts
  - TCP/IP
  - X.25
  - SNA 3270
- Third party gateways to hosts
  - SNA
  - AS 400
  - DECNet

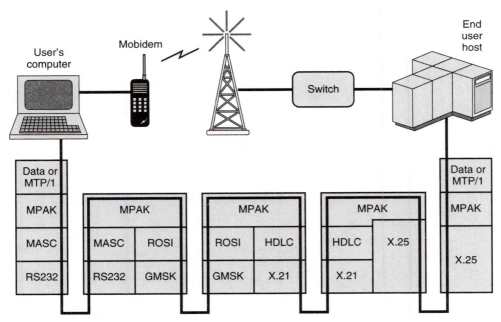

**Figure 5.5** Mobitex protocol layers.

# ARDIS/Modacom Network Technologies

The Mobile Data network provided by Motorola is called Modacom in most parts of the world. In the US it is called ARDIS. At first, it was the IBM field engineering network built for IBM by Motorola. Since that network was so extensive, IBM and Motorola decided to form a separate company, called ARDIS, and offer service on the network not just to the IBM field engineers, but also to the general public. Since then, IBM has sold its share in the network to Motorola.

The ARDIS/Modacom network configuration is depicted in Figure 5.6.

As with RAM/Mobitex, the network intelligence is concentrated in the hub. The hub is connected to the Radio Frequency Network Control Points, which control the base stations that cover the areas of service of the network. The customer has his end user host connected to the nearest RF NCP via private lines that he pays for. The mobile users have their computers communicating to the network via the radio and modem combination that is called the InfoTAC.

From its roots as a network for field engineers, ARDIS registers its users on a specific frequency, because a field engineer usually works in a specific region and does not service accounts in different cities. Today, roaming from one city to another is provided. The MAC protocol is slotted ALOHA, like RAM/Mobitex. Two to six channels exist per city, with 25 KHz spacing between channels. More frequencies are available for expansion.

Interestingly, the new ability of the modems to switch frequencies when roaming from one city to another is not used to switch channels when in the same city. As a result, if one of the fre-

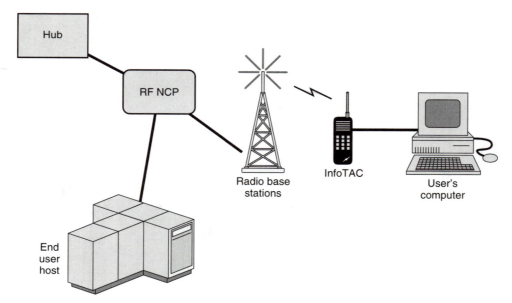

**Figure 5.6**   ARDIS/Modacom network configuration.

quency channels in a city is very heavily loaded and another is lightly loaded, customers on the heavy channel cannot make use of the available capacity on the lightly loaded channel. This situation has the same effect as trunk group splintering that occurs when we have multiple carriers in a given geographical area. If one operator has many customers, the other does not. The users in the successful operator's network receive a poorer grade of service than the ones using the network of the less successful operator, and as a whole, less traffic is carried by the sum of the two.

The protocol of ARDIS/Modacom is also open, although apparently in practice it is not as easily accessible as is RAM/Mobitex. And in fact, many more third party products are available for RAM/Mobitex than for ARDIS/Modacom. Its terminal interface has three options:

- MDC 4800, the original ARDIS protocol
  - 4800 bps
  - FSK
- RD LAP 19.2, announced after CDPD announced they would provide 19.2 Kbps
  - 19.2 Kbps
  - Four level FSK
- RAM/Mobitex
  - 8 Kbps
  - GMSK

The last option means that a user can buy an InfoTAC even if they want to use the RAM/Mobitex network. This strategy from Motorola is interesting.

The MDC 4800 protocol is quite robust. It uses error detection and correction and uses 16 bits for every 32 bits of information. It is a convolutional code and can correct up to 28% of the errors. Whether using that much overhead for error correction is a good tradeoff or not is an engineering decision. The alternative would be to allow more retransmissions. The net effect may be more actual throughput, especially when the connections are good. This much error detection and correction is justified for an extremely poor channel. When the channel is good, the extra bits do not contribute much since very few errors occur. The bits are interleaved, standard practice when error correction is used. Error correction works better when the errors do not occur in runs. Every packet is acknowledged. NACKs are automatically retried up to four times. Finally, an error message is displayed to the application.

In the US, ARDIS has been in operation much longer than RAM/Mobitex, especially taking into account the time that it was the IBM field engineering network. The coverage of ARDIS is more than that of RAM/Mobitex at this point in time. In other parts of the world, RAM/Mobitex has the lead. It is being implemented in many countries in Europe as well as Asia. ARDIS/Modacom is close behind. The first ARDIS/Modacom network outside the US went into service in Germany, before the RAM/Mobitex network began installation there. Now, ARDIS/Modacom is being installed in other countries in Europe and in Asia. In Asia it has different names.

RAM/Mobitex and ARDIS/Modacom are direct competitors. We also have CDPD being deployed in the US. CDPD uses slightly different technology. In addition, we now have narrow band

PCS licenses awarded, and those companies are rolling out two-way paging networks. First, let us discuss CDPD, and then paging.

## Cellular Digital Packet Data Network Technologies

CDPD is a standard that was developed by a consortium of companies that includes IBM, six of the seven Regional Bell Operating Companies, McCaw Cellular, and others. This group of giants grasped what seemed like a very clever idea and came together to quickly formulate an open standard for providing packet data service that is derived from existing cellular networks. In this section, we discuss the following aspects of CDPD:

- Network technologies
- Architecture
- Network components
- Data security
- Subscriber equipment

First, let us discuss how CDPD works and its potential for success. The basic idea was proposed by Dr. Vic Moore, a scientist at IBM. CDPD is based on the traffic engineering fact that a trunk group of circuit switched traffic that is designed to meet a given blocking criterion for the voice and other circuit switched traffic will have gaps of empty channel capacity in it. These gaps are not long relative to the length of an average voice call, but for data they are huge. Why not design a piece of equipment that can accept demand for data traffic, and carry it in these gaps without interfering with the voice traffic?

Figure 5.7 shows an example.

Figure 5.7 illustrates a cellular system with four channels that are designed to carry voice or other circuit switched traffic. As discussed above, gaps occur as shown among the lighter shaded calls that were placed on the four channels at random. Data traffic is being presented to the CDPD equipment, whose job it is to find the gaps in the voice channels without interfering with the voice traffic at all. The voice traffic has absolute priority. Four data requests are shown. The first one comes in, the CDPD equipment scans the channels, finds a gap, places the data packet in it, and completes the transmission. A second data packet comes in, the CDPD equipment scans the channels, and they are all busy. It waits until it finds channel C free and sends the packet to completion there. A third packet comes in, and channel B is available. This packet is long. Before it is completed, a voice call comes. CDPD jumps out of the way and scans again and finds channel A free, so it completes the call there, and sequences the packet fragments. In this way, the data traffic, which is of much shorter average duration than the voice traffic, can utilize the gaps in the circuit switched traffic and gain additional efficiency on the circuits. The data traffic is store and forward, so it is not critical if some delays occur, as long as the average response time is acceptable.

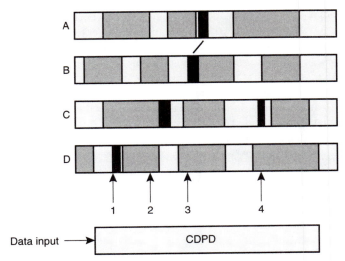

**Figure 5.7** CDPD traffic example.

The CDPD equipment has to be intimately tied to the circuit switching equipment to be able to find the gaps and jump out of the way when a voice call comes in. This functioning requires a close working relationship between the CDPD provider and the cellular carrier. Looking at who comprises the CDPD consortium, we see that they are the cellular carriers themselves. So they are in essence deriving a packet service from their own cellular systems and obtaining additional revenue from the idle times in the voice circuits.

On the surface, this idea seems too good to be true. What are its limitations? Are we getting something for nothing? What would happen if the voice traffic became heavy? The gaps would become smaller. If they become too small the statistics of the situation state that the blocking experienced by the voice traffic would be very heavy. The voice customers would be in an uproar before the gaps became that small. Before the gaps became significantly smaller, the blocking experienced by the voice customers would exceed 20% or so.

What would happen if the data traffic became heavy? That would fill the gaps because the data traffic has a much shorter average holding time and different statistics. It waits for the gaps so it can pack them more fully. What would the operator do then? Build more channels. But this problem is a very nice one to have. The data business is doing so well that she needs to build more channels to handle the new customers. This situation is in contrast to other packet networks such as ARDIS/Modacom and RAM/Mobitex, where they have to spend a tremendous amount of capital before they reap much profit. They have to provide significant coverage before large customers agree to use the service. With CDPD, the initial investment is relatively small, and when they start having significant business, they can expand the capacity. So apparently CDPD is still a very good idea.

One theoretical drawback to CDPD is that it is a fairly complex system. Would we design it that way if we were designing it from the start? Probably not. We would have had to build a combined circuit and packet switched network, and we might have been tempted to fill the gaps in the circuit switched traffic with the packet traffic just like CDPD does. But we probably would have come up with a more elegant solution.

In GSM Phase 2+, a packet service is being proposed. This packet service would also be derived from the GSM allocations and overlay the existing circuit switched traffic. It may be similar to CDPD in general structure. It is once again a packet service that is coming after the fact rather than from the start. If it is too slow in coming, CDPD has a good chance of being implemented in those countries that have implemented GSM Phase 1.

The services provided by CDPD are:

- 19.2 Kbps
- Connectionless service
- Point-to-point
- Multicast
- Broadcast
- Security
  - Authentication of users
  - Authorization
  - Encryption of data

As soon as CDPD announced a data rate of 19.2 Kbps, both RAM/Mobitex and ARDIS/Modacom announced plans to upgrade to 19.2 Kbps. This upgrade is not easy. The channel spacing for both packet radio carriers is such that they both have to change the modulation scheme from binary to four level. The upgrade is gradual.

The basic service of CDPD is connectionless. A user can build a connection-oriented service on top of that if he so desires. All three modes of point-to-point, multicast, and broadcast are available. The security has one additional part that is not usually broken out separately, and that is authorization. This function insures that the user is requesting a kind of service he is signed up to receive.

The investment in cellular in the US at one point was $18 billion. At that point, the number of customers was about 20 million. The investment per user at that stage was about $900. The attractiveness of CDPD is the ability to leverage that investment. It requires relatively small modifications to the equipment at the cell site to accomplish the hopping around the voice channels. The amount of investment is certainly less than putting in a whole separate network.

Figure 5.8 shows the architecture of CDPD. It is based on the version 1.0 of the standard. It does have its own terminology, so a short time is required to outline it.

The user's computer accesses the network via a CDPD modem that is called a Mobile End System. The M-ES talks to the Airlink Network using the A-Interface. The Airlink Network is the collection of CDPD units that are added to the cellular base stations. Those units are connected to the Mobile Data Intermediate Systems, which are the controllers of the units in the base stations. They are at the same level as the base station controllers in a cellular network. The MD-ISs are

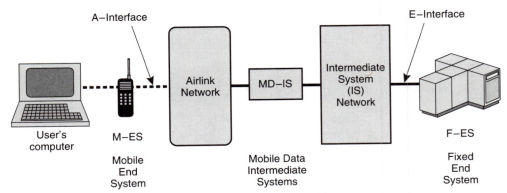

**Figure 5.8**    CDPD network architecture.

then connected to the public switched network, which are referred to as the Intermediate Systems. The end user hosts and other fixed systems are called Fixed End Systems and communicate to the ISs on the E-Interface.

The End Systems definitions are summarized as follows:

- Logical end points of communications
- Each ES has at least one Network Entity Identifier (NEI)
- M-ES
  - Mobile End System
  - Communicates with CDPD via the A-Interface
- F-ES
  - Fixed End System
  - Communicates with CDPD via the E-Interface
  - Sees a M-ES as any other ES

The Air Link network is depicted in Figure 5.9.

The CDPD units in the base stations are called Mobile Data Base Stations. They are controlled by the Mobile Data Intermediate Systems. By equipping the cellular base stations with MDBSs and adding the control functions at centralized locations, the CDPD provider can roll out a nationwide network with good coverage in a relatively short time. Close to 10,000 cellular base stations exist across the US. The number of base stations ARDIS has is about 1500. RAM/Mobitex has about 1000.

The functions of the AirLink network is summarized as follows:

- Overlays existing cell site equipment
- Accepts and forwards traffic to and from M-ESs

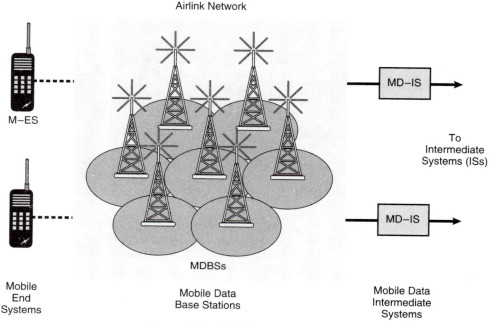

**Figure 5.9**   CDPD Airlink network.

- Over the A-Interface
  - At the PHY and MAC layers
- Manages channel allocation
  - Including interoperation with voice channels
- MD-IS: Mobile Data Intermediate System
  - Uses and controls MDBSs
  - Controls mobile data link
  - Manages mobility
  - Does not perform complex routing decisions; they are included in the functions of the ISs

Two types of Airlink channels exist—a forward channel from the MDBS to the M-ES (down link), and a reverse channel from the M-ES to the MDBS (up link). Both channels are specified in Telecommunications Industry Association standard IS-553. The data stream carried over the channel pair is assigned a Channel Stream Identifier (CSI). The channel stream retains its identity during hops around voice traffic. Several channel pairs can be active at any one time in one cell. So the MDBS communicates with the M-ES via this channel pair to instruct the M-ES which channel to transmit on at any point in time.

Figure 5.10 shows the CDPD switched network.

The Mobile Data Intermediate Systems that control the MDBSs are connected to the collection of Intermediate Systems to which the Fixed End Systems communicate.

The functions of the Intermediate Systems are:

- Perform network layer functions
- Route datagrams among F-ESs and MD-ISs
- Support
  - Internet Protocol (IP)
  - Connectionless Network Protocol (CLNP)
- Can be composed of several administrative domains (service providers)
- Connection oriented communications are provided by transport layer in end system

CDPD supports both the TCP/IP protocols as well as the international set of equivalent standards. Later we see how different administrative domains, or service providers, are coordinated depending on whether they are one of the CDPD consortium members or not.

The components of a service provider network are depicted in Figure 5.11.

A number of servers are connected to the Intermediate Systems, such as the Directory Server, the Accounting Server, the Authentication Server, and the Network Management Server. These servers provide critical network functions, and are the basis for future value-added services.

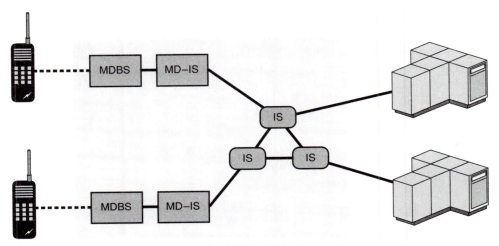

**Figure 5.10**   DPD switched network.

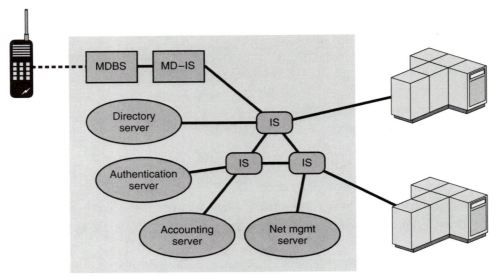

**Figure 5.11** CDPD service provider network components.

Many believe that the majority of revenue in the future will come not from the air time we charge customers, but from the value-added services they order. Note the announcement by AT&T that they will offer free Internet access. This philosophy is probably what they have in mind.

The switched network with multiple service providers is shown in Figure 5.12.

The service providers who are members of the CDPD consortium communicate via the internal I-Interface. A service provider who is not part of consortium must use the external E-Interface like any other Fixed End System.

Next, let us discuss how data security is achieved in CDPD. The three components of data security are authentication, authorization, and Airlink encryption. Authentication is an MD-IS function. The M-ES supplies identification information. The MD-IS validates the authentication information against information resident in the service provider's data base. Authentication is part of Mobile Data Link Protocol.

Authorization, following authentication, is also an MD-IS function. It controls access to CDPD specific resources. The MD-IS obtains the following information from the M-ES:

- Identity
- Capabilities subscribed to
- Limitations imposed
- Billing status

This information is maintained in the Subscriber Directory Profile. This directory is a DSA (Directory Systems Agent). It uses DMI (Definition of Management Information, X.721).

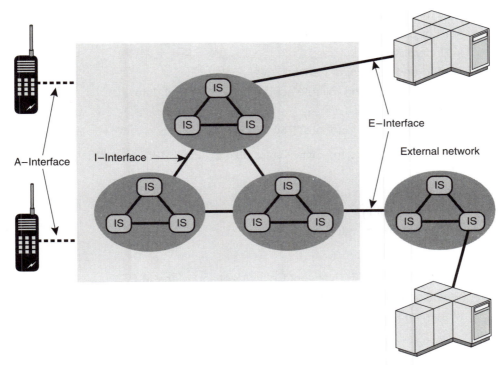

**Figure 5.12**   Network configuration with multiple service providers.

The Airlink encryption service is defined for all non-broadcast airlink connections. The MD-IS provides the encryption to data units destined to a M-ES. It is part of the Sub Network Dependent Convergence Protocol—SN DCP. This is the protocol for the CDPD channel stream sub network. The information is maintained in the Subscriber Directory Profile. This directory is a DSA (Directory Systems Agent). It uses DMI (Definition of Management Information, X.721).

The Mobile End System provides the user with applications, support services, and management services. It uses standard protocols where possible. Protocols for widely used applications are specified, such as virtual terminal. Support services include:

- Data services
- MAC functions
- Link layer functions
  - Reliable sequenced data delivery to MD-IS
  - "Unreliable" unsequenced delivery of data to MD-IS
  - Broadcast delivery of data

- Sub network convergence functions
  - IP or CLNP packetization
  - Encryption
- End-to-end delivery of network level packets
- Optional end-to-end reliable sequenced delivery of data via
  - TCP
  - ISO Transport Protocol (TP4)

Management services are for controlling and configuring M-ES support services. Radio resource management includes:

- Acquiring CDPD channel
- Channel hopping
- Initiating a cell transfer

Security services include:

- Maintaining the NEI (Network Entity Identifier) of the M-ES
- Providing authentication information to the MD-IS
- Managing keys for encryption

Registration services are NEI registration with the network initially and upon cell transfer, and NEI deregistration.

The M-ES components appear in Figure 5.13.

The Mobile Application Subsystem (MAS) is independent of CDPD. It contains the applications and may also contain transport level functions. The Subscriber Unit (SU) provides the CDPD interface. That is where the A-Interface is implemented. The Subscriber Identity Module (SIM) defines the identity of the M-ES user, similarly to the GSM SIM. It also defines access rights of the M-ES user(s).

M-ES functional profiles are defined for:

- General applications
- Vertical market applications
- Virtual terminal applications: Telnet
- CDPD AT profile, which is useful when a physical division exists between the MAS and the SU

In summary, CDPD is an important standard that has been defined by some of the major players in the industry. Figure 5.14 compares it with the other two packet switched services in the US.

ARDIS has been in operation longest. CDPD projects installing the CDPD equipment in the cellular base stations quickly. Most of the members of the consortium are able to offer service

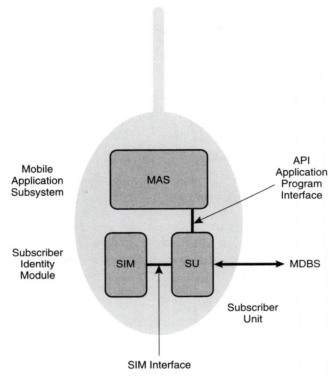

**Figure 5.13**   Mobile End System components.

|  | **RAM/Mobitex** | **ARDIS** | **CDPD** |
|---|---|---|---|
| Metropolitan areas | 100+ | 400+ | 700+ |
| Base stations | 800+ | 1300+ | 9000+ |
| Power (watts) | 2 | 3 | 0.6–1.2 |
| In-building penetration | yes | more | some |
| Data rate (Kbps) | 8 >> 19.2 | 4.8 >> 19.2 | 19.2 |

**Figure 5.14**   Comparison of packet radio services.

within about 12 months of start of deployment. The transmitted power of CDPD is about half as much as that of RAM/Mobitex and ARDIS/Modacom. They do have more cell sites, so whether their coverage will be better or not as good remains to be seen. ARDIS/Modacom does have the best in building coverage, primarily because they do have the highest power transmitted by the portable. Finally, the data rate of ARDIS started out at 4.8 Kbps. RAM/Mobitex started out later with 8 Kbps. They both are upgrading to 19.2 Kbps in the US.

# A Wireless Metropolitan Area Network

Before going to the next section on data over cellular and related services, let us point out one innovative service called Metricom. It can be called a Wireless Metropolitan Network. It uses spread spectrum technology, in particular Frequency Hopping Spread Spectrum, to provide connectivity within a dense urban area. The technology is very similar to a Wireless LAN technology, but the data rate is on the order of 100 Kbps, and the range is 1/4 to 1/2 mile. In a Wireless LAN, that data rate is about 1 Mbps and the range is 50 meters, so Metricom chose a different set of parameters more in tune with a MAN rather than a LAN.

The cell sites can be wired together or they can be connected wirelessly. If they are connected wirelessly, they use up much of the available spectrum since all their transmissions among themselves are essentially repeats of mobile to base transmission; but they are on the air and so share the same bandwidth.

Metricom supports TCP/IP, so it is very well tuned to the Internet. The network can grow in a meshlike fashion. The more cells it has, the more coverage it has. As mentioned, the cells can relay traffic to each other at the expense of bandwidth. This approach, in fact, is a good way at the start, since when the traffic does grow, Metricom can, at that point, lease wired facilities to connect the base stations, take the traffic among the base stations off the air, and make the bandwidth available for mobile-to-base traffic.

# Data Over Cellular and Related Services

The data rates available through cellular and PCS appear in Figure 5.15.

Data over digital cellular is now 9.6 Kbps in most parts of the world. Ironically, data over analog cellular is 14.4 Kbps with analog modems, because modems are doing an exceptional job of extracting the most out of the analog cellular channel just like they are doing with the wired network. Some time was required to reach this level of performance on the wired network. A much shorter time passed before that technology was applied to the cellular network.

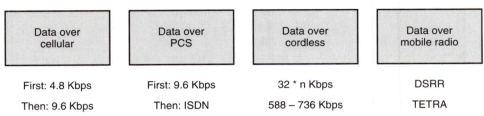

**Figure 5.15**  Data over cellular and related services.

Cellular modems added the capability of handling the poor error performance of the cellular network and the handoff between cells as follows: During handoffs, modems stop and restart the transmission without dropping the connection as a wire line modems would. During fades, the modem corrects errors and may ask for retransmission. The most popular data over cellular protocols are:

- Microcom MNP 10
- ATT ETC
- V.24 and V.34

Data over digital cellular is limited by the way channels are allocated. At present, a voice grade channel is allocated for data and hence the limitation to 9.6 Kbps. In the future, we hope to see allocations of multiple voice channels to data so that we can exceed the 9.6 Kbps limit and begin thinking about wider bandwidth applications in the wide area. Some companies are doing just that with GSM. They are proposing this service in Phase 2+ of GSM as Fast Speed Circuit Switched data. They can put together as many voice grade channels as one whole carrier of GSM can support. This improvement should result in data rates on the order of 100 Kbps. Unfortunately, TDMA cellular in the US has a carrier that has an aggregate data rate of about 48 Kbps, so after overhead we probably cannot expect much more than a 30 Kbps data rate at most by combining all three TDMA channels on one of the FDMA channels. Combining several FDMA channels is possible but would be rather complex.

GSM has a feature called Short Message Service or SMS, which is derived from the signaling channels. The message can be up to 140 characters long and can go in both directions not just to the mobile. So a page can be acknowledged. It has a variant called SMS Cell broadcast. The broadcast message can be up to about 90 characters long and can be sent to all phones in a geographical area. It is derived from the signal that lets a mobile know that it has a call coming, so it can be broadcast over a cell. Its applications are, for example, to warn the people in a particular cell of a bad traffic situation or a weather condition.

Data over PCS starts at 9.6 Kbps. At this stage, the data is put through the voice codec. This action simplifies the equipment requirement at the network end. The data is essentially sent through as voice grade. In the future, we should be able to use one of the voice channels that runs at 32 Kbps, or multiples of voice channels up to the maximum size of the carrier. That maximum will depend on which PCS standard the operator implements and could range from as little as the 30 Kbps for TDMA, to a high of 500 Kbps for DECT.

DECT has spectrum allocations in Europe of 20 GHz between 1.88 and 1.9 GHz. It provides integrated voice and data services. It is targeted at low cost implementations, uses low power, and has short range. Its primary application is for Wireless PBXs, but it can also apply to public access, wireless loops, and residential cordless. Its data services are:

- 32 Kbps for one voice grade channel
- Multiples of 32 Kbps for several voice grade channels
- A maximum for the whole carrier of
  - 736 Kbps without error handling
  - 588 Kbps with error handling
- Support for logically connectionless 'datagram' service
- Connection times of about 50 ms
- Support for multicast and broadcast
- Support for virtual circuits
- Authentication and security services

In addition to providing data rates close to those of Wireless LANS, DECT also provides LAN-like connectionless service and multicast and broadcast. But can it serve as a LAN? It has a connection time of 50 ms, which is very fast for a circuit switch, but is that fast enough for LAN traffic? To answer that question, let us look at LAN user needs. The average traffic packet in a LAN is about 600 bytes long. At Ethernet speed, that takes about 50 ms to send. The connection time of DECT would mean that to send an average packet, getting a channel would take as long as transmitting the average packet. This speed may be satisfactory for some applications, but for many, a faster access time would be desirable. Even in Europe where DECT was developed, a high performance Wireless LAN standard has been developed to supplement DECT. It is Hiperlan.

DECT has a good chance of becoming a worldwide standard for Wireless PBXs. Figure 5.16 shows the topology of a Wireless PBX.

Most Wireless PBXs today provide only voice services. They have not tapped the hidden treasure that lies in the DECT data services. When they do, we will have an excellent foundation for multimedia services in the office. Advanced handheld phones, notebook computers, and other portable devices with access to DECT will be able to use its wide bandwidth to give users superior integrated multimedia mobile services in the office.

The last item in Figure 5.15 is Mobile Radio. No standards have existed for Mobile Radio until recently. ETSI recently finished defining two standards for Mobile Radio, Digital Short Range Radio for private applications, and Tetra for public applications. The DSRR standard has not been widely implemented. The Tetra specification is being used for both public mobile radio applications, as well as for providing virtual Private Mobile Radio systems. This latter application

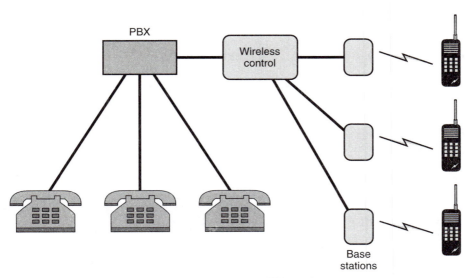

**Figure 5.16**    Wireless PBX topology.

is still to be proven, especially for challenging applications such as police or other emergency groups. The challenge is for a public system to provide all the channels a police department needs in case of an emergency in a specific location.

Many such groups prefer to have a private network in order to insure that they will indeed have the circuits when they need them. Unfortunately, these circuits are not used at other times, and so the system does not use the spectrum efficiently. If we can devise a system that can guarantee providing the needed circuits in times of emergency, and yet allow other users to make use of them at other times, we would be able to make a big leap towards meeting the demands of many diverse groups from a single efficient infrastructure.

The Tetra specification provides:

- Speech and data within closed user groups such as
  - Vehicle fleets
  - Emergency services
- Packet data
- Support for mobile-to-mobile communications
- Connection-oriented as well as connectionless service

The Tetra technology is summarized by:

- 4 TDMA channels per 25 KHz allocations
- 36 Kbps modulations rate

- 19.2 Kbps net bit rate
- < 300 ms call set up time
- Slotted ALOHA random access protocol

It provides both circuit switched as well as packet switched data. The call setup time of 300 ms is fast for a Wide Area Network service. The random access scheme is the same as the scheme used by ARDIS/Modacom and RAM/Mobitex. The beauty of Tetra is that it provides both circuit switched channels for voice and long message data, as well as packet channels for transaction traffic. This is on par with what GSM Phase 2+ hopes to have.

## Comparison of Packet Radio Networks to Data Over Cellular and Paging

Figure 5.17 plots the functionality of data over cellular, packet radio networks, and paging relative to the costs of the services.

Arguably, data over cellular provides the greatest functionality. It does provide a guaranteed channel for the duration of the connection, so it is best suited for longer messages. Its cost is largest if the message is short. Packet radio provides a service that is attuned to shorter messages. Paging is for the shortest messages.

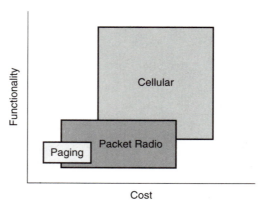

**Figure 5.17** Cost/performance comparison of Mobile Data options.

# Cell Size Classification

We have discussed a great many cell sizes. Figure 5.18 suggests some names and applications for each kind of cell size.

Cell sizes larger than 50 kilometers in radius are the realm of satellite systems. The next three categories encompass cellular systems of varying applications. The large cell systems are for rural areas with cell sizes from 10 kilometers to 50 kilometers in radius. Most cellular systems have a radius from 1 to 10 kilometers in size and serve urban areas. Mini cells that have radii that range from 100 meters to 1000 meters can be used to provide service to dense urban areas. Both cellular systems as well as high tier PCS systems can be used in these cases. This area is one of overlap between the different systems. Micro cell systems serve office campuses and office buildings. The cell sizes are in the 10 meter to 100 meter range. These are quite small cells for a cellular system; this area is where low-tier PCS systems shine, and cordless systems are most suited. This is where wireless PBXs will be applied.

This cell size applies to Wireless LANs as well. The kind of Wireless LANs that have this kind of cell size are usually radio based. Infrared Wireless LANs also exist. Their range is smaller and fits in the pico cell category. These systems serve a single room, not only because their range is limited, but also because infrared cannot penetrate walls. We are still not at the end.

One more category will become very prevalent—the femto cell category for private, point-to-point infrared systems. A standard was developed by the Infra Red Data Association. The association was led by HP, and produced the first phase of the standard for very short range, 2 meter or less transmission between two end systems. This kind of system is very low cost and will be found in the majority of notebook computers in the future.

| Cell type | Cell radius | Coverage | Services |
|-----------|-------------|----------|----------|
| Huge cell | > 50 Km | Continents | Satellite |
| Large cell | 10–50 Km | Rural | Cellular |
| Cell | 1–10 Km | Urban | Cellular |
| Mini cell | 100–1000 m | Dense urban | Cellular/DCS/PCS |
| Micro cell | 10–100 m | Office campus | DECT/PCS/Radio LANs |
| Pico cell | 2–10 m | Single room | IR LANs |
| Femto cell | < 2 m | Private short range | IRDA |

**Figure 5.18**  Cell size classifications.

# Summary

In this chapter, we focused on the technologies behind Mobile Data networks. We presented the structures of the RAM/Mobitex network and the Motorola ARDIS/Modacom network. The two are very similar in structure. They both have a central hub where most of the network intelligence is located. The base stations are connected to the hub via a network of wired circuits that may be leased from a private line provider. The protocols used on both packet radio networks are similar. They both use slotted ALOHA at the MAC layer and use fairly robust error detection and correction codes over the air channel. The data rates are comparable.

CDPD has an innovative approach. It derives a packet service from the gaps between circuit switched cellular calls. The gaps exist because of the statistics of voice and other circuit switched calls. The gaps are small relative to the length of voice call, but are quite sizable relative to an average data message. By providing equipment that can utilize these gaps without impacting the service quality experienced by the voice calls, CDPD can provide a packet service using much of the same cellular equipment of existing cellular networks. The CDPD providers are themselves cellular providers, so in essence they are deriving additional service revenues from the same licenses, and the same cellular network infrastructure. GSM Phase 2+ will also have a packet service that is designed after the fact to add this feature to already implemented circuit switched cellular networks. Tetra, a Public Access Mobile Radio standard that is developed by ETSI, actually provides both a circuit switched and a packet switched service definition from the start.

Metricom uses Wireless LAN technology, namely FHSS, to provide what might be called a Wireless Metropolitan Area Network. The data rates are about one tenth as high as for typical Wireless LANs, and the range is about 10 times are large.

Data over cellular can provide about 10 Kbps initially, rising to 100 Kbps or more as faster speed circuit switched data services are defined in the standards. The majority of data traffic today is carried by analog cellula because many people have cellular phones. A cellular modem is relatively inexpensive and the air time is not prohibitively expensive even for short messages. Many service providers are providing combined circuit switched and packet switched services by combining a cellular modem with a CDPD modem. This provides the user with both options so that he can optimize his performance cost relative to the kind of data he needs to transmit.

# 6 *Wireless LAN Technologies*

Currently Wireless LAN products are based on spread spectrum techniques, both Frequency Hopping Spread Spectrum (FHSS) and Direct Sequence Spread Spectrum (DSSS). Several MAC alternatives are possible for handling the special requirements of Wireless LANs. Power management is critical and may require special provision in the MAC protocol for mobile applications. Interconnection with backbone networks allows roaming within a campus environment as well as in the wide area. In this chapter, we discuss:

- Technology trends
- Wireless LAN wish list
- FHSS system engineering
- Multipath and its effect on data rate
- Modulation alternatives
- Frequency hopping pattern selection
- Preamble for FHSS PHY
- MAC protocols for Wireless LANs
  - Listen Before You Talk MAC protocol
  - Integrated CSMA/TDMA MAC protocol
  - Reservation/polling MAC protocol
- Power management
- Interconnection with backbone networks
- Mobility within the same network
- Mobility among different networks and Mobile IP
- Name and directory services
- The PCS model for mobility

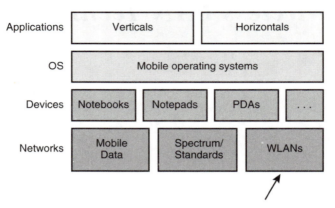

**Figure 6.1**   Focus on Wireless LANs.

Referring to Figure 6.1, we now focus on the Wireless LANs area of the networking layer in the Mobile Computing chart.

## Technology Trends

In this section, we discuss technology trends in the cellular and PCS industries and in the electronics industry in general that can affect the progress of technology in the Mobile Data and Wireless LAN markets.

Many of the cellular and PCS products are crowded around 1 GHz and 2 GHz of the frequency spectrum. Several years ago, silicon could not operate effectively much above 1 GHz. For this reason, most systems of that era were below 1 GHz. Using higher frequencies meant having to use Gallium Arsenide, which was more expensive at the time. Now, silicon is faster, and Gallium Arsenide, has become more cost effective, so we are able to build circuits at higher frequencies economically.

The next step in the march up the frequency spectrum in search of greater bandwidth is the use of Microwave Monolithic Integrated Circuits or MMICs. These circuits operate in the 10 and 20 GHz range of frequencies. They are available for defense applications, and are just beginning to appear in commercial applications. One example is Motorola's Altair system.

Most mobile Wireless LAN systems today provide data rates between 1 Mbps and 2 Mbps. Some of the non-mobile Wireless LAN systems that are aimed at the wire replacement market provide 10 Mbps. Infrared wireless LAN products also provide data rates in the range of 1 Mbps to 2 Mbps or 4 Mbps. Research is being done at higher data rates both in microwave radio as well as in infrared.

As for the MAC layer, CSMA seems to be a good choice for Wireless LANs at this time. Its advantages are:

- It is simple and robust
- It has very fast access time when the traffic is light
- It does not require a coordination function
- It supports ad hoc networking relatively simply

Its disadvantages are:

- Its maximum capacity is limited to a fraction of the data rate in real applications
- Its efficiency drops drastically for high offered traffic

Options for alleviating these shortcomings include wireless specific CSMA algorithms.

Comparing the Mobile Data and Wireless LAN environments to the cellular and PCS environments, we find that the cellular and PCS environments are much more challenging in the following areas:

- Near/far problem of 80 dB dynamic range or more
- Long path length multipath
- Interference with many other users
- Handoff among cells for fast nodes of 60 mph or greater

Solutions used by cellular and PCS include:

- Agile power control
- Equalization
- RAKE filters
- Long pseudo random codes
- Soft handoff using the same frequency but different codes

Some of these solutions could be used for Mobile Data and Wireless LAN systems as well.

## Wireless LAN Wish List

What is the ideal Wireless LAN product from a user's point of view, without being limited by what is possible at the present point in time? If we were to forget technology limitations, spectrum limitations, production costs, and other real-world issues, what would we want in a Wireless LAN? If this question is posed to a group of prospective users, especially those who have no experience with the technology, the list may look like this:

- High speed, at least as fast as today's ethernet, possibly faster in the future
- Low cost, perhaps not much more than today's Ethernet
- Coverage wherever the users are throughout the building or campus
- No use of the battery of the mobile computer, or at least minimal impact
- No susceptibility to interference that may be present in the area where it will be used, for example from door openers, or microwave ovens
- Easy installation, use, and management
- Easy repair and upgrading
- PCMCIA form factor
- No external antenna to break off or otherwise be in the way
- Works in the presence of other Wireless LAN systems in the area, for example, another company nearby within radio range

After looking at Wireless LAN technology in the rest of this chapter and after the available products in Chapter 7 are presented and compared, we will return to the above list to see how achievable these wishes are.

## FHSS System Engineering

In this section, we consider the system engineering aspects of an FHSS Wireless LAN system. We discuss the design of the radio, the transmitter, and receiver specifications; the modulation options and their respective merits; frequency hopping pattern design and selection; and FHSS preamble for acquiring and maintaining synchronization. First, let us discuss what the design goals for such a system may be. Here is a high-level list:

- Form factor
  - PCMCIA card
- Performance
  - 1 Mbps
  - 50 m range
- Technology
  - 2.4 GHz ISM band
  - FHSS
  - 15 channels to allow cellularization

- Power consumption
  - 10 ma at 5 v in standby mode
  - Price
- End user list price < $500

Before addressing the details of the design, let us discuss some of the methods used for dealing with radio propagation indoors. Radio propagation is far from ideal in an indoor environment because of obstructions such as furniture, partitions, and walls of various construction. Some walls are fairly transparent to radio propagation below about 10 GHz; some walls are not. Their passivity to radio propagation depends on the amount of metal in the walls, and how well that metal forms an electromagnetic shield. Radio engineers sometimes model the environment indoors as a channel that has different attenuation curves, depending on the nature of the obstruction. One such model assumes the following:

- First 3 meters
  - Square law
- Greater than 3 meters, open office environment
  - Inverse third law
- Greater than 3 meters, through inside walls
  - Inverse fourth law
- Through outside walls, and through floors/ceilings
  - Inverse sixth law

These attenuation functions appear in Figure 6.2.

With this kind of model, a power of about 100 milliwatts should yield a range of about 50 meters in most indoor environments, including propagation in open office environments having

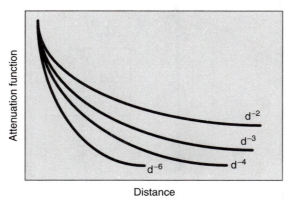

**Figure 6.2**   Attenuation functions for indoor propagation.

partitions of various heights, as well as through inside walls of moderate construction. Propagation through outside walls and through floors and ceilings is limited. However, this limitation is not always bad. It means that we have to use different access points on different floors of a building, but it also means that we can reuse the channels on different floors. The situation usually dictates that we cannot rely on an access point to provide coverage on more than one floor, but we cannot count on an access point not to interfere with the access point on the next floor, or even with the access point two floors away.

What does this restriction mean about the design of an indoor environment? Figure 6.3 illustrates an example of laying out an office complex with several buildings, each with multiple floors. One of the buildings is across a public roadway.

On the first floor of the large four-story building we would start with channel one. Will one access point be enough for this floor? The radius of coverage of the radio is 50 meters, so the size of the floor could be up to 100 meters, or about 300 feet on the side. This is a good size floor and may cover most floors of most buildings, but of course not all. Suppose that the four-story building has floors that are smaller than 300 feet on the side, except for the part of the first floor that consists of perhaps a cafeteria or a library.

On the second floor, we cannot count on obtaining adequate coverage from the access point on the first floor. At the same time, we cannot count on having no interference from that access point, so we would use another access point with another channel, channel 2. How about on the third floor? We could perhaps reuse channel 1, but using a third channel would be more conserva-

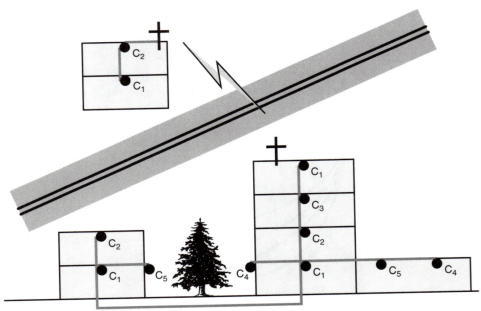

**Figure 6.3**   An example of an office campus layout.

tive. In a real case, we would do a site survey to find out for sure. By the time we are on the fourth floor, we should be able to reuse channel 1. In the cafeteria, we have to use other channels since we have a mixture of inside walls, and outside walls with windows. In the courtyards we need different channels from the channels inside the building, but perhaps we can reuse the channels that were used in the cafeteria since several walls exist in between, including an outside wall, and a fair amount of distance. In the building to the left we can reuse the first two channels, and in the building across the public roadway we can reuse those channels. Again, a site survey is required to insure that this design would indeed yield a satisfactory propagation environment.

So for this simple office complex, we require five channels to do the three-dimensional cellularization design. These have to be distinct channels that use different frequency space or different time space, or in the FHSS system we are considering here, different frequency hopping patterns, as we will discuss shortly.

What about connecting the building across the street? We can trench from the building on the right to the building to the left because it is within the property of the office complex. We cannot dig a trench across the public roadway. So we have two options. We can obtain private lines from the phone company and pay on a monthly basis, or we can use a point-to-point microwave or laser communications system. This latter option is shown in the Figure 6.3.

Many point-to-point systems are available from vendors of microwave radios and laser systems. These systems are not a specific subject of this book. However, almost all Wireless LAN product lines include a point-to-point option. These options are covered in Chapter 7.

## Multipath Radio Propagation and Its Effect on the Data Rate

Next let us focus on another aspect of the indoor environment that can degrade performance—multipath. Multipath is a problem in outdoor environments as well; in fact, it can be more of a problem outdoors than indoors because the path lengths are longer. Figure 6.4 illustrates a sample situation in an indoor environment.

In the example shown in Figure 6.4, line of sight exists between the transmitter and the receiver so we have a direct path. This is not always the case because of line of sight obstructions such as partitions, furniture, or walls. The next strongest signal is the one that is reflected from the floor; it is also often missing. Next is the signal that is reflected from the ceiling. A number of other signals arrive at the receiver as well. The rule is that angle of incidence equals the angle of reflection. Of course, not all the signals arrive at the receiver; one such example appears in Figure 6.4.

How does this multipath propagation affect the performance of the system? In certain situations it can actually help. As we can see, more energy arrives at the receiver than would if no multipath existed. Those reflected signals would have propagated away from the receiver. Let us examine the structure of the composite received signal. Figure 6.5 illustrates a bit stream composed of a one followed by a zero, and the composite received signal.

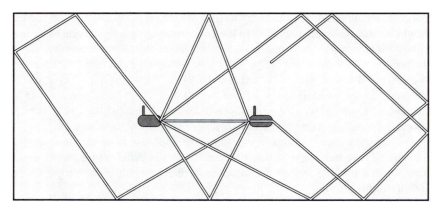

**Figure 6.4** Multipath example indoors.

The top of Figure 6.5 shows the transmitted one zero bit stream. The one is positive; the zero is negative. This transmission occurs in most systems to keep the DC component to a minimum. Having a small DC component allows the use of low pass filters to eliminate some of the noise. The middle part of Figure 6.5 shows the received signals in the case when the delays are short relative to the propagation time of one bit. In this case, the sum of the received signals is actually a bet-

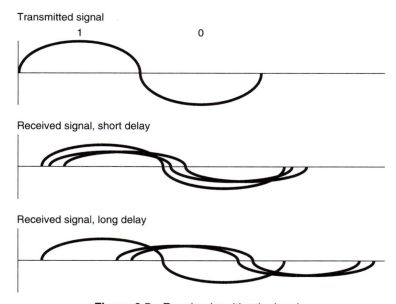

**Figure 6.5** Received multipath signals.

ter signal than the direct signal alone. When the path length differences are short compared to the propagation time of one bit, multipath improves the situation.

When is multipath a problem, and what kind of a problem does it cause? The next part of Figure 6.5 shows that when the path length differences are a significant portion of the propagation time of one bit, the situation is different. Now the reflections of the first bit arrive over a large part of the direct signal of the second bit. This kind of multipath causes Inter Symbol Interference or ISI.

Under what conditions does this occur in the Wireless LAN systems we are considering here? Suppose the bit rate is 1 Mbps. Then the bit duration is 1 microsecond. Electromagnetic propagation travels at the speed of light, or $3 \times 10^8$ meters/second, so one bit is roughly 300 meters long. Can we get path length differences that are significant portions of 300 meters indoors? That would be a fairly large path length difference. What if we wanted to transmit at 10 Mbps? The bit length would then be 30 meters, and such a path length difference could happen often. So for data rates of 1 Mbps or perhaps 2 Mbps, multipath improves the received signal. For data rates higher than 2 to 4 Mbps, multipath causes ISI and degrades the error performance of the system.

Propagation experiments conducted for small buildings and for large buildings show that for small buildings, the maximum delays are on the order of 100 nanoseconds, and for large buildings, the delays are on the order of 250 nanoseconds. Therefore, the conclusions drawn above about the maximum data rates possible without multipath degradation are borne out by experimental data.

What if we would like to transmit at higher data rates? Then we would have to do additional functions to mitigate the effect of multipath. The options are adaptive equalization or RAKE filtering. Both these techniques are fairly expensive, and almost all present products avoid using them by keeping the data rate below 2 Mbps. The situation for outdoor systems such as Mobile Data systems and cellular systems is worse. The path length differences are much longer, and ISI cannot be avoided even at the slower data rates of the outdoor systems. For this reason, most cellular systems use a form of adaptive equalization or RAKE filtering.

# Modulation Alternatives

For a given spectrum bandwidth, the data rate possible is determined by the modulation technique. The level of modulation can yield one bit per second per hertz of bandwidth, or two bits per second per hertz, or more. The lower-level modulation systems are simpler and less expensive to implement; the higher-order systems are more complex, more expensive to implement, and require greater sensitivity receivers.

The basic digital modulation techniques for radio systems are Frequency Shift Keying and Phase Shift Keying. Infrared systems use baseband transmission techniques such as On Off Keying or Pulse Position Modulation. The possible variations on these techniques are many. Choosing just the right technique is an art as well as a science and can lead to very long and interesting discussions. Such discussions take place in standards committees all the time! Many of the techniques are close in performance. Choosing the right technique depends on how well it fits within the spectrum mask specified by the regulatory agency that allocates the bandwidth, and other performance criteria such as ability to reduce the effect of ISI.

When a regulatory agency allocates bandwidth, they do not specify that absolutely no transmission shall take place outside the allocated bandwidth. This restriction is physically impossible for real signals. Every real signal actually has components, albeit very small, at all frequencies. The regulatory agency specifies a spectrum mask below which the signal must fit. The mask specifies that most of the energy of the signal, typically 99%, fits within the nominal bandwidth, and that beyond that the signal falls off sharply, perhaps down by 50 dB or even 80dB at further frequencies from the center of the band allocated. We show some frequency shapes later in this section.

The next consideration regarding multipath performance has to do with how smooth the pulse shape is. The smoother it is, the less degradation due to multipath occurs.

Now, let us discuss three modulation schemes that are well suited for an FHSS Wireless LAN system and summarize their merits:

- CPFSK - Continuous Phase Frequency Shift Keying
- GMSK - Gaussian Minimum Shift Keying
- GFSK - Gaussian Frequency Shift Keying

A four-level CPFSK system can have a compact spectrum shape given by:

- 20 dBc @ ± 0.5 MHz
- 45 dBc @ ± 2 MHz
- 60 dBc @ ± 30 MHz

The term dBc means dB relative to the center frequency. This is illustrated in Figure 6.6.

The nominal bandwidth of the signal is 1 MHz. ninety-nine percent of its energy is contained within the 1 MHz bandwidth. Outside that bandwidth, the signal falls off sharply, as shown in Figure 6.6. Other signals occur in those other frequencies; the amount of energy contributed by this signal is small enough so as not to interfere—it adds slightly to the background noise for the other signal. In fact that is what background noise is partially composed of—the tails of other transmitted signals.

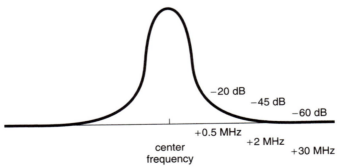

**Figure 6.6** Spectrum shape of CPFSK.

This modulation technique yields a data rate of 1 Mbps, and thus it yields one bit per second per Hertz. As we see, 1 Mbps is desirable from the point of view of not requiring complex circuitry to mitigate the effect of multipath. In addition, two other reasons explain why it is desirable. First, the maximum bandwidth of the signal allowed by regulatory agencies for FHSS signals in the 2.4 GHz ISM band is 1 MHz. Obtaining 1 Mbps within this bandwidth is fairly straightforward and cost-effective. The other reason 1 Mbps is desirable is that it is the minimum that IEEE 802.11 equipment can provide.

Next, let us consider 0.39 GMSK modulation. This modulation can also have a 20 dB band-width of 1 MHz, which has about 99% of the energy contained in that bandwidth. The frequency deviation is 25% of the bit rate, or 250 KHz. The 3 dB point is at 39% of the bit rate. Figure 6.7 shows the 7 pole filter that can realize this modulation.

The last modulation example to consider is GFSK, Gaussian Frequency Shift Keying. The modulation parameters to be chosen are:

- M: Number of levels
- BT: Bandwidth/Time product
- Pulse shape
- h: Modulation index

With a two-level system, BT = 0.5 and h = 0.36, 1 Mbps can be achieved within a 1 MHz spectrum that is down 20 dB at the 1 MHz edge. The choice of BT or 0.5 also minimizes ISI. The choice of two levels allows the use of a noncoherent receiver that is economical.

The block diagrams for a two-level radio and a four-level radio appear in Figure 6.8 and 6.9, respectively.

The cost comparison between the two systems can be summarized as follows. The four level system needs:

- More complex filters in receiver and transmitter
- Four-level slicer
- Digital Signal Processor or very large gate array demodulator
- Center frequency tolerance more critical
- Deviation control more critical

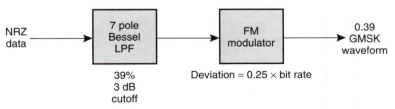

**Figure 6.7**   0.39 GMSK modulator block diagram.

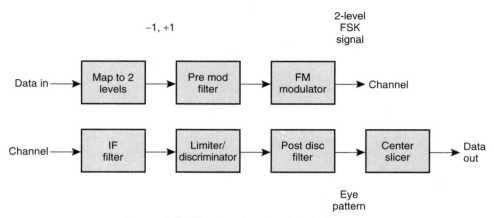

**Figure 6.8**   Two-level system block diagram.

- Phase distortion more critical
- Longer preamble and sync

The transceiver specifications for an FHSS radio have to include not only transmitted power levels and the receiver input levels, but also switching times between transmitting and receiving, and hop settling time. Typical values for an FHSS radio are:

- Transmitted power
  - Maximum of 1 w set by FCC part 15.247
  - 250, 11, 50, 10, 1 mw optional levels

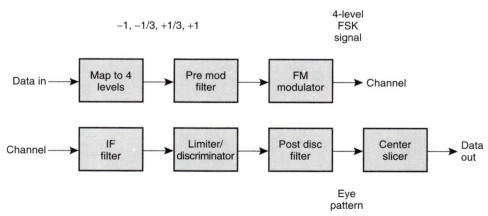

**Figure 6.9**   Four-level system block diagram.

- Receiver
  - Maximum input level: -20 dBm
  - Minimum input level: - 80 dBm @ 10-5 BER
- Switching time TX to RX: 100 microseconds
- Hop settling time: 300 microseconds max
- Frequency stability: 50 ppm
- Antenna port impedance: 50 ohms.

When the channel is below usual performance levels, specifying lower data rates is possible, such as 800 Kbps, 500 Kbps, and 250 Kbps. The bit error rate with an $E_b/N_o$ of 16 dB is on the order of $10^{-5}$.

## Frequency Hopping Pattern Selection

For FCC part 15.247 @ 2.4 GHz, 83 MHz is available. The maximum signal bandwidth is 1 MHz. Seventy-nine frequency slots must be used equally on a random basis. With these rules in mind, what is a good frequency hopping pattern? The objectives of a good pattern are to:

- Provide minimum interference among patterns used for
  - Different networks
  - Different cells in the same network
- Avoid two patterns on the same frequency at the same time
- Minimize two patterns on the same frequency at adjacent times
- Maximize frequency separation in adjacent times to reduce
  - Error runs due to interferers
  - Coherent bandwidth of fading

Remember that a channel in an FHSS system is a hopping pattern, not a frequency slot. FDMA has a different frequency slot for each channel; whereas, in FHSS, the pattern defines a channel. The total number of channels possible for a given number of frequency slots depends on a good selection of patterns that are most different from each other.

Let us consider a simple example with just six slots to find how good a pattern we can obtain. Theoretically 6! permutations of the six slots are possible, or 720 possible permutations. These have patterns on the same slot at the same time. These patterns are certainly not acceptable since those frames, where patterns collide, will be garbled and will have to be retransmitted. Of the 720 permutations, only six patterns have no two patterns on the same slot at the same time. Those six are shown below:

- 1 2 3 4 5 6
- 2 3 4 5 6 1
- 3 4 5 6 1 2
- 4 5 6 1 2 3
- 5 6 1 2 3 4
- 6 1 2 3 4 5

These patterns avoid having any two patterns on the same slot at the same time. They would work; however they would require fairly tight band pass filters and time guard bands, since patterns are on adjacent frequency slots at the same time, and on adjacent time slots on the same frequency.

To avoid this situation we have to eliminate the second, fourth, and six patterns. This elimination makes the band pass filters and time guard bands not so critical and expensive. The result is:

- 1 2 3 4 5 6
- 3 4 5 6 1 2
- 5 6 1 2 3 4

So for six slots, we were able to obtain about three good patterns. If we were to work this out for 79 slots, the number of good patterns would be in the range of about 20 good patterns, or FHSS channels. This is the number that is specified by IEEE 802.11, as we discuss in chapter 8. Most vendors provide 15 hopping patterns in their present products.

## Preamble for FHSS PHY

Next, let discuss the preamble that is required for an FHSS radio. The purpose of the preamble is to power up the transmitter and stabilize it, and to acquire synchronization. The basic elements of the preamble are a ramp up period, an idle pattern, and a synchronization word. Typical lengths for these elements are:

- Ramp up: 8 bit periods
- Idle pattern: 72 bit periods
- Synchronization word: 16 bit periods

The purpose of the ramp up period of 8 bits is to power up the transmitter and stabilize it. Controlling the rate of the power increase in the ramp period avoids power splatter in other channels. As a point of reference, Digital European Cordless Telephone uses a ramp up period of 10 bits. DECT does not specify a rate of power increase, an action that can further limit spurious emissions in other bands. A possible specification is for the transmitter to be off at the start of the first bit, no more than 1 mw at the end of the first bit, within 3 dB of steady state at the end of the 7th bit, and within 1 dB of steady state at the end of the 8th bit. Further, the ramp up should not exceed 1 volt per microsecond.

The purpose of the idle pattern is for the receivers to sense the presence of the signal, to do any diversity measurements and antenna selection if diversity is provided, and to synchronize to the carrier and clock of the incoming signal. This preparation must be done with no prior knowledge as to when packets occur. Seventy-two bits are sufficient to perform antenna diversity selection and bit synchronization, and for the receivers to stabilize prior to receiving a unique word for word synchronization. A zero/one pattern is most appropriate for the idle pattern since it has the most number of transitions and thus eases synchronization. Such a pattern also has the minimum DC offset.

Finally, the unique word has the purpose of providing word synchronization and to point to the first bit of the MAC payload. The length of the unique word is chosen to minimize overhead while maintaining a low rate of false alarms. A 16 bit synchronization word represents a good balance. To summarize this example, we have:

- Ramp up: 8 bit periods
- Idle pattern: 72 bit periods (0,1 pattern)
- Unique word: 16 bit periods (word 4657)
- Total: 96 bit periods

As we have seen, building an FHSS radio is complex. This complexity is required because the ISM bands are not dedicated to Wireless LANs; they are used on secondary basis. Someone else has the primary usage of the bands. Wireless LANs, and indeed anyone else who would like to use these bands, must spread the spectrum by frequency hopping or direct sequence in order not to present any noticeable interference to the primary license holders. Next, we consider the engineering issues of a Direct Sequence Spread Spectrum system.

# DSSS System Engineering

The parameters in this section are based on one of the early DSSS Wireless LAN systems. The system is designed to operate at the 900 MHz ISM band. A later version works in the 2.4 GHz ISM bands for the parts of the world that do not have the 900 MHz band available. The maximum power allowed for a DSSS system in the US is 1 watt. The maximum power allowed in other countries at 2.4 GHz and other bands is 100 mw. This design uses 250 mw in the US and 100 mw in other parts of the world.

A simple way of achieving diversity is through the use of polarization diversity at the receiver. This works because when signals are reflected they change polarization. Thus, when a signal is transmitted in vertical polarization, it changes to horizontal polarization when it is reflected. Since much of the received energy is reflected at least once, as we saw above in the discussion on multipath, this kind of diversity provides a good way of obtaining different signals.

Specifying the operating range of a radio is not a matter of giving one single number. The range depends on the kind of environment. If we are in free space, we obtain the maximum range. For indoor environments with open space we can obtain a very different number. Going through inside walls yields yet another number, and going though outside walls or floors and ceiling yields the smallest number, because the attenuation function is dramatically different for the different situations, as we discussed above. For this system, the different numbers vary widely as illustrated below:

- 800' outdoors
- 250' indoors, open space
- 100' through walls

The data rate of this system is 2 Mbps. Provision for falling back to 1 Mbps exists if the channel is not as good as expected. The bit error rate is $10^{-5}$ for $E_b/N_0$ of 16 dB. $E_b/N_0$ is the energy per bit divided by the noise density. The channel availability is 99.5%.

Even at 2 Mbps, multipath should not cause a problem. The bit duration at 2 Mbps is 500 nanoseconds. The maximum typical delay for small buildings is 100 nanoseconds. For a large building it can be as high as 250 nanoseconds, which would cause ISI, so the performance of this system could degrade if the walls are very far apart.

The modulation chosen for this system is Differential QPSK. Differential modulation requires less accurate carrier tracking than coherent detection. It can use 50 ppm crystal accuracy at 2.4 GHz to allow a low-cost implementation.

The data rate of 2 Mbps must be spread by a factor of at least 11 to satisfy the FCC part 15 for DSSS. Therefore, a chip rate of 22 Mcps would be required. To avoid running at such a high rate, choose quadrature modulation. So that we can run at half that rate at 11 Mcps. The bandwidth of this signal is still 22 MHz, due to the roll-off of the filters. The specific shape is given by:

- 22 MHz allocated
- 30 dBc @ ± 11 MHz
- 55 dBc @ ± 50 MHz

With this bandwidth, the maximum number of independent channels at the 900 MHz band is one. The maximum number of channels in the 2.4 GHz band is three, in contrast with 15 to 20 channels for FHSS. This contrast is one of the major differences between FHSS and DSSS, and one of the reasons most vendors are favoring FHSS at this time. We develop a comprehensive comparison of the two systems shortly.

The transceiver specification for this system is given by:

- Transmitted power
  - Maximum of 1 w set by FCC part 15.247
  - 250, 11, 50, 10, and 1 mw optional levels
- Receiver
  - Maximum input level: - 20 dBm
  - Minimum input level: - 76 dBm @ $10^{-5}$ Bit Error Rate
- Switching time TX to RX: 10 microseconds
- Adjacent channel rejection: 50 dB
- Antenna port impedance (if exposed): 50 ohms

The block diagram of the transmitter for this system is illustrated in Figure 6.10.

The RTS and CTS packets required to deal with hidden nodes are inputs to the transmitter control along with the transmitter clock and the data. The data is scrambled, often to avoid runs of errors. When a problem occurs on the channel, it affects a series of bits in a row. By scrambling the information bits, that series of bits is not actually in order when it is descrambled at the receiver.

Next is the DQPSK modulator, followed by the spreader. The spreader applies the chip stream, which is at a rate of 11 Mcps. The resulting chip stream is multiplied by the local oscillator, which is in the 900 MHz band or the 2.4 GHz band, and the resulting RF signal is transmitted on the channel through the antenna. The system is managed by the management function. A training sequence generator provides the sequence that is needed by the receiver to achieve and maintain synchronism.

The block diagram of the receiver for the system appears in Figure 6.11.

The received signal is first filtered and power amplified. Next, it is mixed down from RF frequency and filtered. Then amplitude variations are removed by an Automatic Gain Circuit. The correlator applies the same pseudo-random code that was used at the transmitter to despread the signal. The code must be synchronized with the transmitter; the resulting signal is used at this point to perform the carrier sense function in CSMA. It cannot be done at any earlier point in the system. Clock is recovered at this time as well. The data is sent down to a differentiator to extract the data from the differential data received. Then it is put through a four-level decision unit and descrambled to recover the original bit stream. Management is performed by the management circuits shown.

Once again we see that having to spread the spectrum to meet the secondary usage criteria results in complex circuitry. If we did not have to use spread spectrum, the radios could be a great deal simpler, and better performance could be obtained at lower cost. To do this improvement, we have to have spectrum that is dedicated to this market. This bandwidth has been allocated; it is the Unlicensed PCS spectrum that is discussed in chapter 8. No systems use this new spectrum at this point in time since it is not cleared of incumbent users as yet.

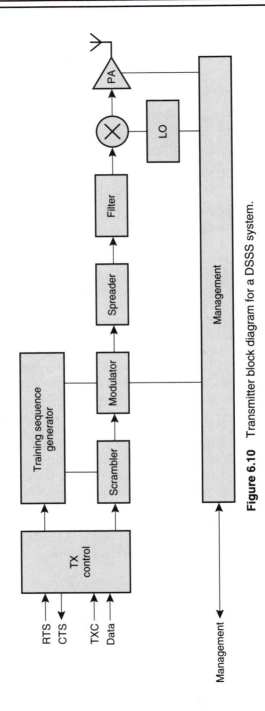

**Figure 6.10**   Transmitter block diagram for a DSSS system.

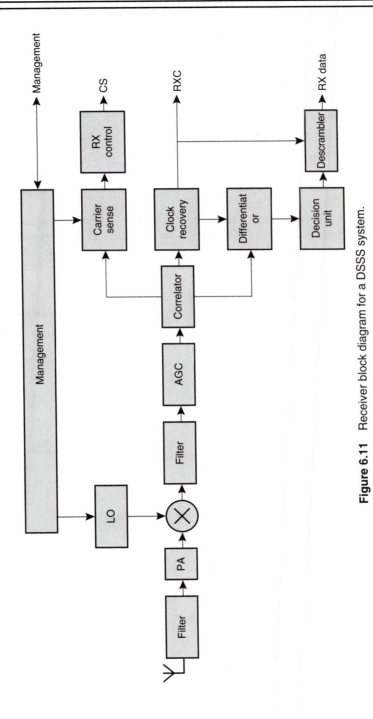

**Figure 6.11**    Receiver block diagram for a DSSS system.

## MAC Protocols for Wireless LANs

In this section we discuss three MAC protocols for Wireless LANs:

1. Listen Before You Talk MAC protocol
2. Integrated Wireless LAN MAC protocol
3. Polling MAC protocol

Before starting, let us define some terms. Figure 6.12 depicts the network architecture of a Wireless LAN.

The distribution system is the backbone network that has all the servers and other resources connected to it. Access Point 1 serves Basic Service Set 1, which has nodes A and B. Access Point 2 serves Basic Service Set 2, which has nodes C, D, and E in it. An ad hoc network also exists, which is not served by an access point. Figure 6.12 serves to illustrate the different possibilities that can occur in a Wireless LAN.

The MAC protocols that are presented in this section are characteristic of some of the products that are available on the market. Some were proposed to the 802.11 committee and demonstrate the advantages and disadvantages of the different schemes.

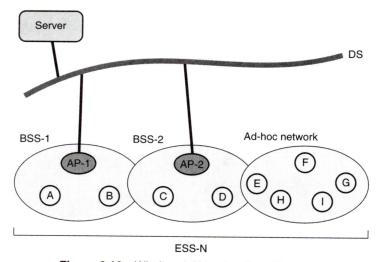

**Figure 6.12** Wireless LAN network architecture.

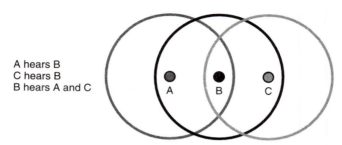

**Figure 6.13**  Hidden nodes.

## Listen Before You Talk MAC Protocol

The first MAC, the LBT protocol, is basically a nonpersistent CSMA protocol. It differs from CSMA protocols that are used in wired LANs in two ways. First, an RTS packet is transmitted before data is transmitted to the intended receiving node. The receiving node transmits a CTS packet that is heard by all nodes within radio range of the receiving node. This communication avoids collisions at the receiving nodes from any nodes that may be hidden from the transmitting node and are not able to hear its transmission. The RTS/CTS scheme avoids the hidden node problem illustrated in Figure 6.13.

After the RTS/CTS packet, the transmitting node transmits the data. Then, and this point is where this protocol also differs from CSMA protocols for wired LANS, the data is acknowledged at the MAC layer because the performance on the wireless link is much poorer than on typical wired networks. By providing ACKs at the MAC layer, the performance is brought up to par with wired networks. The result is an error performance that is expected by network layers above this wireless MAC.

## Integrated CSMA/TDMA MAC Protocol

The next MAC to be discussed is an integrated MAC protocol that is a hybrid of reservation and random access. The frame is segmented into:

- Two reservation intervals for isochronous traffic
- One interval for random access traffic

The boundary between the random access traffic and the isochronous traffic part can be moved adaptively by a control function. This can be made to work with or without an Access

Point. With an access point, the control function is in the Access Point. Without an access point, the control function is distributed among the nodes of the ad hoc network. We discuss more about that in Chapter 8.

The time frame of the integrated MAC appears in Figure 6.14.

The reservation-based sections of the frame are for traffic that requires guaranteed bandwidth. This is isochronous traffic such as voice and video that does not work well with random access MACs such as CSMA because the packets get lost too frequently, and arrive out of order some of the time. Put another way, the variance of arrival of the packets is too large for isochronous traffic. In the reservation part, a user can get a virtual circuit and has it until she is finished. This process is like circuit switching.

Another use for the isochronous part is to improve the performance of the system when the traffic becomes heavy. As we have discussed, CSMA has very poor behavior when the traffic becomes heavy. All the users are essentially colliding and hardly anyone gets through. This problem can be remedied with the integrated MAC. When the traffic becomes heavy and the throughput begins to degrade, the control function can begin to require that users request channels, and all must use the reserved part. This is the combined TDMA/CSMA protocol discussed in chapter 2.

The original intent of 802.11 was to provide a system that served both random as well as isochronous traffic. This requirement was called the time bounded service, referring to the variance of the arrival times of the packets. This requirement was delayed until a later phase of the protocol in the last minute, so the initial release of the protocol serves only random traffic.

The components of the integrated MAC protocol are a reserved part from the Access Point to the Mobile Station, a reserved part from the Mobile Station to the Access Point, and a random part. This protocol can support ad hoc networks by replacing the Access Point with a distributed coordination function as is discussed in Chapter 8. The random part is slotted ALOHA with Listen Before you Talk. This a variation on classical CSMA, and an improvement over slotted ALOHA alone, since the user must listen before using a slot.

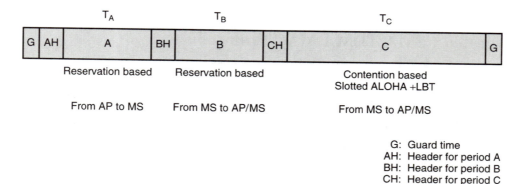

**Figure 6.14**   Integrated MAC frame structure.

The headers of the three parts of the frame contain the information below:

- Header AH
  - Length of TA, TB, TC
  - BSID = Unique ID of the Access Point
  - NET_ID = Network ID
  - NEXT_FREQ / NEXT_CODE / NEXT_CHNL
  - < Si, Wi > = Access Point transmits Si packets to user Wi

The network ID can be used to identify a network within the available radio channel that would filter the traffic out from other identified networks, for example, to isolate two different companies that are sharing the radio spectrum but do not wish to share traffic. The next items are assuming the underlying physical layer is an FHSS PHY.

The header for the next part of the frame contains:

- The length of TB, TC
- < Si, Vi, Wi > = User Vi transmits Si packets to user Wi

The vectors indicating traffic source and destination are for power savings. By putting this information in the header, sleeping nodes only have to wake up for the header to see if they have any traffic coming to them.

The header for the last part of the frame contains:

- The length of TC
- K = Current estimate of users actively attempting transmission in random access section

A subset of this protocol is used by one of the products to be discussed in Chapter 7. The subset is essentially TDMA with a random access part that is used for users to request channels in the TDMA part. This setup is not unlike cellular systems. They too have a random access part of the frame for users to request channels.

# Reservation/Polling MAC Protocol

Next, we discuss a reservation/polling protocol. Why discuss such a protocol? The company that uses this protocol has been working with a stock trading application. In such an application, the fairness of the MAC is of utmost importance. If something important happens in the market, every trader wants to access the system at the same time and they want to be insured that the first there is first served. A random access scheme would be intolerable. To make this point further, the first order from a stock exchange for a Wireless LAN system went to another nontraditional Wire-

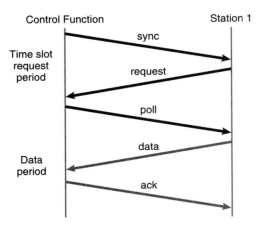

**Figure 6.15** Reservation/polling protocol.

less LAN product, the IBM product that uses essentially a TDMA protocol. TDMA has a very slow average access time compared with CSMA, but it is fair, and that is what the stock traders need.

The reservation/polling protocol is depicted in Figure 6.15.

When a node has a packet to send, it first sends a request to the control point. Its request is queued along with all other users, and the control point polls the users in turn. The data transmission is acknowledged, and all transmissions go through the access point. No ad hoc networking is possible.

# Power Management

In this section, we discuss how to provide power management features in the MAC to help nodes that are running on batteries and must sleep as much as possible. First, let us look at two kinds of mobiles, a notebook computer and a palm-top type of computer. The notebook computer uses relatively large batteries that have the following characteristics:

- Battery life
  - 2 to 4 hours now
  - 4 to 8 hours future
- Energy capacity
  - 500 to 1500 mAh

Most Wireless LAN adapters draw current from the computer battery, unlike most Mobile Data devices, which have their own battery. How much is the mobile user willing to give up from his precious computer battery? Not much. Most Wireless LAN products strive to keep the power budget of the Wireless LAN adapter below 20% of the total power capacity of the computer battery. If this budget is the case, then the power budget for wireless is 100 to 300 mAh. For over two to four hours, the result is an average current in the range of 25 ma to 150 ma.

The design point for palm-top computers is much more stringent. Palm-tops run from AA batteries. The flatter form factor palm-top computers run from AAA batteries. The characteristics of these batteries and their expected life are given by:

- AA batteries have a capacity of 2000 mAh
- AAA batteries have a capacity of 250 mAh
- Batteries in palm-top computers are expected to last for weeks

Suppose that the battery life is four weeks, and that the palm-top computer is on for 20 hours in the week; the battery provides 80 hours of service. If the impact of the Wireless LAN adapter is less than 20%, then the current available for the Wireless LAN adapter is 0.6 to 5 ma—not very much.

In order to achieve these low budgets, the Wireless LAN adapter must sleep as much as possible. The following states are defined for the Wireless LAN adapter:

- Transmit state
  - Transmitter is turned on
- Awake state
  - Receiver is powered on and ready to receive
- Doze state
  - Transceiver dozing

The way the power savings scheme works is with the help of the Access Point. The AP knows the power management modes of the nodes that are associated with it. The AP buffers traffic for dozing nodes. The AP informs nodes of traffic for them in special broadcast packets called TDIMs, or Traffic Delivery Information Messages. The frame header includes which stations have data to receive in the frame, how much data to receive, and when it will be delivered. The stations need to wake up only when they are transmitting, or when they have data specifically intended for them. They wake up during the frame header to check the TDIM to see if they have traffic destined for them. If they don't, they go back to sleep until the next header. If they do have traffic destined for them, they go back to sleep, wake back up when it is due, receive it, and then go back to sleep. Palm-top computers, which must be especially conservative, do not wake up every frame. They remain asleep as long as they wish, and wake up to check the frame header as seldom as they wish. The tradeoff is that they do not receive their traffic as quickly as if they woke up more often, but they do save battery life.

# Interconnection with Backbone Networks

Now is the time to address the very important topic of connecting to backbone networks. We address two aspects: First, connecting within the same network, done below the network layer using MAC layer bridges. Secondly, we address mobility between different networks, done at the network layer via new protocols such as Mobile IP. Next we discuss naming and directory services for dealing with the need for a huge number of addresses to satisfy the growing interest in the Internet, and PCS-like structures for dealing with same issue in the worldwide telephone network.

## Mobility within the Same Network

Figure 6.16 presents the situation in which mobile nodes are roaming in areas that are covered by different access points but that are in the same network.

Each access point contains three components:

- A Wireless LAN interface to communicate with the nodes in its service area
- An interface card to the backbone LAN, for example Ethernet

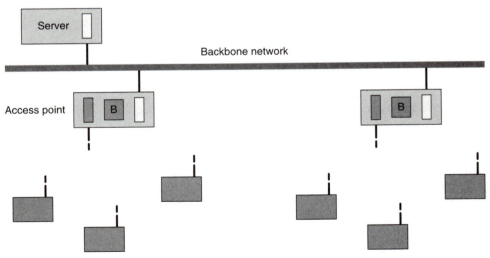

**Figure 6.16**   Mobility within the same network.

- A MAC layer bridge to filter the traffic between the wireless subnet and the backbone

This filtering is essential to prevent all the traffic on the backbone from being repeated on the wireless subnet. Bridging is used to filter traffic from different wired segments of a large LAN. In Wireless Networks it serves the same purpose and is much more critical since the capacity of the Wireless LAN can be quickly exhausted. Before discussing how wireless bridges work, let us review briefly how wired bridges work, and how they are different from repeaters and routers. The basic idea is that wireless bridges work the same way as wired bridges except they have shorter timers for aging out nodes.

Repeaters copy bits between cable segments. They simply extend the reach of a cable; they do no filtering of the traffic whatsoever. Every packet that comes on one interface is repeated on the other interfaces connected to a repeater, thus extending the electrical length of the cable.

Bridges isolate traffic between the interfaces to which they are connected. They relay traffic onto a cable segment only if they know it is destined for a node on that cable segment. Routers, gateways, and protocol converters operate at higher protocol levels. In particular, routers operate in a large system, having several networks, each with a distinct network identity. Routers look at the network address in the packets and route them according to tables that are generated in the routers and updated as the network changes.

Bridges perform their functions mostly automatically. When a bridge is first installed, it acts as a repeater. It promiscuously repeats all packets it receives on all LAN segments to which it is connected. Then, as traffic goes through it, it watches the packets and begins to form a table of which nodes are on which LAN segment. It does so by looking at the source address in the packets. Next time it receives a packet, it looks at the destination address and examines its table. If the destination address is in its table, then it forwards the packet only on the LAN segment where that node is at that point in time. If the destination address is not in its table, it has to send the packet on all LAN segments until it sees a packet with that source address and notes from which LAN segment it came.

The entries in the table are not kept forever. Nodes can be turned off, or may have moved, and sending those packets on the LAN unnecessarily would be useless. For this reason, bridges have a timer that ages out old entries in the table if it has not heard from a given node for some time. Those timers for wired LANs are on the order of hours. This area is where bridges for Wireless LANs differ from bridges for wired LANs. Wireless bridges age-out entries in the table much faster. The age-out timers in wireless bridges may be on the order of minutes, to allow for mobile nodes moving out of range of one access point and into another.

What if the age-out timer is too short? This problem means if a node is quiet for awhile but still in the same wireless subnet, it will be aged out. The bridge must then repeat traffic destined for it on all LAN segments connected to it until it hears from the node. What if the age-out timer is too long? This problem means that the node could have been turned off or left the service area of the Access Point, and traffic for it is still being sent on this Wireless Subnet and wasting capacity on it. Meanwhile, the node could be in the service area of another Acess Point that is sending its traffic on the second subnet. The right choice balances these two factors and is usually on the order of minutes.

Additional functions of bridges include:

- Buffering between different speed LANs
- Changing frame formats between incompatible LANs
- Adding or deleting fields within the frame, e.g. 802.3 has a data length field and 802.4 doesn't

Within 802, six LAN standards and 2 bridging protocols exist, as you see in Figure 6.17. The Wireless LAN standards are:

- 802.3 - Ethernet
- 802.4 - Token bus
- 802.5 - Token ring
- 802.6 - Metropolitan Area Networks
- 802.9 - Integrated voice and data networks
- 802.11 - Wireless LAN networks

802.2 is where the Logical Link Control functions such as addressing are specified. 802.1 is where MAC bridging functions are specified. The TCP/IP protocol is superimposed on the chart as well. Internet Protocol is at layer 3, the network protocol. Transport Control Protocol is at layer 4, the transport layer.

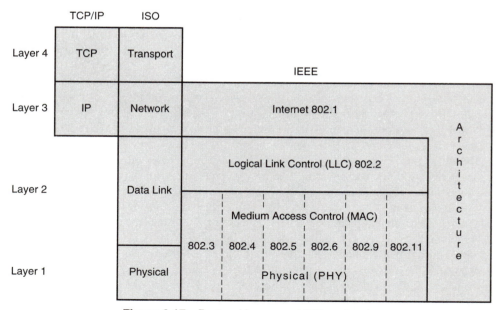

**Figure 6.17**   Protocol layers and 802 protocols.

Within 802 are two MAC layer bridging protocols:

- Spanning tree bridges
- Source routing bridge

Spanning tree bridges and source routing bridges both construct tables of which LAN segment nodes are at any point anytime and age them out if they have not heard from them. The biggest difference between them from an implementation point of view is that source routing bridges place a greater burden on the nodes. Most bridges use the spanning tree option.

Constructing the spanning tree is an iterative process that ends up with a distributed database of where all the nodes in the network are and the best way to reach any given node. The topology of the network is not in any one bridge, but taken together, the topology takes shape. The way this topology is formed is as follows. Each bridge broadcasts its identity, and all other bridges about which it knows. A distributed algorithm exists for selecting a root bridge and a tree that reaches every other bridge, and minimizes the number of hops from each bridge to the root. The tree is continuously updated as bridges come and go.

Source routing bridges rely much more on the source node, which keeps a table of where other nodes are, and constructs a view of the network topology. It includes the route the packet is to take in the header. These calculations must all take place in the node, thus placing a heavy load on its resources. For this reason, most LANs and especially Wireless LANs use the spanning tree type of bridge.

# Mobility among Different Networks and Mobile IP

Now let us focus on mobility among different networks, in particular the Mobile IP protocol. We discuss the goals, definitions, and general operation of Mobile IP, and provide the specifications of various packets.

The goals of Mobile IP are:

- Mobility is handled at the network layer
- Transport and higher layers are unaffected
- Applications do not need to change
- The infrastructure of non-mobile routers are unaffected
- Non-mobile hosts are unaffected
- Continuous operation occurs across multiple networks
- Security is as good as with existing networks

The Internet is huge and contains a tremendous number of nodes and routers. Implementing mobility has to be gradual and cannot disturb any nodes or routers that do not wish to implement mobility at an early stage of the development, or ever. In the Internet, nodes are known as hosts. To minimize the impact on the Internet and on applications, Mobile IP specifies that mobility is to be handled at the network layer and not disturb higher layers. Further, routers that do not wish to implement mobility do not have to change in any way. And hosts that are not mobile do not have to change in any way.

The basic objective of Mobile IP is to provide hosts that are mobile the ability to move from one location to another and take with them a mobile IP address. At present, the IP address is associated with a fixed network location much like a phone number. The phone number is associated with a jack in the wall in a specific physical location; it does not travel with the person. By the same token, today's IP address reflects a physical location served by some host that is not mobile. For hosts to be mobile, a new set of IP addresses are provided; these Mobile IP addresses move with the mobile host. The job of Mobile IP is to configure a way of finding where those Mobile IP addresses are at any point in time, and to deliver packets to them without disrupting the whole Internet in the process. The security requirement of Mobile IP is not to degrade the present level of security of the Internet. This is called "weak security," perhaps humorously!

The operation of Mobile IP is fairly simple. Two options were considered, similar in nature to the two kinds of bridges discussed above. One option is handled mostly in the routers; the other places more of the job on the nodes. The one chosen is the one that assigns the job mostly to the routers. Basically, it is a forwarding mechanism. Packets destined for a mobile host first go to its home network. If the node is not there, its home router places the packet in another envelope with its forwarding address on it.

To understand in more detail, let us first make some basic definitions:

- Mobile Host: A host that moves from place to place invalidating historical Internet design assumptions about static placement of computers
- Home Address: An address used to identify an MH no matter where it may currently be located
- Home Network: The logical network where an MH's Home Address resides
- Care of Address: An Address used to locate an MH at some particular instant

Thus, a mobile host obtains a Mobile IP address from a new pool of IP addresses. This Mobile IP address is associated with that node's home address. This setup is akin to a cellular phone user having his cellular phone associated with a Home Location Register in his hometown. When the user is away from home, she has to somehow obtain a Care of temporary address while she is visiting in that area. This situation is similar to the cellular user being registered with a Visitor Location Register when roaming away from his home location. The Care of Address is temporary while the user is in the location served by the foreign router. The Home Address is permanent. It is the address known by the Internet community.

The new software that implements the mobile capabilities in the routers are agents. They are defined as follows:

- Home Agent: An agent that redirects or tunnels packets from a Home Network to the Care of Address of an MH
- Foreign Agent: A specialized forwarding agent that
  - Offers a Care of Address
  - Maintains and performs mapping between that address and the Home Address of an MH in its care

These are some of the functions routers must implement if they wish to become Foreign Agents. They have to offer visiting nodes Care of Addresses. They also must let the Home Agent in the Home Network of the mobile host know that it has the node in its care so the Home Agent can perform the forwarding function.

As one might guess, situations arise where inefficient triangle routing, or worse, back and forth routing can occur. An example is shown in Figure 6.18.

A fixed host sends a packet to a node that is normally in San Francisco. The node is visiting in Boston. The mobile node has a Care of Address in Boston, and its Home Agent in San Francisco is aware of this fact. All other hosts are not aware of it, though. The fixed host in Washington addresses the packet to the mobile node's Home Address, which routes the packet to the mobile host's Home Network in San Francisco. The Home Agent reenvolopes or encapsulates the packet and sends it to Washington. This process is triangle routing.

Triangle routing is not too bad if it involves just one or two packets. If it involves many packets, then it results in a waste of network bandwidth. To remedy the situation, if many packets are going from the fixed node in Washington to the mobile node while it is visiting in Boston, the Foreign Agent in Boston sends a message to the fixed node in Washington and asks it to use the mobile node's Care of Address instead of its Home Address. The packets then go directly from Washington to Boston instead of via San Francisco.

An analogy exists with the telephone network, but it is not quite the same. In the telephone network most calls are connection-oriented, as opposed to connectionless, since they are in the Internet. The setup of the calls in the telephone network takes place over a high-speed packet net-

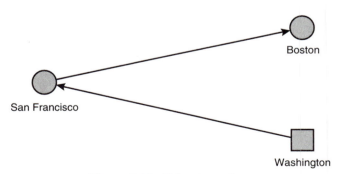

**Figure 6.18**   Triangle routing.

work, the Common Channel Signaling network. The calling party signal goes to the called party's Home Location Register. The HLR informs the calling party of the Visitor Location Register serving the cellular user he is calling. This communication takes place over the CCS packet switched network. When the time comes to set up the trunk to carry the user traffic, it is set up the shortest way.

Figure 6.19 illustrates the operation of Mobile IP.

Mobile host B is away from its Home Network. It is adopted by Foreign Agent 1. Foreign Agent 1 is an Internet router that has implemented Mobile IP. It provides the Foreign Agent function and has provided Mobile Host B with a Care of Address while it is in the serving area of Foreign Agent 1. All packets destined for Mobile Host B are tunneled or encapsulated and sent to Foreign Agent 1, which delivers the packets to Mobile Host B. When Mobile Host B moves to another serving area, for example, one served by Foreign Agent 2, then that Foreign Agent provides Mobile Host B with a new Care of Address while it is in the serving area of Foreign Agent 2 and informs the Mobile Host's Home Agent of the new adoption. Packets destined to Mobile Host B now become tunneled to Foreign Agent 2 for delivery.

How does a Mobile Host find a Foreign Agent that has the Foreign Agent software? Two ways are possible. The first is through advertisements. Foreign Agents send out service advertisements that announce their willingness to provide Care of Addresses to visiting Mobile Hosts. If the Foreign Agent does not wish to broadcast advertisements so as not to load the network or its own resources, then the Mobile Host can send out a solicitation packet asking if a Foreign Agent is in the vicinity.

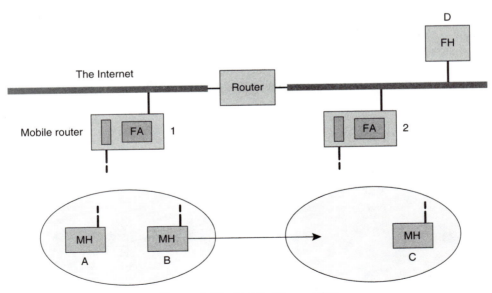

**Figure 6.19** Mobile IP operation.

To understand the operation of Mobile IP at a deeper level, we can examine the structure of the different packets that make up the protocol. That structure is presented below at a point in the development of Mobile IP and is subject to change.

- Advertisement packet
  - Type, code, checksum
  - Care of Address
  - Foreign Agent incarnation number (in case it crashes)
  - Advertisement interval
- Solicitation packet
  - Type, code, checksum
  - MH's IP address
  - MH's MAC address
- Registration
  - MH to Foreign Agent
  - Foreign Agent to Home Agent
  - Registration ACKs
- MH to Foreign Agent registration packet
  - Type, code, checksum
  - Home Agent's address
  - Sequence number
  - Previous Care of Address
  - MH authenticator to Home Agent
  - MH authenticator to Foreign Agent
  - MH's IP address
  - MH's MAC address
- Foreign Agent to Home Agent registration packet
  - Type, code, checksum
  - Care of Address
  - Sequence number
  - MH authenticator to Home Agent
- Home Agent to Foreign Agent registration ACK packet
  - Type, code, checksum
  - MH's IP address
  - Sequence number

- Care of Address
- Cache time-out: How long MH can trust Home Agent to keep track of its whereabouts
  - Foreign Agent to MH registration ACK packet
    - Type, code, checksum
    - MH's IP address
    - Sequence number

Next we discuss naming and directory services that are needed to deal with the growing Internet in a scalable way.

## Name and Directory Services

The existing directory services appear in Figure 6.20.

Novell has Bindery in version 3.x and Network Directory Service in version 4.0. Banyan has StreetTalk. DNS was born out of the explosive growth of the Internet and the need to find the IP number for a given host name. Previously, host names were stored in a HOSTS.TXT file kept on the hosts and updated from a central site. The DNS approach uses a distributed, hierarchical name space. Each site maintains its own database for its own machines. The collection of these databases makes up the distributed directory.

The DNS components are:

- Hierarchical name space and associated resource records
- Name servers that search the data
- Resolvers that query the name servers on behalf of client applications

DNS operation is illustrated in Figure 6.21.

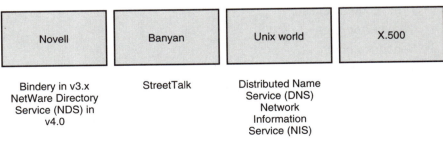

| Novell | Banyan | Unix world | X.500 |
|---|---|---|---|
| Bindery in v3.x NetWare Directory Service (NDS) in v4.0 | StreetTalk | Distributed Name Service (DNS) Network Information Service (NIS) | |

**Figure 6.20**   Naming and directory services.

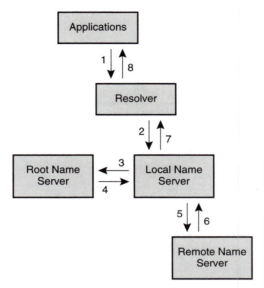

**Figure 6.21**    How DNS works.

The way DNS works is as follows. The application needs to send a packet to a server, so it asks the Resolver. The Resolver queries the Local Name Server. If the Local Name Server has the location of the destination host, it provides it to the Resolver. If not, it sends a query to a root name server that directs it to the Remote Name Sever that has the required address. The Local Name Server obtains the address from the Remote Name Server and adds that address to its cache of addresses in case this user or another user requests the same address in the near future.

This kind of scheme is distributed, hierarchical, and most importantly scalable as the Internet grows. It has similarities to the telephone network and future Personal Communications Services structures, so let us examine those next.

## The PCS Model for Mobility

In cellular and PCS networks, each person has a unique number that goes with her wherever she goes, similar to the Mobile IP home address. This address or universal phone number is stored in the user's Home Location Register, which is located in the server at the office of the cellular provider that provides the user her server back in her hometown. When the user is visiting a foreign location, she is automatically registered with a Visitor Location Register that informs the user's Home Location Register of the adoption, so calls coming to the user are routed directly to

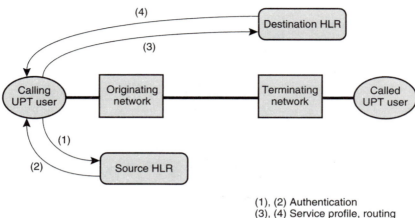

(1), (2) Authentication
(3), (4) Service profile, routing

**Figure 6.22** PCS call flow.

the switching center served by this VLR. This process is illustrated in Figure 6.22, which shows the call flow.

The HLRs and VLRs are essentially a distributed database of all the users in the future worldwide cellular and PCS network. They contain a wealth of information, in particular the names, services subscribed to, universal phone numbers, and present location of all the cellular and PCS subscribers throughout the world. The present location of the users is kept confidential except from government agencies who need them.

The HLRs and VLRs are the roots of future Value-Added Services. The next step may be a Yellow Pages service that allows a user in a foreign location to find the nearest Chinese restaurant, or tennis players of his own ability. The dimensions of the future are boundless. These value-added services hold the potential for future revenue growth.

## Summary

In this chapter, we explored various aspects of Wireless LAN technologies. We began the chapter with a summary of technology trends, particularly in the radio field, as they relate to the cellular market, and contrasted them to the Wireless LAN market. Many of the developments in the cellular and PCS markets can be useful in the Wireless LAN market. We develop a wish list that a user may desire in a Wireless LAN.

Next, we analyze FHSS systems. First, we provide a list of systems design goals, followed by a system engineering discussion that deals with details of the radio. The next section shows how multipath can cause Inter Symbol Interference, and that in contrast to cellular systems, Wireless

LANs avoid the problem of multipath by keeping the data rate below about 2 Mbps. Cellular systems do deal with it through equalization or rake filtering. Wireless LANs avoid the cost of these sophisticated techniques.

Various modulation techniques are analyzed including CPFSK, 0.39 GMSK, and others. Next, the philosophy behind frequency hopping pattern selection is presented. For the approximately 80 frequencies available in the 2.4 GHz ISM bands, about 15 to 20 channels, or frequency hopping patterns, are possible. Finally, the preamble required to achieve and maintain synchronization in an FHSS system is studied. The result is that a preamble of about 96 bits is found to be sufficient for the job.

Moving up the protocol stack, the next topic is Wireless LAN MAC protocols. Three protocols are studied. The Listen Before you Talk protocol is essentially nonpersistent CSMA. It is the one used by the majority of Wireless LAN products. All the products use different variations of it since they were developed before the standard was finalized. The standard is also based on this basic LBT MAC. The other two protocols are an integrated CSMA/TDMA protocol and a Reservation/Polling protocol. These two protocols are used by two Wireless LAN products and interestingly are the ones favored by the stock trading applications since they are very fair algorithms, even though they do not have the fastest response time.

The next topic is power management. Two design points are studied, the notebook computer model, and the palm-top computer model. One has a battery with average life time ranging from two to four hours moving towards four to eight hours, the other using AA or AAA batteries that are expected to last for weeks. Ways of saving battery life are presented, including sleeping almost all the time except when the computer has something to transmit or something to receive. The MAC support needed to implement these power saving features are outlined.

Interconnection to backbone networks is discussed for mobility within the same network, as well as for mobility among different networks. For mobility within the same network, spanning tree MAC level bridges are favored. These bridges are very similar to their wired LAN cousins with the exception that the age-out timers are much shorter, on the order of minutes instead of hours in length. Mobility among different networks is presented in light of Mobile IP. The protocol is essentially a tunneling or encapsulation scheme. It relies on some of the routers in the Internet to implement Home Agents and Foreign Agents to take care of Mobile Hosts. The Home Agents reenvelope packets destined for a Mobile Host that is away from home.

Finally, this chapter deals with naming and directory services, such as DNS, which are hierarchical, distributed name spaces that provide a scalable structure that can handle the growth of the Internet, including Mobile Hosts, in a way similar to the cellular and PCS networks.

# 7 *Wireless LAN Products*

Wireless LAN products serve office buildings and campuses and provide relatively high data rates as compared to Mobile Data networks in the wide area. A number of products are now available. How do they work? How well do they perform? How much do they cost now and what are they likely to cost in the future? In this chapter we discuss:

- Choosing a Wireless LAN
- WaveLAN
- Digital Ocean Grouper
- Digital Equipment Wireless LAN
- Solectek AIRLAN
- Proxim RangeLAN 2
- Xircom Netwave
- IBM Wireless LAN
- Motorola Altair
- Windata
- RadioLAN
- Photonics
- Spectrix
- InfraLAN
- Comparison of Wireless LAN products

First, we start with a discussion of the issues that need to be addressed in choosing a Wireless LAN product.

# Choosing a Wireless LAN

The types of questions one might ask when considering acquiring a Wireless LAN are:

- What are the applications? Is mobility required?
- What level of performance is acceptable?
- Will infrared satisfy the needs?
- To what backbone networks do we need to connect?
- With what Network Operating Systems do we need to work?
- Is it secure?
- How easy is it to install? To use? To manage?
- How much does it cost?

The majority of future applications of Wireless LANs are expected to be for mobile computers. At the same time, the wire replacement applications will continue be an important niche market. The cost of both kinds of adapters are about the same. Not all manufacturers provide an adapter that fits in a portable device; they meet only the needs of the niche wire replacement market. Other vendors provide both solutions, a Network Interface Card as well as a PCMCIA solution. In the future, most manufacturers will likely provide only the PCMCIA solution. Desktop computers will probably have such an interface. For those desktop computers that do not have such an interface, an adapter is already available that converts between the NIC physical interface and the PCMCIA interface.

The next question to ask is what data rate is acceptable. Users probably would like not to see any difference between the wired network and the Wireless Network, as discussed in the previous chapter. This possibility is not available in the near term. In fact, Wireless Networks are not likely to ever be able to match the bandwidth of wired networks. Whenever Wireless LANs achieve a jump in performance, wired networks will likely experience a jump in performance as well, keeping the size of the gap about the same over time.

Infrared systems have the potential of being less expensive; however, their range tends to be shorter and they require line of sight. Infrared Access Points can cover a campus if a sufficient number of them exists. Is this possibility a feasible solution for the situation being considered? Are the Access Points sufficiently inexpensive, and is their installation sufficiently simple to make the whole system more cost-effective than a radio system? Or perhaps the application is a one-room scenario like a stock trading room or similar situation.

To what backbone networks must we connect, and to what Network Operating Systems must we connect? Most products support Ethernet at this time. Some have mentioned future possible support for Token Ring; two products support Token Ring now. Most products support a "short list" of NOSs, including Novell, TCP/IP, and Microsoft NOSs.

Security is a highlighted problem for Wireless Networking applications of all types. Security is an option in most products. Interestingly, even though it is available, many users elect not to use it. Perhaps the implementation of the security options is not satisfactory. In many cases, it is a problem of administration of passwords and keys.

Ease of installing, using, and managing the devices includes a range of questions such as: How easy is updating the software? Are complex site surveys required? Are training classes required for users? Hopefully the answer to the last question is no. The equipment should be practically transparent to the user.

Finally, the issue of cost could be a determining factor in making the decision to purchase a Wireless LAN. As is typical with a new industry, the price of Wireless LAN nodes is on the order of $400 or more at the present time. By the time Access Points and other equipment are added in, the cost per node could be about $500. For many vertical applications, this is justifiable, but for the large-volume horizontal applications, this price is hard to justify. For this reason, initial applications of Wireless LAN products are in the vertical markets. Horizontal markets, and their accompanying large volumes, have to wait for the price to drop to the range of what Ethernet used to be some years ago, around $200 per user complete. Achieving this level is no easy task for the industry. One major factor that would help is the availability of a standard. This is becoming a reality soon, and shortly after the standard is complete we should have chip sets available that make manufacturing Wireless LANs cost-effectively easier.

Figure 7.1 illustrates some, not all, of the Wireless Networking products available. This list is not exhaustive, but rather it is a partial list used for the purpose of illustrating different products that use different technologies.

The chart organizes Wireless LAN products according to whether they use radio or infrared, and according to whether they come in the PCMCIA form factor and therefore provide mobility, or

| | Mobile | Wire replacement |
|---|---|---|
| **Radio** | Lucent WaveLAN | Motorola Altair |
| | IBM Wireless LAN | |
| | Proxim RangeLAN | Windata |
| | Telxon | |
| | Symbol | RadioLan |
| | Xircom Netwave | |

| | | |
|---|---|---|
| **Infrared** | Photonics | InfraLAN |
| | SpectrixLite | Radiance |

**Figure 7.1**    Sample Wireless LAN configurations.

they come in a larger form factor that does not fit in a portable computer. The most popular configuration is a radio Wireless LAN in PCMCIA form factor. Here we have products from AT&T, IBM, two small companies, Proxim and Xircom, and two medium-sized companies that are active in the retail industry, Telxon and Symbol. The mobile infrared products include Photonics and Spectrix, both small companies.

The large form factor products include one from Motorola that is different from the others in that it uses the 18 GHz band and not spread spectrum technology in the ISM bands. Windata and RadioLAN *do* use the ISM bands. Windata uses the 2.4 and the 5.7 GHz bands; RadioLAN uses the 5.7 band but not the spread spectrum option. They use the little-known low-power option. They also position themselves as a wire replacement option at the present time even though they plan on having a PCMCIA option in the near future. The wire replacement infrared products include InfraLAN, which started out as a Token Ring plug-compatible product but has generalized to include Ethernet point-to-point as well as traditional Ethernet subnet, as will be discussed later in this chapter.

In the next sections, we present a summary of each product. The first ones covered are explained in detail; subsequent products are described more briefly in reference to the earlier products. The products are presented roughly in the order in which they appeared on the market in each of the categories. First, we discuss mobile radio Wireless LANs, followed by wire replacement radio products, and then we discuss the infrared products. For each product we present:

- Product line
- Topology
- How it works
- Protocols supported
- Performance

After presenting most of the products, we compare them relative to various criteria.

# Lucent WaveLAN

One of the first Wireless LAN products to appear on the market is the WaveLAN, which is now provided by Lucent Technologies. When it was first introduced the company was NCR. The product line includes the components you see in Figure 7.2.

The original product has an ISA/Microchannel card with a cable that connects to a flat antenna that is the size of a small cigarette pack. The PCMCIA product comes with a small external box that has a small retractable antenna. This is a common initial implementation for the PCMCIA products. The reason is to keep the sensitive RF section of the radio a bit removed from the hostile RF environment inside the PCMCIA cage of the computer. The PCMCIA cage is shielded, but still it is in the middle of a notebook computer that is full of electronic equipment that is running at

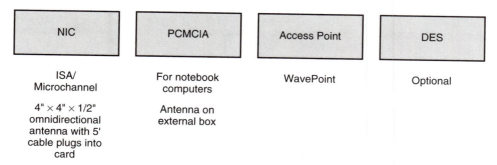

**Figure 7.2** AT&T WaveLAN product line.

high clock frequencies. Putting sensitive RF equipment in such an environment is a challenge. Most manufacturers have plans to evolve to such a one-piece solution in the future. Xircom, which has been making small form factor products longer than most other vendors, did introduce the first product that is one piece with only the antenna external to the PCMCIA card.

The rest of the AT&T product line includes the Access Point and an optional encryption chip. The Access Point is a standalone device that is the size of a small box. When this product was first introduced (this fact applies to most of the Wireless LAN products) they did not have a standalone Access Point. Instead, a server was used as an Access Point. The server was equipped with the same node hardware, with a radio, the backbone interface card that was mostly Ethernet, and software that implemented bridge or router software.

The topology of the AT&T product appears in Figure 7.3.

As shown in Figure 7.3, we have desktop computers with NICs, and portable computers with PCMCIA cards. With no other hardware, these computers could communicate in an ad hoc Wireless LAN manner. Most of the mobile products can.

With the Access Point, the nodes can communicate directly or through the access point. The Access Point extends the range, and more importantly provides access to all the resources on the backbone. The Access Point contains three components:

- A Wireless LAN adapter to communicate with the wireless nodes
- A wired adapter to communicate over the backbone
- MAC layer bridging software to filter traffic from the backbone to the wireless subnet

The system engineering of the AT&T product is summarized by:

- The radio
  - 902-928 MHz ISM band
  - 2.4-2.483 GHz ISM band
  - 250 mw power output in 900 MHz band, 100 mw in the 2.4 GHz band

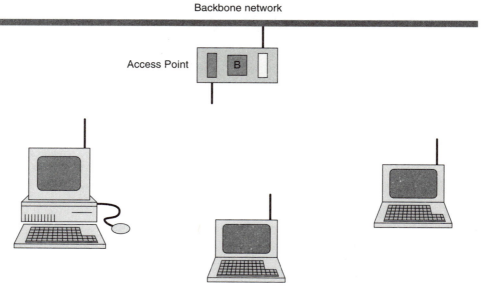

**Figure 7.3**   AT&T Wireless LAN network topology.

- Modulation
  - Direct sequence spread spectrum
  - DQPSK
- MAC
  - CSMA/CA
- Protocols supported
  - Novell NetWare 2.x and 3.x
  - TCP/IP
  - LAN Manager
  - Windows for Workgroups
  - Banyan VINES

Initially, the product was introduced in the 900 MHz band only in the US, because the 900 MHz band is not available in Europe or most of Asia. Interestingly, the AT&T product was developed in the Netherlands at NCR's offices there. The reason for the choice of 900 MHz probably had to do with ease of finding cost-effective silicon components at that frequency at that time. They could have used Gallium Arsenide, but those components were still expensive then. Later, the product was modified to work at the 2.4 GHz band and at a lower power of 100 mw, to fit the requirements of the worldwide market.

The modulation chosen for the product is DQPSK, and the spectrum technique is direct sequence. Why direct sequence? Spread spectrum technology grew out of defense applications. Such applications used direct sequence spreading for applications such as anti-jamming and undercover transmission. The early Wireless LAN manufacturers favored direct sequence because components and technology were more available for it than for frequency hopping. The MAC used is CSMA/CA, and the protocols supported include the "short list."

The WavePoint Access Point's functions are summarized below:

- MAC layer transparent bridge (IEEE 802.1D)
- Filtering/forwarding
- Automatic learning and aging
- Spanning tree algorithm
- SNMP management
- Radio path diagnostics
- Access control
- Net ID

It performs basic MAC layer transparent bridging functions including filtering, forwarding, and automatic learning of which nodes are on the wireless subnet and which nodes are on the backbone. It ages the nodes with timers appropriate for Wireless LANs. It uses the spanning tree algorithm specified by 802.1D. Further, it provides an SNMP agent in the Access Point. Most later Wireless LAN products also do so in the Access Point. They do not provide such an agent in the nodes, however. The Access Point is the focal point for access control. The nodes must convince the Access Point they are authorized to use the network before they are granted access.

Radio path diagnostics help the network administrator keep the network running satisfactorily. A network ID can be used to isolate traffic from one group to another, for example two different departments in a company, or two companies that are sharing the same radio space. The network ID does not increase the overall capacity of the system; it just provides isolation of the traffic. The network ID also does not provide true security because it is too easy to break. To provide true security, the encryption option needs to be implemented. This fact is also true of the spread spectrum nature of the product. Spread spectrum does not provide true security except against the most casual intruder. Any intruder with the same make of product can listen. The products from the same company typically use a finite number of spread spectrum codes that are public.

The WavePoint is $7'' \times 14'' \times 1.6''$, or $10 \text{ cm} \times 40 \text{ cm} \times 5 \text{ cm}$ in size. It can be placed on a table or hung from the ceiling or the wall. It supports all physical types of Ethernet:

- 10BaseT, twisted pair Ethernet
- 10Base2, thin wire Ethernet
- 10Base5, thick wire Ethernet

The Lucent Wireless LAN product line includes a point-to-point product that can provide a range of up to 5 miles by using directional antennas where they are permitted. Most Wireless LAN products provide such a point-to-point solution for interconnecting LANs in different buildings wirelessly. This, for example, could eliminate the need for private lines from the phone company to interconnect the LANs in different buildings, especially if the buildings are on opposite sides of a public highway. The range of the point-to-point products varies depending on the power levels and the antenna directivity used. Directive antennas are not always allowed in all countries since they focus the energy in a particular space and in a sense defeat the idea of secondary usage that requires that the secondary users not interfere with the primary users.

The point-to-point products are discussed here since they are provided by the same companies that provide Wireless LAN products. In addition to these point-to-point solutions, a whole set of other companies specializes in point-to-point solutions and telephone company bypass products that are not covered in this book.

Before discussing the performance of this product and the other products, we need to put the discussion in perspective by comparing it to similar calculations for a wired LAN that uses a similar CSMA protocol. As discussed in Chapter 3, the throughput of a LAN using CSMA has a theoretical maximum for multiple users of about 65% of the data rate. Furthermore, near that maximum, the response time has a steep knee. Therefore, the expected performance of CSMA LANs is typically 30% of the data rate. For Ethernet, this is in the range of 3 Mbps. For the AT&T Wireless LAN product, we would expect 30% of 2 Mbps, or about 0.6 Mbps, and this rate is indeed the case as tested by an independent laboratory.

Next, we discuss a number of products that OEM the AT&T product and add value to it in various ways.

## Digital Ocean Grouper

The Digital Ocean Grouper is produced in alliance with AT&T for the Apple product line, including Macintoshes, PowerBooks, and Newtons. It supports Ethernet as well as LocalTalk, Apple's physical layer LAN.

## Digital Equipment Wireless LAN

Digital Equipment Corporation also OEMs the Lucent product and adds significant value to it. The product line as presented by DEC appears in Figure 7.4.

Just like the AT&T product line, the DEC Wireless LAN product line includes PCMCIA form factor LAN adapters as well as standard Network Interface Card adapters for desktop applica-

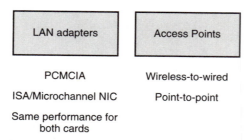

**Figure 7.4**   DEC Wireless LAN product line.

tions. To connect to backbone networks, wireless-to-wired Access Points are available. To connect remotely located LANs together point-to-point Access Points are available.

The main component of the wireless infrastructure is the wireless-to-wired Access Point. The Access Point connects a wireless subnet to the wired network and all the services available on it. At present, Ethernet is supported—thin wire, thick wire, or 10baseT.

Full roaming is supported, so a user can walk within the same Wireless Subnet, or to other subnets while maintaining the wireless connection. Within the same Wireless Subnet, which may include several Access Points, a spanning tree algorithm is used to forward the packets to the Access Point serving the user at any point in time.

If the user moves to a different subnet, an early implementation of the Mobile IP protocol is used to forward the packets to the network and the Access Point that is serving the user at that instant. This area is one where DEC adds significant value.

A point-to-point Access Point is provided. This Access Point product allows the connection of two remotely located LANs. The connections use private products and avoid costly private lines that must be paid for on a month-to-month basis. To extend the range of the radio, special antennas are used. The software that makes the connection possible is called "Remote Wireless Network Connect."

The protocols supported by the DEC Wireless LAN product include:

- Pathworks V4.1
- Novell NetWare 2.x and 3.x
- TCP/IP
- LAN Manager
- Windows for Workgroups
- Banyan VINES

The Wireless LAN performance of the DEC product is essentially the same as the AT&T product.

Next let's discuss how many users this kind of throughput can support. DEC suggests that users generate traffic at the rates shown below:

- Light: 16 Kbps
- Medium: 32 Kbps
- Heavy: 64 Kbps

The 2 Mbps raw data rate provides about 0.6 Mbps of throughput, so we can support between 10 and 40 users, depending on how heavy their individual traffic is. This number of users is not large. The traffic engineering of Wireless LANs is further complicated by the fact that the users move about, so not only do we not know how much traffic each user generates, but we do not know how many users are present in a given location at any point in time, and the number could vary greatly. This variable is a challenge to the MIS manager of a Wireless LAN.

The products for US and Europe/Asia are summarized in Figure 7.5.

The product in the US differs from that available in Europe due to different regulatory environments. The 900 MHz band is not available in Europe. The European model has a lower range at the higher frequency. The DES option is currently available only in the US.

Another area where DEC truly adds value is in the products that provide connectivity from remote locations away from the office back to the office. Digital's Wireless WAN products are software packages for mobiles and for their VAX line of computers. They allow the user to roam away from the private LAN and still be able to connect back to services on the LAN. Both products use TCP/IP. The products are:

- DECtransporter for MS-DOS/MS-Windows
  - A TCP/IP package
  - Enables cellular connection with appropriate modem, or a wired connection with appropriate modem
- DECtransporter for OpenVMS VAX
  - A TCP/IP to packet radio network gateway
  - Enables connection to a private network over a public packet radio network such as Mobitex or ARDIS

Figure 7.6 illustrates these capabilities.

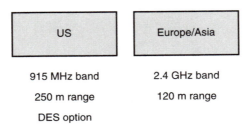

Figure 7.5   DEC's Wireless LAN products for the US and other parts of the world.

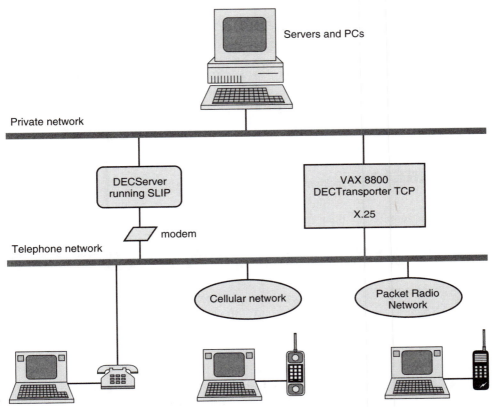

**Figure 7.6**   DEC's remote connectivity configurations.

If the user is in a hotel room, for example, and he has his notebook computer and a wired modem, he could call a number back in the office that would access a modem pool and a server running Serial Line IP and thus connect to the backbone. Serial Line IP is a form of IP that allows access over phone lines. If the remote user does not have access to a wired phone, but does have a cellular phone and a cellular modem, then he can call the same number and access the same SLIP server. If the user has a packet radio modem such as a RAM/Mobitex Mobidem, or an ARDIS/Modacom InfoTAC, he connects with an X.25 server that connects him to the backbone.

What is especially useful about this collection of options is that it provides the user with economical wired circuit switched access, and two wireless options—a circuit switched cellular option that is most suitable for long transmissions, and a packet switched option that is most suitable for short messages.

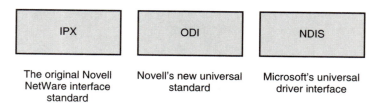

**Figure 7.7**   Protocols supported.

## Solectek AIRLAN

Solectek is another company that OEMs the AT&T Wireless LAN product line. The way they specify compatibility with existing interfaces appears in Figure 7.7.

IPX is the original Novell NetWare interface standard. ODI and NDIS are driver interface standards that are de facto standards that most vendors follow. ODI is Novell's new universal standard. NDIS is Microsoft's universal driver interface.

## Proxim RangeLAN 2

The next product line is the Proxim product line. Figure 7.8 shows the product line.

The product line includes a PCMCIA card that has a small external package with a small retractable antenna like the AT&T product. However, Proxim's external package is a bit smaller than the AT&T product. Proxim also has an ISA card with a 5″ antenna attached to the board. The Access Point is a MAC level bridge that is built first for Ethernet and eventually for Token Ring.

The topology of the Proxim product is similar to that of AT&T's and is shown in Figure 7.9.

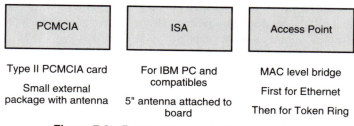

**Figure 7.8**   Proxim Wireless LAN product line.

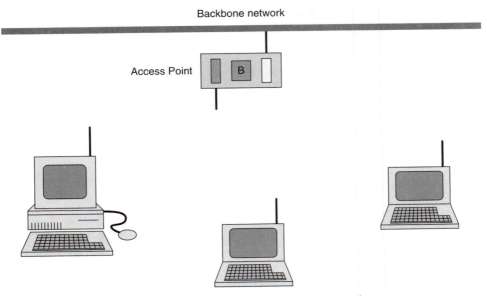

**Figure 7.9**   Proxim Wireless LAN network topology.

The technology of RangeLAN 2 is summarized by:

- Frequency hopping spread spectrum
- 2.4 to 2.483 GHz ISM band
- 15 independent channels
- RangeLAN CSMA/CA protocol
- 100 mw transmitted power
- GaAs semiconductors
- Power from computer's internal battery

Proxim provides 15 independent channels or frequency hopping patterns. The MAC protocol is CSMA/CA and has a special design to make it more suitable for Wireless LANs. The transmitted power is 100 mw worldwide, even though in the US the maximum allowed is 1 watt. Proxim elected to use Gallium Arsenide semiconductors because of their better characteristics and not much greater cost. Like all the Wireless LAN products to date, the Proxim product is powered by the computer's internal battery.

The RangeLAN2 Access Point has the following capabilities:

- MAC layer bridge
- IEEE 802.1(D) spanning tree protocol

- Support for roaming from one bridge to another
- Transparent access to wired Ethernets
  - 10Base5 (Thick) 15 pin AUI
  - 10Base2 (Thin) BNC
  - 10BaseT (Twisted-Pair)
- SNMP agent provided
- Protocols supported
  - Novell NetWare 2.x, 3.x, 4.x
  - Novell NetWare Lite
  - LAN manager
  - Windows for Workgroups

This set of capabilities is becoming fairly standard among Wireless LAN suppliers.

The performance of the Proxim RangeLAN 2 is a raw data rate of 1.6 Mbps. The quoted range is 800′ to 1000′ outdoors, and 300′ to 500′ indoors. The range is highly dependent on the environment, as discussed earlier.

Considering an example of installing a Wireless LAN is interesting. The Proxim ISA equipment comes in the following package:

- Interface card
- Antenna
- Software
- Manual

The installation process for the node is as follows:

- Hardware installation
  - Confirm default setting on card
  - Install card in computer
  - Screw antenna onto connector in back of card
- Software installation
  - Copy configured IPX.COM driver to hard disk
  - Load the IPX driver and DOS shell, NETX
  - Copy the LOGIN.EXE file

The installation is quite simple.

Looking at the initial Wireless LAN product from Proxim is also interesting. It was called RangeLAN, and had the following specifications:

- Direct sequence spread spectrum
- 902 to 928 MHz
- Three independent channels
- RangeLAN CSMA/CA protocol
- 100 mw transmitted power
- 242 Kbps data rate

The initial product was DSSS at the 900 MHz band, like the AT&T product. This product had the lower data rate of 242 Kbps and only three independent channels. In migrating to Range-LAN 2, Proxim moved from DSSS to FHSS, from 900 MHz to 2.4 GHz, and from 242 Kbps to 1.6 Mbps. The industry seems to be moving toward FHSS from DSSS for the reasons cited above.

## Xircom Netwave

The Xircom product line is depicted in Figure 7.10.

The CreditCard Netwave Adapter is a PCMCIA card with integrated antenna that extends outside the computer. As mentioned, Xircom was the first to provide this one-piece design, and it is a challenge to provide. The external antenna is physically vulnerable if the computer is handled somewhat roughly. The Pocket Netwave Adapter is a palm-sized adapter that connects to the PC via the parallel port. It draws power from the keyboard port and is intended for desktops or notebooks with no PCMCIA slot.

The Netwave Access Points support roaming, and contiguous Access Points use different hopping patterns like the other Wireless LAN products.

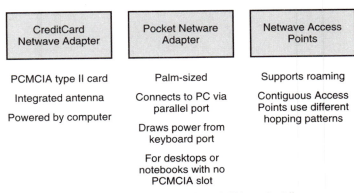

**Figure 7.10**   Xircom Wireless LAN product line.

The Xircom network topology appears in Figure 7.11.

Xircom does not produce an ISA card; however adapters that accept PCMCIA cards and fit into the ISA slot are readily available.

The Xircom technology is summarized below:

- FHSS implementation
- 50 mw power output
- Use of 78 1-MHz slots in the 2.4 to 2.4835 GHz band
- Hop every 0.1 s
- Synchronized system
- Hopping sequence that defines network
- Hopping sequence that avoids runs of errors

The output power is half as much as the maximum allowed worldwide, most likely due to the one-piece design. The power management features of the Xircom product hinge on the Access Point. Netwave adapters power down when the PC enters sleep mode. The Access Points store traffic for a sleeping node.

The Access Point is also the focal point of authentication and security, which is optional. Stations accessing the network are authenticated by the Access Point, and authenticated stations are provided a key for data privacy.

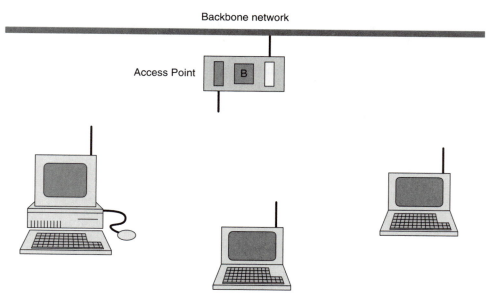

**Figure 7.11**   Xircom Wireless LAN network topology.

Xircom provides two kinds of ad hoc networks:

- Public ad hoc networks
  - Anyone in range can join a public ad hoc network
- Named ad hoc networks
  - One station must start a named network
  - Other stations join if they specify the name
    - Optional encryption is available

Ad hoc networks can be extended by the use of an Access Point.

A word at this point about independent collocated operation is in order. This capability allows different companies to have Wireless LAN products within radio range of each other and both operate without interference. That is the collocated aspect. The independent aspect means that they do not have to meet to do any frequency planning or other coordination. This option is possible if the product provides multiple channels, as they all do. Independent collocated operation is possible by using a different network ID. This ID is used to filter the traffic between the companies. It does not create additional capacity, nor does it provide security. The capacity is basically shared via the CSMA protocol.

The data rate of the Xircom product is 1 Mbps, with a stated range of 750′ in open spaces and 150′ indoors. The nominal range needs to be tested in a site survey to insure adequate coverage. The Xircom product may provide a bit less range than the other products due to its lower power of 50 mw.

# IBM Wireless LAN

Next is a product by IBM. The unique aspect of this product is that its MAC is TDMA as compared to all the others, which use CSMA. The technology of the product is summarized by:

- FHSS in the 2.4 GHz band
- 100 mw power output
- Antenna receive polarization diversity
- TDMA MAC layer
- Requirement of Access Point
- Ethernet and Token Ring compatibility
- SNMP agent

The other difference is that an Access Point is required to administer the TDMA channel allocation and Token Ring is supported along with Ethernet. The average response time of this product is likely to be longer than the other products that use CSMA. However, the TDMA MAC is first-come-first-served, which may appeal to certain applications such as the stock trading application. TDMA also has good behavior when the traffic is heavy. The IBM product is a bit more expensive than the rest. The stated data rate is 1 Mbps.

A network administration function called the Wireless Network Administrator (WNA) provides:

- Authentication and privacy
  - Users are registered with WNA and provided security keys
  - Registered stations are authenticated by Access Point
  - Optional encryption is available
- Interference management through change of hopping pattern

## Motorola Altair

Now we shift to the wire replacement market and discuss the Wireless LAN products whose form factor does not allow them to be used in mobile computers at this time. The first is the Motorola Altair product. We will see that the topology of this product, along with the Windata to be discussed next and the InfraLAN product to be discussed with the infrared products, are similar. They may be considered to be half wireless since they require the desktop computers to be connected to a shared user module by cable. The user module then communicates to a control module that can be mounted in the ceiling. These products save the need for having to drop cable from the ceiling to each computer. Instead, the computers are wired to the shared user module, which is placed in the general vicinity of the computers.

The unique aspect of the Motorola product is that it uses licensed spectrum at 18 GHz in the US and at 17 GHz in other parts of the world. Motorola is experienced in obtaining spectrum worldwide, and has obtained spectrum for this product worldwide. Even if the product does not penetrate the market significantly, obtaining this spectrum in itself is a major accomplishment for Motorola. The other forward-looking aspect of the product is its use of the much higher band. In the future, we will have to go to higher bands for greater spectrum. Motorola has the jump on producing technology that works at the higher frequencies. They leverage their experience with defense electronics and the use of Monolithic Microwave Integrated Circuits or MMICs, which is a key technology for systems that operate at the higher frequencies.

The product is described by:

- Not spread spectrum
- In the 18 GHz band
- Low power - 25 mw

- Comprised of a control module and a user module
- 8 × 11.5 × 3 inches in size
- Antenna internal to module
- Packaging similar for both modules

The topology appears in Figure 7.12.

Up to eight desktop computers can share a user module. The computers must have an Ethernet card. From there, the product is plug-compatible with Ethernet. The control module is connected to the Ethernet backbone network and provides access to all the resources on the backbone at Ethernet speeds.

To shield the user from licensing administration woes, Motorola handles it for the customer. This converage includes if the customer moves and therefore needs to obtain a different license for the new location.

Altair is approved in over 20 countries. In the US, Motorola has obtained 600 licenses to cover metropolitan areas with 30,000 or more populations. Each license has a radius of 17.5 miles. The maximum number of licenses in any geographic area is five.

Motorola also has a point-to-point product called the VistaPoint, which works through the window. A green light shines when connection is achieved. The maximum range is 500′, and the data rate supported is 3.5 Mbps in each direction.

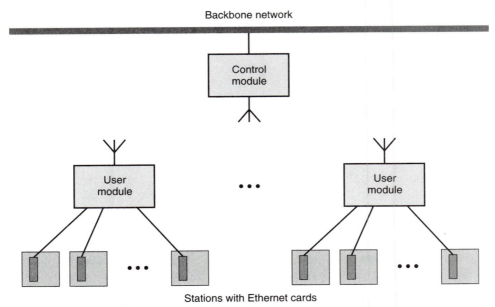

**Figure 7.12**    Motorola Wireless LAN network topology.

# Windata

The Windata Wireless LAN product line is summarized in Figure 7.12.
The network topology appears in Figure 7.14.

The Ethernet transceiver is a desktop unit that is shared among up to eight users. It is plug-compatible with Ethernet. The FreePort Wireless Ethernet hub can also be desktop or rack-mounted. It has a horizontal coverage antenna with a range of up to 80 meters. It can control up to 62 transceivers. The hub functions include:

- Connectivity of transceivers
- Synchronization
- Access security
- Power control
- Network management

The radio uses the two higher ISM bands—the 2.4 GHz band for the down link, and the 5.7 GHz band for the up link. It is a DSSS radio with 16-level PSK. The hubs transmits at 1 watt. The transceiver has adaptive power control that adjusts the power from 0.02 milliwatt up to 650 milli-watts. The network management system is an application that can run on the system adiminstrator's PC and communicates with agents in the hubs. It uses SNMP and has the following functions:

- Enabling and disabling transceivers
- Adding and deleting access to stations
- Monitoring performance
- Checking status of radio link

The data rate of the system is 10 Mbps. It is plug compatible with Ethernet. The maximum range of the cell is 250′.

Two point-to-point products are available, called Airport I and Airport II. They both provide 8 Mbps in each direction. They operate window-to-window. Airport I has a range of up to 1000′, and Airport II has a range of up to 1.8 miles.

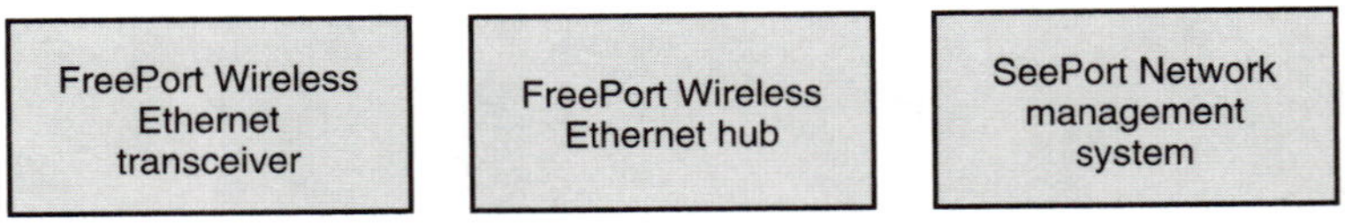

**Figure 7.13**  Windata Wireless LAN product line.

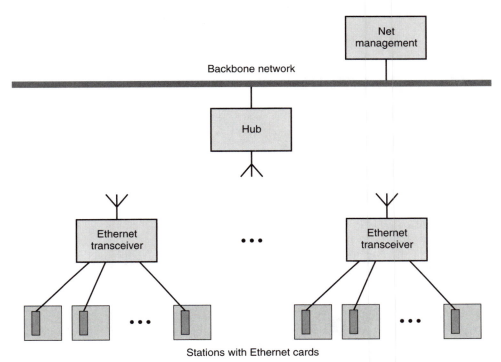

**Figure 7.14** Windata Wireless LAN network topology.

# RadioLAN

RadioLAN is a system that has been announced but not shipped at this time. The name of the company is the same as the name of the product. The capabilities below are based on the announcement. It provides 10 Mbps and is priced aggressively. Its range is about 150′. It uses the 5.7 GHz band exclusively. It is positioned initially as a wire replacement market for replacing wired Ethernets. The product line includes:

- ISA card
- Parallel port version
- RadioLAN/10 Access Unit
- Radio transceiver
- Base station

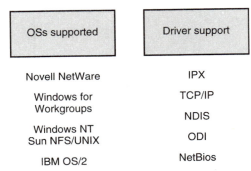

**Figure 7.15** RadioLAN OS and driver support.

A PCMCIA version is planned. DES is an optional security capability. The operating systems and the driver interfaces supported appear in Figure 7.15.

The name of the operating system that operates the RadioLAN product is RadioLINK. It manages the Wireless Network and provides wireless operations management, including monitoring and dynamically adjusting the radio network. It can elect a dynamic master. It operates the system in CSMA when the traffic is light; when the traffic is heavy, it switches to TDMA. It can also set up a dynamic relay function.

The system provides MIBII support. When a software upgrade is available, the upgrade can be shipped to the customer via modem. Once there, it can be loaded to the Access Points via the network.

## Photonics

Photonics builds an infrared product for the PC as well as for the Macintosh. The product for the PC is called Collaborative and includes:

- PCMCIA II card
- ISA card
- Collaborative parallel option
- Access Point
- External transceiver

The product for the Macintosh is also called Cooperative and includes:

- External device for Macs, PowerBooks, and Newtons
- Access Point

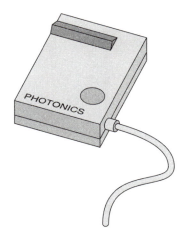

**Figure 7.16**  Photonics IR transceiver.

The transceiver is about three inches in size and is placed next to the computer and tilted towards the ceiling as you see in Figure 7.16.

The system uses diffuse infrared technology. The transceivers illuminate a common spot on the ceiling, so they don't need to be within LOS of each other. They use 250 mw or less of consumed power.

The diffuse infrared energy fills the room as Figure 7.17 shows.

The size of the room served is about 30′ on the side. The topology of the network appears in Figure 7.18.

**Figure 7.17**  Diffuse IR.

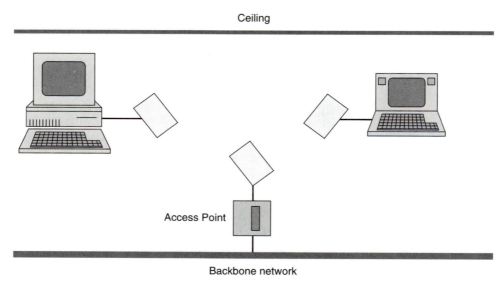

**Figure 7.18**   Photonics network topology.

Ad hoc networking is supported. If access to the backbone is required, an Access Point uses a transceiver and a backbone network interface to provide the access shown in Figure 7.19. Roaming among Access Points is also supported.

The Collaborative PC software supports:

- Novell NetWare
- Novell Lite
- Microsoft LAN Manager

The system provides a data rate of 1 Mbps.

## Spectrix

Spectrix also provides a diffuse IR Wireless LAN product. Spectrix works extensively with the Chicago Board of Trade on a stock trading room application, and its system is particularly suited for that application. An Access Point is required. Figure 7.19 depicts the topology of the system.

Access Points are positioned in the ceiling in every room. The Access Points are connected to a server that has bridging software and a connection to the backbone. The details of the network configuration appear in Figure 7.20.

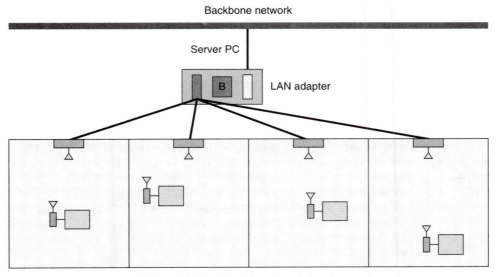

**Figure 7.19**    Spectrix network topology.

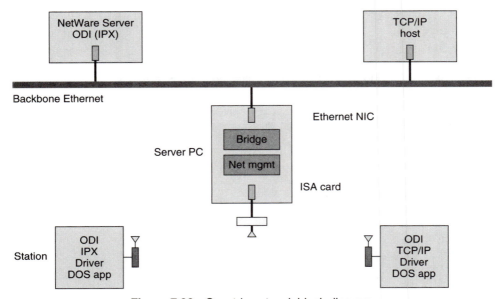

**Figure 7.20**    Spectrix network block diagram.

The Spectrix system provides 4 Mbps and range of about 50′. The MAC layer is a simple polling protocol that relies on the required Access Point. The MAC is chosen to make sure it is first-come-first-served, as required by the stock trading application.

# InfraLAN

The initial InfraLAN product supported only 802.5 Token Ring networks; now the product line includes support for Ethernet, point-to-point, as well as an Ethernet hub topology. The transceivers must be within line of sight of each other. They are depicted in Figure 7.21, and are about the size of a large flashlight.

The Token Ring product topology is depicted in Figure 7.22.

A number of stations share a user module. The stations still have a Token Ring adapter. The user module is plug-compatible with Token Ring and has a ring-in and a ring-out transceiver that points at the other transceiver. The beam width is fairly narrow. One of the user modules is con-

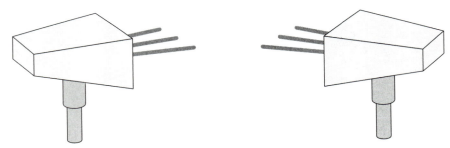

**Figure 7.21**   InfraLAN directed IR transceivers.

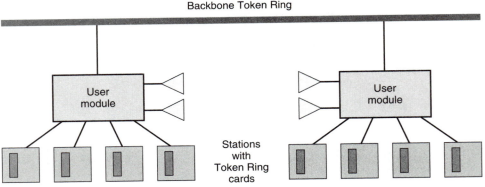

**Figure 7.22**   InfraLAN Token Ring topology.

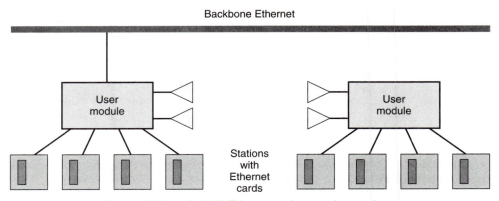

**Figure 7.23** InfraLAN Ethernet point-to-point topology.

nected to the backbone network to provide access to the services on it. The user modules basically replace the Token Ring cables. If an obstruction passes between the transceivers, it could knock one or both of the directions of transmission out, so care must be exercised in placing the transceivers in such a way that they will not both be interfered with at the same time.

The topology for the Ethernet point-to-point product is similar to the Token Ring point-to-point product (see Figure 7.23).

The topology for the Ethernet hub network appears in Figure 7.24.

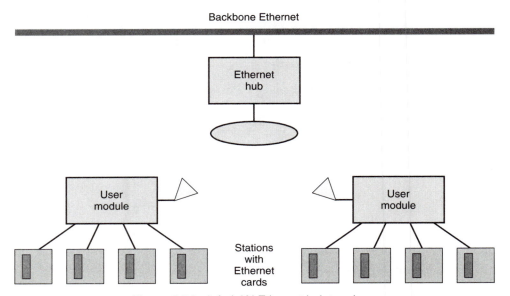

**Figure 7.24** InfraLAN Ethernet hub topology.

The performance of the products for the different configurations is:

- Range - 80' LOS
- Token Ring - 4 and 16 Mbps
- Ethernet - 10 Mbps

The performance is essentially the same as observed on a wired network with a similar protocol.

## Comparison of Wireless LAN Products

Figure 7.25 shows the Wireless LAN products we discussed above, along with others we did not discuss in detail. The products are classified according to whether they are for the mobile market or for the wire replacement market, and whether they use radio or infrared. The ability to support the PCMCIA product qualifies a product as being mobile.

Scanning Figure 7.25, we see that three of the companies—Lucent, IBM, and Motorola—are large. Two of the companies—Symbol and Telxon—are medium in size and focus on the retail market. The rest of the companies are small. This industry is one where small companies can pro-

|  | Mobile | Wire replacement |
|---|---|---|
| **Radio** | Lucent WaveLAN | Motorola Altair |
|  | IBM Wireless LAN | |
|  | Proxim RangeLAN | Windata |
|  | Telxon | |
|  | Symbol | RadioLAN |
|  | Xircom Netwave | |
| **Infrared** | Photonics | InfraLAN |
|  | SpectrixLite | Radiance |

**Figure 7.25**  Wireless LAN products.

vide viable products. The challenge is to stay in business long enough until the market develops beyond the early adopter stage and significant revenues that allow profitability begin to flow.

Figure 7.26 compares the mobile Wireless LAN products.

The comparison shows that most of the products provide between 1 and 2 Mbps with the exception of Spectrix, which provides 4 Mbps. The difference between 1 and 2 Mbps is probably not perceptible at the end-user level. With that difference, looking at the specific implementation of the MAC is more important in determining what the ultimate performance would be.

The frequency of operation is in the 2.4 GHz band, which is internationally available. The Lucent product is available at both 900 MHz as well as 2.4 GHz. The technology used is all FHSS except for the Lucent product, which was one of the first introduced and has remained with DSSS. The range of the products is nominally close to the 50 meter number with slight variations. The variations may point to the Lucent product as having a slightly larger range and the Xircom product as having a slightly shorter range. All the products support ad hoc networking and do not require an Acess Point, with the exception of the IBM product and the Spectrix product. Interestingly, those two products are the first to be tried by the stock market trading floor applications.

The range of the infrared products is on the order of 10 meters instead of 50 meters for the radio products. The number of Access Points required by infrared is much larger than for radio, and an Access Point is needed in every room where coverage is required. The two products shown use OOK and PPM modulation techniques that are discussed in detail in Chapter 3.

Figure 7.27 is a comparison of the wire replacement products.

These products have a form factor that does not allow them to fit inside a mobile computer. The network topology of these three products is similar. A number of stations share one user module and are connected to it via a cable. The user module communicates with a control module that is connected to the backbone network. Thus, these products avoid having to run a separate cable

| Product | Data rate | Frequency | Technology | Range | Access Point |
|---|---|---|---|---|---|
| Lucent | 2 Mpbs | 900 MHz | DSSS | 50 m | Optional |
| IBM | 1 Mpbs | 2.4 GHz | FHSS | 50 m | Required |
| Proxim | 1.6 Mpbs | 2.4 GHz | FHSS | 50 m | Optional |
| Xircom | 1 Mpbs | 2.4 GHz | FHSS | 50 m | Optional |
| Photonics | 1 Mpbs | IR | PPM | 10 m | Optional |
| Spectrix | 4 Mpbs | IR | OOK | 10 m | Required |

**Figure 7.26**   Comparison of Wireless LAN products—mobile.

| Product | Data rate | Frequency | Technology | Range | Access Point |
|---|---|---|---|---|---|
| Motorola | 10 Mpbs | 18 GHz | Narrowband | 15 m | Required |
| Windata | 10 Mbps | 2.4, 5.7 GHz | DSSS | 50 m | Required |
| InfraLAN | 4, 16, 10 Mbps | IR | OOK | 25 m | Required |

**Figure 7.27**  Comparison of Wireless LAN products—wire replacement.

down from the ceiling to each station, but still require a cable from the station to a user module that may be situated in the middle of the stations sharing it. The user module can be located on a desk, a table, or other convenient place in the middle of the users sharing it.

The Motorola system uses the 18 GHz band. Motorola has obtained licenses in over 20 countries for this product. The maximum range between the control module and the user module is about 15 meters. The radio uses fairly low power. The Windata network is another product that has continued to use DSSS. It also uses both the 2.4 GHz band and the 5.7 GHz band. It uses one of the bands for the up link and the other for the down link.

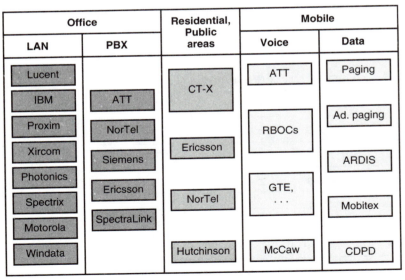

**Figure 7.28**  Wireless map.

All three products require an Access Point, so they do not support ad hoc networking. Ad hoc networking is not a strong requirement for desktop wire replacement configurations.

Returning to Figure 7.28 from chapter 1, we have now completed discussing the left hand column of the figure.

In Chapter 8, we discuss the spectrum allocations and the standards for Mobile Data and Wireless LAN.

# 8
# *Wireless Spectra and Standards*

At present, Wireless LANs must rely on spread spectrum technology to use the ISM bands. New spectrum allocations such as for Unlicensed PCS make possible the use of simpler radios and higher data rates. To allow communications among products from different vendors, many standards groups across the world are converging on technology choices. In this chapter, we focus on:

- ISM bands
- Unlicensed PCS
- Unlicensed PCS etiquette basics
- IEEE 802.11 standards
- The 802.11 MAC standard
- The 802.11 FHSS PHY standard
- The 802.11 DSSS PHY standard
- The 802.11 IR PHY standard
- Hiperlan
- Mobile Data standards
- Wireless ATM

In this chapter, we focus on the middle block in the networking layer of Figure 8.1.

## ISM Bands

The ISM bands provide FCC Part 15 use, which means secondary use. In order not to interfere with the primary user who *does* have the license for the band, the Wireless LAN provider must use spread spectrum techniques. In this section, we discuss the specifics of the spread spectrum techniques.

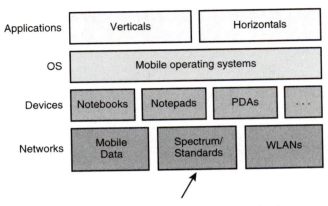

**Figure 8.1** Focus on spectra and standards.

Figure 8.2 lists the bands.

A 26 MHz band is available at 900 MHz; this is the band that the early products used. This band is also popular with many other applications, including some cordless phones, door openers, and many other devices. It is becoming quite crowded because it is not limited to Wireless LAN users. Anyone can use it as long as they abide by the Part 15 rules of the FCC. Those rules state that the maximum power is 1 watt, and either FHSS or DSSS must be used, as detailed later in this chapter.

Most manufacturers favor the 2.4 GHz band because it is not as crowded as of yet, and it is also available internationally. Also, much more bandwidth is available there, 83.5 MHz. But one of the disadvantages of the 2.4 GHz band is that microwave ovens radiate in that region. Some field trials have shown that if a number of microwave ovens are on the same floor and they are all on, they could significantly interfere with a Wireless LAN product operating on the same floor. This possibility is the risk of using the ISM bands, but these bands are the only choice at this time until we get the Unlicensed PCS bands cleared, as we will discuss shortly.

| Band (GHz) | Bandwidth | Power Level | Spread Spectrum |
|---|---|---|---|
| 1. 0.902–0.928 | 26 MHz | 1 w | FHSS, DSSS |
| 2. 2.4–2.4835 | 83.5 MHz | 1 w | FHSS, DSSS |
| 3. 5.725–5.85 | 125 MHz | 1 w | FHSS, DSSS |
| 4. 24.0–24.25, and in 1,2,3 | 250 MHz | 50 mv/m @ 3 m | Not Applicable |

**Figure 8.2** The ISM bands in the US.

At 5.7 GHz, even more bandwidth is available, 125 MHz. Some manufacturers have started to use this band. In the future, we will see more suppliers make use of the additional bandwidth in this higher band. The Hiperlan standard uses this band, as well as the 17 MHz band, which is available in Europe.

A higher band is also available—the 24 GHz band where 250 MHz is available. At this time, the only way to use this band is with the low-power option, which is not a well-known option in the ISM bands. This option is specified by field intensity at a particular distance. This field intensity equates to about 3 milliwatts for a typical implementation—a very low power level. Systems that use this option usually have a very short range. One example is RadioLAN; another is an early implementation of a Wireless PBX by Ericsson.

The specific rules for FHSS are depicted in Figure 8.3.

The signal bandwidth must be less than 1 MHz. This limitation has led most Wireless LAN vendors to keep their data rate below 1 or 2 Mbps. Providing higher data rates in this bandwidth is difficult. Even with 2 MHz, a higher level of modulation must be used that results in more expensive radios. The other constraint is multipath, which becomes a significant problem for most buildings if the data rate exceeds 2 Mbps.

The signal bandwidth is limited to 500 KHz in the 900 MHz band. This restriction is one reason why the early vendors chose DSSS. At that time, finding components that operated cost-effectively at 2.4 GHz was difficult, so they chose the 900 MHz band. At 900 MHz, if they chose DSSS, they had 26 MHz to use and could provide about 2 Mbps. If they used the FHSS option, they would have had to limit the data rate to 0.5 Mbps, or perhaps 1 Mbps.

The number of frequency slots is 79. The product must use at least 75 of those slots in any 30-second interval, and must not spend any more than 0.4 seconds in any one slot. Most products hop every 0.1 seconds and use all the slots. As discussed in Chapter 7, most products provide up to 15 channels through the use of orthogonal frequency hopping patterns. How well this works remains to be seen in large-scale implementations. This number of channels may cause more self-interference than anticipated theoretically. It may also be more vulnerable to the primary user, or may interfere with the primary user unacceptably. Time and experience will show the real capacity of this band.

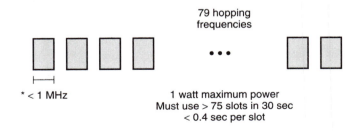

**Figure 8.3** Frequency Hopping Spread Spectrum rules.

Figure 8.4 illustrates the rules for DSSS.

The DSSS rule is to spread the signal by a factor of at least 11. The product can have any data rate, as long as the signal is spread by this factor. Therefore, to provide 2 Mbps, the resulting chip rate must be at least 22 Mcps, as illustrated in Figure 8.4. This is already a high clock rate and requires fast components. The bandwidth of such a signal is nominally around 20 MHz. The spreading factor is large enough to drop the spectral density of the signal so it does not interfere with the primary user, as long as too many DSSS users are not in the same area. However, the spreading factor is not large enough to extract any channels from the code. In other words, a spreading factor of 11 is not enough to produce any CDMA channels. The CDMA systems use a spreading factor of at least 50. With a spreading factor of 11, we can only obtain one channel. If we tried to use another code for another channel, it would be too correlated with the first and would interfere with it.

As a result, with a bandwidth of around 20 MHz, we can obtain only two or three independent channels with DSSS in the 2.4 GHz band. This is what is commonly available. The 802.11 standard discussed later in this chapter suggests two channels that are movable around possible interference spots.

Why could we not extract more overall capacity from DSSS, as we apparently can from FHSS? The question is of today's technology level and cost. To obtain as much capacity from DSSS as we apparently obtain from FHSS, we would have to increase the data rate to perhaps 15 Mbps. With quadrature modulation and a spreading factor of 11, this would result in a chip stream running at about 75 Mcps. With fairly tight filters this could fit in the 2.4 GHz band, but would require clock rates of 75 GHz. Such components are available but are quite expensive, and require high power. Further, many tolerances would become very tight, such as synchronization. Thus, extracting more capacity from DSSS is theoretically possible, but with today's technology implementing such a DSSS system would be much more expensive than an FHSS system.

The specifics of the low-power options are detailed in Figure 8.5.

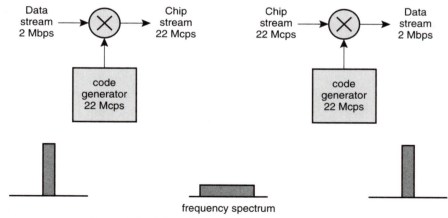

frequency spectrum

**Figure 8.4**    Direct Sequence Spread Spectrum rules.

| Fundamental frequency | Field strength of fundamental | Field strength of harmonics |
|:---:|:---:|:---:|
| 0.902–0.928 GHz | 50 mv/m | 500 uv/m |
| 2.400–2.4835 GHz | 50 mv/m | 500 uv/m |
| 5.725–5.875 GHz | 50 mv/m | 500 uv/m |
| 24.0–24.25 GHz | 50 mv/m | 500 uv/m |

**Figure 8.5**  Low power in FCC ISM bands.

The field strength of the fundamental as well as the harmonics is specified. The low-power option is available in all three bands used by FHSS and DSSS as well as at the higher 24 GHz band.

Next, we outline the ISM bands in Europe and other parts of the world. The allocation by CEPT, the regulatory agency for Europe, is very similar to the US allocation. It also provides secondary usage for non-protected, non-interfering use. It also allows DSSS and FHSS, as well as the low-power option. It provides bandwidth in five bands, Figure 8.6 shows.

The first difference between the CEPT allocation and the FCC allocation is that the power levels are less—100 mw instead of 1 w. Many manufacturers are electing to use the 100 mw internationally, including the US. The second difference is that the bands are different, but do coincide, especially at the 2.4 GHz band. This fact is illustrated in Figure 8.7.

The bands available in Japan also appear in Figure 8.6. The 2.4 GHz band has been made available in many other parts of the world as well. The higher bands will probably also become available in other parts of the world as products begin to penetrate those areas.

The bands in the higher frequencies are compared in Figure 8.8.

As you can see, each regulatory agency apparently tried to find bandwidth where the other one had bandwidth, so we have as much overlap as possible. Further, we can see that abundant bandwidth occurs at the higher frequencies. These frequencies are more difficult to use at present

| Band (GHz) | Bandwidth | Power Level |
|:---:|:---:|:---:|
| 1. 2.4–2.4835 | 83.5 MHz | 100 mw |
| 2. 5.785–5.815 | 30 MHz | 100 mw |
| 3. 17.1–17.3 | 200 MHz | 100 mw |
| 4. 24.11–24.14 | 30 MHz | –28 dBw/MHz |
| 5. 61.0–61.5 | 500 MHz | –28 dBw/MHz |

**Figure 8.6**  CEPT allocation for the ISM bands.

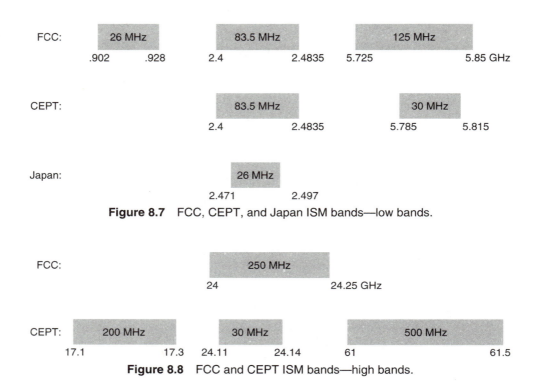

**Figure 8.7**   FCC, CEPT, and Japan ISM bands—low bands.

**Figure 8.8**   FCC and CEPT ISM bands—high bands.

due to technology, but we already have experimental radios at 60 GHz, so hopefully they will become a cost-effective reality in not too long a time.

A physical limitation exists at the higher bands, however. The propagation begins to behave more and more like visible light. It does not penetrate walls, and so must be line-of-sight. At those frequencies, the energy falls off rapidly, anyway, so the cell sizes will be very small. Seeing how future very high frequency systems are configured will be interesting.

## Unlicensed PCS

Several years ago, Apple started to petition the FCC for bandwidth where Wireless LANs could have primary usage. Why hamper such an important industry by forcing it to use complex spread spectrum techniques? The name of the service at that time was Data PCS. This was an inaccurate name because PCS itself provided both voice and data. The intent behind Apple's petition was some sort of local high-speed service such as Wireless LANs. Apple rallied the computer industry and received enthusiastic support from most computer companies.

The FCC considered the petition and decided that combining this activity with other systems that were of a private nature (most notably Wireless PBXs) made sense. It asked Apple and the computer companies to join forces and propose how to use this band jointly. The forum expanded to include the telephony companies that provide PBXs today and are interested in providing Wireless PBXs in the future, such as Nortel, Ericsson, AT&T, and many others. At first, some euphoria existed in the group, but soon the proposal became difficult. The two groups seemed to have cross interests, and lack of trust developed. The end result was simply to divide the band in two equal segments. The resulting allocation appears in Figure 8.9.

10 MHz is allocated to what is called asynchronous traffic, and 10 MHz divided into two sub-bands is provided to what is called isochronous traffic. The asynchronous band is earmarked for Wireless LANs. The isochronous band is aimed at Wireless PBXs and other customer premises equipment.

The bands are unlicensed, meaning that a notebook computer could roam from one part of the country to another and not have to be concerned with having a different license to operate in different parts of the country. This mobility makes the implementation of a private system that is implemented in different parts of the country easier. It also makes ad hoc networking possible. A group of people can simply turn on their computers and use the unlicensed band wherever they please.

As with the rest of the PCS spectrum, the UPCS allocation is on top of existing users. The FCC did find higher bands for these incumbents to move to, but it left the move up to the new service providers to arrange and pay for—an interesting delegation of responsibility by the FCC. Clearing the bands became the responsibility of the Wireless LAN industry and the Wireless PBX industry, as well as paying the incumbents to relocate to the higher frequencies. They had to negotiate with the incumbents the cost of relocating their services to higher frequencies, an arduous task at best.

This approach is the way the FCC chose to operate for the whole PCS band, a critical industry for the country. The PCS industry took on the task and has been successful, with minor problems in negotiating agreements for the incumbents to move.

UPCS does not have this luxury. For a manufacturer to offer a UPCS product, they need to have the whole band cleared nationwide first. The other challenge is that UPCS does not belong to a single entity as do the PCS allocations. In order to act, the industry has to organize and agree on its actions. Such an organization was formed and is called UTAM, the Unlicensed PCS Ad Hoc Committee for 2 GHz Microwave Transition and Management. The FCC delegated UTAM to coordinate the use of unlicensed PCS devices. All manufacturers of unlicensed PCS equipment are required to participate in UTAM. UTAM is the organization that is responsible for clearing the bands.

But how does it get started? The cost of relocating the incumbents is significant. A rough estimate of the cost spread out over devices that use this band is $20 per device. This is the cost each

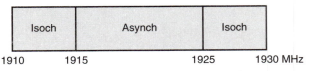

**Figure 8.9** UPCS spectrum allocation.

vendor has to pay UTAM to use the band. The money is used to relocate the incumbents. For the Wireless PBX industry, which is more accustomed to dealing with FCC, the task was arduous but not insurmountable. Led by Nortel, the bands are slowly becoming clear. Nortel's leadership comes not only in the form of people, but also significant money to clear the bands sufficiently to attract other vendors to begin contributing.

For the computer industry, which is not accustomed to the FCC and which is more fragmented, this hurdle became insurmountable. The result is that 10 MHz of spectrum is not being aggressively pursued at this time. Instead, Apple is back to the FCC requesting yet more bandwidth, this time at 5 GHz where very few, if any, incumbents exist. This is the band that Hiperlan is aiming at, so it is a promising band to renew the efforts of the computer industry.

# UPCS Etiquette Basics

Any unlicensed band is in danger of becoming a garbage band, such as the citizen's band became. To insure that the UPCS band does not become such a band, an etiquette was developed. The word *etiquette* implies politeness, but this particular etiquette does not depend on politeness. Any product that uses the UPCS band must adhere to the etiquette through type approval testing. The purpose of the etiquette is to make the band usable for all unlicensed users of the band. It specifies the limits to transmission in four areas:

- Power
- Bandwidth
- Transmission time
- Channel access mechanism

The first two areas are typical regulatory limits. The third area insures that no one user monopolizes the channel. The fourth area insures that the channel access algorithm allows users equal chance of accessing the medium.

The power limits are specified by:

- $P \leq 10\text{-}4\sqrt{\text{Bandwidth}}$ watts
- $P \leq 3$ mw in any 3 KHz band
- Antenna gain above 3 dB relative to an isotropic antenna, must reduce power dB for dB

Figure 8.10 illustrates the power limits.

As you can see in Figure 8.10, for a signal having a bandwidth of 1 MHz, the power limit is 100 mw. For larger bandwidth signals, the power limit is larger; for smaller bandwidth signals, the power is less. Thus, the power spectral density is maintained at an approximately uniform rate.

| Power (mw) | Bandwidth (MHz) |
|:---:|:---:|
| 17.3 | 0.03 |
| 32 | 0.1 |
| 52 | 0.3 |
| 100 | 1 |
| 173 | 3 |
| 316 | 10 |

**Figure 8.10**   Power limit examples.

The frequency limits are specified by:

- Asynchronous band
  - 500 KHz $\leq$ B $\leq$ 10 MHz (B is bandwidth)
  - If B $\leq$ 2.5 MHz, start at band edges
  - If B $\geq$ 2.5 MHz, start at center of band
- Isochronous band
  - Divided into 1.25 MHz channels
  - Narrower bandwidths are allowed within these channels
  - If B $\leq$ 625 KHz, start at lower end of band
  - If B $\geq$ 625 KHz, start at higher end of band

The asynchronous bands are aimed at wide-bandwidth applications with a bandwidth of at least 0.5 MHz. The larger-bandwidth applications start in the center of the band; the smaller-bandwidth applications start at the edge of the band to provide a good packing algorithm for the whole band.

The isochronous band is divided into 1.25 MHz channels and is split into two sub-bands. The two sub-bands could serve as up- and down-link frequencies if desired for a Frequency Division Duplexing system.

The time limits of the etiquette are as follows:

- Asynchronous
  - T $\leq$ 10 ms
  - Inter-burst transmission time $\geq$ random interval uniformly distributed between 50 us and 375 us
  - Intraburst gap $\leq$ 25 us

- Isochronous
  - Frame time = 10 ms * N, where N is a positive integer
  - Frame repetition rate accuracy ≤ 50 ppm

To insure that no one user monopolizes the band, any transmission is limited to 10 milliseconds. After that period, the user must stop and give other users a chance to access the medium. If no one else wants to use, then this user can use it again. The amount of time to wait is random, to reduce the probability of collisions, and is less for a high-bandwidth user than for a low-bandwidth user so as not to slow down a high-bandwidth user.

The isochronous systems specify a frame, with the idea that the channels will be provided by a control point that will be charged with providing fair access to the medium.

The channel access limits are as follows:

- Asynchronous: Listen Before Talk for at least the longer of
  - 50 u seconds
  - (20/B) seconds
- Isochronous: Listen Before Talk for at least 10 ms

Once again, the asynchronous allows the high-bandwidth user to wait less time. The isochronous requires waiting for at least one frame.

Next let us review the structure of the standards committees in the US and in other parts of the world, and then outline the emerging standards.

# IEEE 802.11 Standard

In this section, we outline the structure of the IEEE standards committees as they pertain to Wireless Networking. The committees of IEEE 802 and their functions are:

- 802.1
  - Overview
  - Architecture
  - Inter-networking
- 802.2
  - LLC
- 802.3
  - CSMA, CD
- 802.4
  - Token bus

- 802.5
  - Token Ring
- 802.6
  - Metropolitan Area Networks
- 802.89
  - Integrated voice and data
- 802.10
  - Security
- 802.11
  - Wireless LANs

The committees of concern to Wireless LANs are 802.11, 802.10 for security, and 802.1 for MAC layer bridging functions required for roaming within the same network. The 802.11 Mission and Scope are to develop a MAC and PHY specification for radio and for infrared, and to provide at least 1 Mbps of data rate to serve unlicensed radio equipment. Initial emphasis is to be placed on the 2.4 GHz ISM bands.

Some selected definitions are helpful in defining the standard:

- MAC Service Data Unit - MSDU
- Coordination Function - CF
- Basic Service Area - BSA
- Access Point - AP
- Extended Service Area - ESA
- Distribution System - DS

The coordination function could be distributed in an ad hoc network, as illustrated in Figure 8.11.

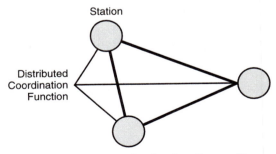

**Figure 8.11**   Distributed coordination function—ad hoc network.

An algorithm determines which of the nodes serves as the coordination function. If that node leaves, then the algorithm specifies how another node is selected to act as the coordination function. If an Access Point exists in the network, it provides the coordination function, as Figure 8.12 illustrates.

The network topology appears in Figure 8.13.

The distribution system is the backbone network with servers and other resources connected to it. The Access Points are also connected to the distribution system and serve Service Areas with nodes in them.

When nodes enter Service Areas and roam through other Service Areas, they need to perform several security functions given by:

- Association
  - Establishing an association between a station and an AP
- Reassociation
  - Handover of a station from one AP to another
- Authentication
  - When a station convinces an AP or other station of its identity
- Privacy
  - Encryption of the data

Authentication can have one of three levels, as Figure 8.14 specifies.

The open level provides access to anyone wishing to access the network. This can serve public applications. The next level is password protected and is probably the one most applications use. The station provides a password to the Access Point, which has a list of the stations that can access the network. The public key authentication level is the most secure. In particular, it insures that no passwords are transmitted in the clear, preventing an intruder from picking up the passwords and later using them to access the network.

For privacy of the data, 802.11 uses the capabilities of 802.10 as much as possible. All stations start out in the clear; the default is stay in the clear. If that is not acceptable to one of the sta-

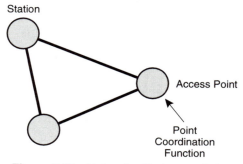

**Figure 8.12**   Network with Access Point.

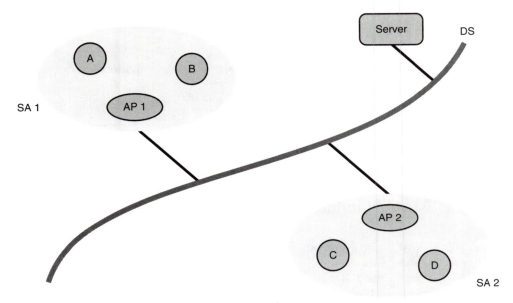

**Figure 8.13**  Network topology.

tions, a key is provided by the Access Point before association takes place. The same key is used for subsequent reassociations.

Next, we summarize the three PHY level standards and the MAC layer standard. The architecture of the standard appears in Figure 8.15.

The PHY is broken down into two sublayers to ease the interface to the common MAC.

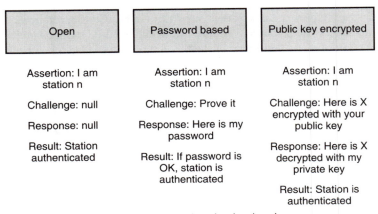

**Figure 8.14**  Authentication levels.

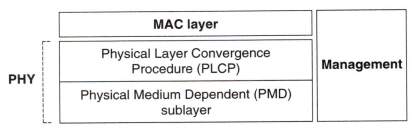

**Figure 8.15**   Architecture of the 802.11 standard.

# The 802.11 MAC Standard

The 802.11 MAC standard provides asynchronous, connectionless service. This service is aimed at providing short response time. A time-bound, connection-oriented service was postponed to a later phase of the standard. It was an original aim of the standard and remained in consideration until the last moment. It was left in as long as it was because of the experience some of the committee members had with FDDI I and FDDI II. Apparently, FDDI I ignored isochronous service, or time-bound service, and was short-lived because of that trait and supplanted by FDDI II. Whether that experience happens with 802.11 or not remains to be seen. More than likely, enough applications in the next few years will require asynchronous service with a relatively simple MAC, to justify a MAC that does not provide the time-bound isochronous service at the expense of greater complexity and cost.

The MAC supports working with and without an infrastructure; thus it supports ad hoc networking. This requirement was also in danger of falling out of the initial standard, but it did survive.

The MAC supports power-saving devices. Part of the MAC header indicates when traffic is due for a sleeping node, to help conserve battery life. A single MAC supports multiple PHYs. This element too was questioned by those who wished to optimize the MAC for a specific PHY, but in the end the single MAC won out, to provide some insulation between the MAC and the PHY so different manufacturers can provide each.

The process that took place in reaching the MAC protocol is interesting. The 802.11 committee depends on volunteer participation from interested parties. Anyone from any country can participate, no matter how large or small. The 802 committees tend to have many more small companies and individuals than the telephony committees and similar international committees. The proposals for the MAC went from 9 to 11. The 11 proposals were provided by:

1.  Xircom
2.  Incent Technologies (NCR at the time)
3.  IBM

4. Spectrix

5. Hitachi

6. University of Taiwan

7. INRIA, France

8. Hughes

9. Rypinski

10. Crowder

11. National Semiconductor

The majority of the proposals came from individuals. Some came from large companies. Four finalists were then selected. Those were:

- AT&T, Telxon, Xircom
- IBM
- Spectrix
- National Semiconductor

Telxon and Xircom joined forces with AT&T. From there the committee voted on a "foundation" MAC. The first one was selected by a wide margin. It was the most complete, and was selected as a foundation upon which the best features of the others would be added as required. We now describe the essence of the resulting MAC.

The MAC frame includes:

- A MAC header containing
  - Control info
  - Addressing
  - Sequencing
  - Fragmentation ID
  - Duration
- Frame body
  - Variable length data
- CRC
  - IEEE 32 bit

Figure 8.16 details the MAC header.

Several address fields are provided. The maximum packet size is huge, especially when compared with Asynchronous Transfer Mode (ATM) cells. More about that at the end of this chapter when we briefly address Wireless ATM. The 32-bit CRC completes the frame.

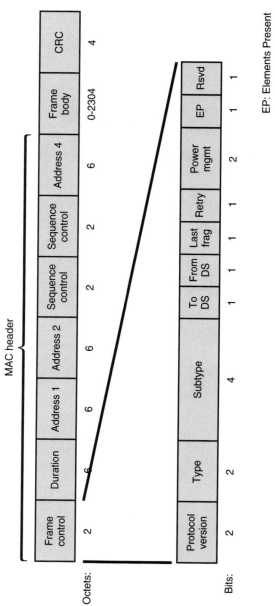

**Figure 8.16** 802.11 General MAC frame format.

The elements of the frame are defined below:

- To DS, From DS: AP present, not ad hoc
- Last fragment: Last fragment or sole fragment
- Retry: This frame is a retransmission
- Elements present: Frame is not empty
- Duration: Duration in microseconds for hidden node handling
- Address fields
  - Source address
  - Destination address
  - AP address
  - Transmitting station address
  - Receiving station address
- Sequence control
- Dialog token: 12-bit transmission ID
- Fragment number: 4-bit fragment number of this transmission
- Frame body: Up to 2304 bytes long
- CRC: Error handling

The power management states are:

- Transmit: Transmitter on
- Awake: Receiver is on
- Doze: Transmitter and receiver off, timer may be on

The AP buffers traffic to dozing stations. The Traffic Indication Map included in each beacon indicates traffic destined for dozing nodes. Dozing stations wake up to listen to TIM in the beacon. AP then sends a Delivery TIM (DTIM) followed by data for that station.

The types of MAC frames are delineated in Figure 8.17.

The Access Point transmits a beacon that includes:

- Time stamp
- Beacon interval
- DTIM period
- DTIM count
- Channel sync info
- ESS ID
- TIM and broadcast indicator

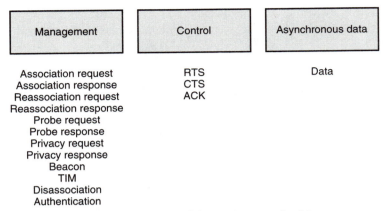

**Figure 8.17**   802.11 MAC frame types and subtypes.

A station can passively scan for the beacon. If it does not find a beacon, the station can actively scan by sending a Probe Request. The Access Point responds with a Probe Response. The station then sends an Association Request. The Access Point sends an Association Response that could use one of the three authentication levels outlined above. If the station roams to another Access Point, it sends a Reassociation Request that a Reassociation Response answers. When a station leaves an Access Point, it sends a Disassociation packet.

The RTS and CTS packets provide improved performance when nodes are hidden from each other, as discussed in Chapter 3.

# The 802.11 FHSS PHY Standard

In this section, we summarize the three 802.11 PHY standards. First, we present the requirements for the PHY, then the FHSS PHY, the DSSS PHY, and finally the infrared PHY. The PHY requirements are as follows:

- FCC Part 15.247 compliant
- Capable of data rate of at least 1 Mbps
- Capable of multiple collocated network operation
- Suitable for low power consumption
- Capable of insuring interoperability between conformant stations
- Operable in modes
  - Peer-to-peer
  - Station-to-AP and AP-to-station

The PHY is divided into the two sublayers you see in Figure 8.15. The Physical Layer Convergence Procedure (PLCP) sublayer simplifies the interface to the MAC. The PHY-specific preamble is included in this sublayer. The Physical Medium Dependent (PMD) sublayer provides a clear channel assessment mechanism, a transmission mechanism, and a reception mechanism. The Physical Layer Management Entity (LME) manages the PHY in conjunction with the MAC LME.

The FHSS PHY is for FHSS products that work in the 2.4 GHz ISM band. It provides:

- 1 Mbps and 2 Mbps data rates
- 79 frequencies in the US and Europe
- 23 frequencies in Japan
- 99% of its energy contained in 1 MHz bandwidth

The modulation parameters are:

- M: Number of levels = 2 or 4
- BT: Bandwidth/Time product
- Pulse shape
- h: Modulation index

The modulation parameters chosen for the 802.11 FHSS PHY appear in Figure 8.18 for the 1 Mbps and 2 Mbps rates.

Figure 8.19 illustrates the frame header for the FHSS PHY.

The first 96 bits are the FHSS preamble. A CRC is provided on the PHY header to improve its chance of correct reception.

The frequency hopping patterns provided in different parts of the world are outlined in Figure 8.20.

In the US and Europe, 66 hop sequences are defined. Two patterns minimize adjacent channel interference. In Japan, 12 hop sequences are defined. Four patterns minimize adjacent channel interference.

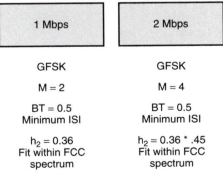

| 1 Mbps | 2 Mbps |
|---|---|
| GFSK | GFSK |
| M = 2 | M = 4 |
| BT = 0.5<br>Minimum ISI | BT = 0.5<br>Minimum ISI |
| $h_2 = 0.36$<br>Fit within FCC<br>spectrum | $h_2 = 0.36 * .45$<br>Fit within FCC<br>spectrum |

**Figure 8.18**   Chosen modulation for the 802.11 FHSS PHY.

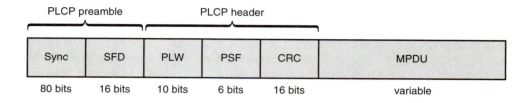

SFD: Start Frame Delimiter
PLW: PLCP Length Word
PSF: PLCP Signaling Field,
including data rate
MPDU: MAC Protocol Data Unit

**Figure 8.19** FHSS PLCP frame format.

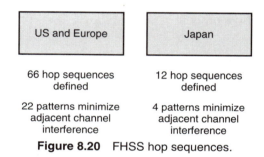

**Figure 8.20** FHSS hop sequences.

## The 802.11 DSSS PHY Standard

The DSSS PHY is for products that operate in the 2.4 GHz ISM band. It is summarized by:

- 1 Mbps and 2 Mbps
- 11 chip spreading factor
- DBPSK for the 1 Mbps data rate
- DQPSK for the 2 Mbps data rate
- 6 overlapping channels identified
- 10 mw to 1000 mw transmitted power

The six overlapping channels appear in Figure 8.21.

The six overlapping channels provide 3 pairs of non-overlapping channels, meaning that a pair of channels can be available in the presence of some interference. Figure 8.22 shows the PLCP preamble.

It has similar functions to the FHSS PLCP frame format.

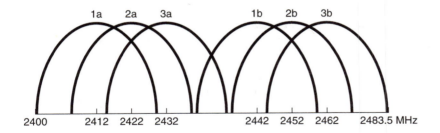

Japan, one channel at 2484 MHz

**Figure 8.21** DSSS channels.

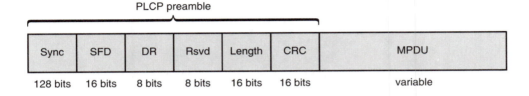

128 bits    16 bits    8 bits    8 bits    16 bits    16 bits                variable

SFD: Start Frame Delimiter
DR: Data Rate
MPDU: MAC Protocol Data Unit

**Figure 8.22** DSSS PLCP frame format.

# The 802.11 IR PHY Standard

The infrared PHY is summarized by:

- Baseband transmission
- 850 to 950 nanometer range of IR
- Diffuse IR for LAN operation

The range of infrared systems can be up to 10 m in typical office buildings, with the possibility of going up to 20 m with sensitive receivers. No regulations from the FCC exist. Some safety regulations must be met, though. The PLCP frame header is shown in Figure 8.23.

The IR Modulation and data rates are given by:

- 1 Mbps: 4-PPM, each group of 2 bits is mapped in one 4-PPM symbol
- 2 Mbps: 16-PPM, each group of 4 bits is mapped in one 16-PPM symbol

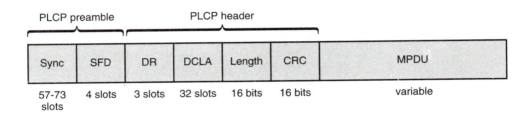

**Figure 8.23**   IR PLCP frame format.

# Hiperlan

Hiperlan is a high-performance Wireless LAN standard that is being developed in Europe in ETSI. ETSI representatives have participated in 802.11 from the beginning, leading to the two standards being complimentary. 802.11 provides data rates in the 1 Mbps to 2 Mbps range. Hiperlan provides higher data rates. The specifics of Hiperlan are summarized by:

- 20 Mbps
- 5.12 - 5.3 GHz = 180 MHz
- 17.1 - 17.3 GHz = 200 MHz
- Range of 50 m
- Non spread spectrum

The band in Europe has been allocated. The band at 5 GHz is available in the US, but just for spread spectrum products. The petition from Apple requests a band where Wireless LANs can be primary. This would fit Hiperlan products nicely.

The initial releases of Hiperlan are called type 1 and use customary CSMA, like MAC protocols. The later versions, type 2, use Wireless ATM.

# Mobile Data Standards

Very few actual standards exist in the Mobile Data area. The only standard that is developed by a standards body per se is the Tetra standard, which was developed by ETSI for Public Access

Mobile Radio. The Digital Short Range Radio was also developed by ETSI for Private Mobile Radio, but is not receiving much acceptance.

We do have de facto standards for data over circuit switched cellular, and de facto standards for packet switched networks. The two competing standards for packet networks are Mobitex and the protocols from Motorola for their ARDIS/Modacom networks. CDPD is also a de facto standard that was developed by an industry consortium for providing a packet service over existing circuit switched services. Other cellular-like services provide data according to their standards. For example IS 136 provides 9.6 Kbps data initially; so does GSM. PCS standards vary and typically provide greater data rates ranging all the way up to almost 1 Mbps for DECT bearer services.

Now we have completed our discussion of the first column and the last column in the map in Figure 8.24.

Next we discuss Wireless ATM briefly.

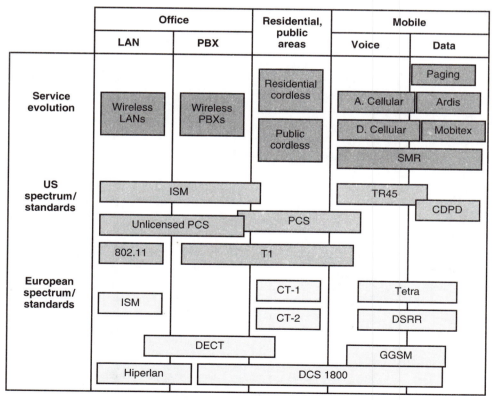

**Figure 8.24**   Wireless map.

## Wireless ATM

ATM, or Asynchronous Transfer Mode, is a cell relay technology for switching and multi-plexing. It uses asynchronous time division multiplexing that is based on undedicated slots sup-porting users' instantaneous needs. It provides point-to-point transmission between two entities and meets the needs of both isochronous services and asynchronous services. It provides extremely short transfer delay for the asynchronous services and provides guaranteed bandwidth and cell order integrity for the isochronous services.

For the isochronous needs, it has:

- Guaranteed delivery
- Cell loss ratio < 1.7 × 10-10
- Cell delay variation < 250 usec

For the asynchronous needs, it has:

- Very short transfer delay
- 150 usec at the 99 percentile level per switch

Even if five switches are in the path, the delay is less than one millisecond. Today, most LANs have an access time on the order of 10 milliseconds. For these reasons, LAN manufacturers are looking at ATM technology for their future high-performance LAN products.

The ATM cell is depicted in Figure 8.25.

It is very short compared to the huge packets that we find in Wireless Networking. Much re-search is ongoing in the Wireless ATM area. As mentioned, we anticipate Hiperlan Type 2 will use Wireless ATM. The present wave of standards use customary CSMA-like protocols.

## Summary

In this chapter we have dealt with Wireless Networking spectra and standards. We started with the ISM bands that are available in the US, Europe, and most other parts of the world now. At this time, the most available band is the 2.4 GHz band. About 80 MHz are available in the US and Europe and other parts of the world. In Japan only 26 MHz are available. Other ISM bands also exist at higher frequencies; some manufacturers are beginning to use them for commercial prod-ucts. At the very high bands that range all the way up to 60 GHz, some experimental radios point the way to future very high-performance systems.

To use the ISM bands, we must use complex spread spectrum technology that complicates the products. The Unlicensed PCS bands provide primary usage for Wireless LANs and Wireless PBXs. The bands for Wireless PBXs are beginning to be cleared. The bands for Wireless LANs are not moving ahead very rapidly due to difficult startup issues such as obtaining initial revenues to

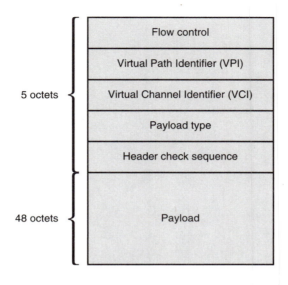

5 octets {

Flow control

Virtual Path Identifier (VPI)

Virtual Channel Identifier (VCI)

Payload type

Header check sequence

48 octets {

Payload

total = 53 octets

**Figure 8.25**   ATM cell.

relocate the incumbents in the band. To preserve the UPCS band from becoming unusable, an etiquette has been specified. The etiquette provides limits on the transmission in the band along four dimensions: power, bandwidth, duration of transmission, and method of access. The etiquette is enforced through type approval.

The IEEE 802.11 standard contains a MAC standard and three PHY standards for FHSS, DSSS, and IR. The specifics of the four standards are summarized. They are focused on the 2.4 GHz band at this time and in the first release provide asynchronous service but not isochronous service. They provide ad hoc networking capability that requires a distributed control function. The data rates provided by the PHYs are either 1 Mbps or 2 Mbps if the channel supports them. The higher data rate is achieved through higher order modulation.

The Hiperlan standard type 1 provides data rates on the order of 20 Mbps. It operates at the 5 GHz band and the 17 GHz band. The new effort by Apple to obtain spectrum at 5 GHz in the US is probably aimed at this kind of high-performance Wireless LAN. The next version of Hiperlan uses a Wireless ATM protocol. Wireless ATM is in the research stage at this time. It is facing some challenges but is proceeding well. We expect to see standards in this area in the near future.

The Mobile Data field relies mostly on de facto standards such the Mobitex protocol from Ericsson and the packet standards from Motorola. Of course, the cellular modem standards are available for carrying data over circuit switched analog cellular. And we have the data over digital cellular standards such as IS 136, IS 95, and GSM. Also, data over other cellular services such as PCS and DECT can range all the way up to almost 1 Mbps, in the case of DECT.

# 9 *Conclusions*

In this chapter, we bring together some of the highlights of the book, and make concluding remarks about Mobile Data and Wireless LANs.

## Who Will Be Mobile?

In the first chapter, we focused on the application layer of the Mobile Computing chart you see in Figure 9.1.

We started by discussing vertical and horizontal applications, in general showing that the dynamics of the market indicate that vertical applications have the greatest potential for early profits and they are more easily justified by their users; whereas horizontal applications garner the majority of the revenues in the future but must be priced much lower to appeal to the mass market, both professional and consumer, as depicted in Figure 9.2.

We presented several vertical market examples including airlines, police, emergency, hospitals, maintenance, retail stores, and stock exchanges. These are but a small sample of what promises to be an expansive industry with applications five years from now that we have not imagined today.

Next, we addressed the major challenges facing the Wireless Networking industry, namely security, bandwidth, software applications, and safety. We discussed these concerns via results of specific interviews with prospective users of Wireless Networking. Then we provided several early case studies of users of the technology. The case studies illustrated applications for Mobile Data services and for Wireless LAN products.

Next we presented an applications/technology matrix showing the private sector applications and the public sector applications and which of the Wireless Networking technologies applied best. Next we discussed horizontal applications, starting with early horizontal applications, followed by what will be pervasive horizontal applications that we will all use. These are illustrated in Figure 9.3.

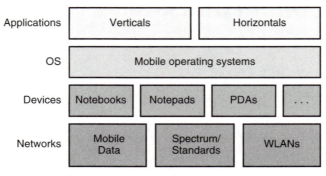

**Figure 9.1**   Mobile Computing chart.

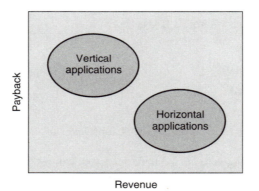

**Figure 9.2**   Vertical and horizontal market dynamics.

Finally, we discussed the position of Wireless Networking relative to wired networks and argued that Wireless Networking is a great adjunct to wired networks that will serve the majority of our needs; but for high-bandwidth multimedia applications, the wired network remains superior.

## Wireless Networking

In the second chapter, we provided an introduction to Wireless Networking. We began by showing the potential of Wireless Networking for simplifying mobile devices while making them more powerful. This trend applies not only to mobile devices but to PCs in general as they achieve

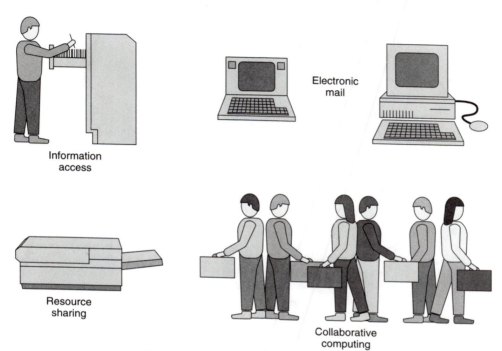

**Figure 9.3** Horizontal office applications.

greater connectivity to the Internet. We defined Wireless LANs as high-throughput, small cell size, low-speed mobility networks that serve asynchronous data traffic well in localized areas, but are not well suited to isochronous traffic such as voice and video. We defined Wireless WANs as medium-throughput, large cell size, high-speed mobility networks that serve voice very well and are ubiquitous, being available wherever users are likely to be located. These definitions appear in Figure 9.4.

We discussed the various kinds of Wireless WANs and their applicability to different kinds of user traffic. In particular, we argued that cellular carries voice well and data fairly well. Paging serves alert traffic very well. Packet data networks serve data very well. Satellite networks serve voice and data well at an expense, and provide positioning services very well. PCS serves voice very well and data well.

We discussed the different kinds of Wireless LANs, including ISM Wireless LANs, infrared Wireless LANs, and Wireless LANs in future Unlicensed PCS bands. We put these services into perspective by presenting several wireless maps. The first map showed the evolution of products and services, as well as the standards and spectra for Wireless Networking activities throughout the world, including not just Wireless LANs and Mobile Data services, but also cellular and PCS. We presented the map of data rate and cell size in Figure 9.5 that compared the services and analyzed their present relationship.

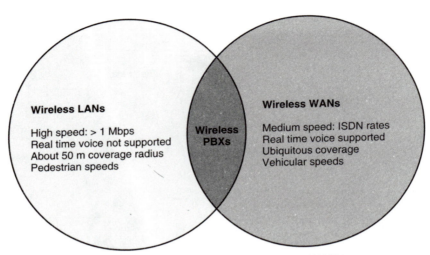

**Figure 9.4**    Wireless LANs and Wireless WANs.

We proposed some qualitative market forecasts for the field of Mobile Data and Wireless LANs, as Figure 9.6 shows.

The whole field is in the early stages of development. Some major questions still could alter the shape of the market in the next few years. The current view is that the development of the services are in the following rough order: Mobile Data over analog cellular, packet radio networks, Wireless LANs, Mobile Data over digital cellular, and two-way paging.

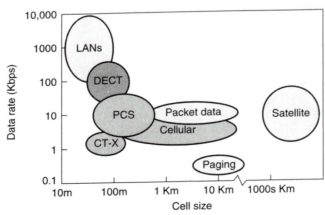

**Figure 9.5**    Relationship of networks.

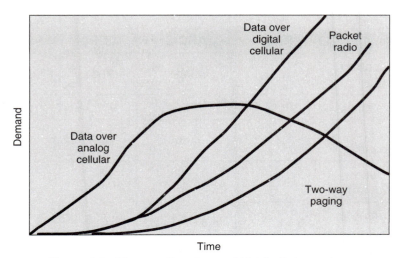

**Figure 9.6**   The growth patterns of Mobile Data services.

# Mobile Data Services

In the third chapter, we discussed and compared packet radio networks, such as RAM/Mobitex and ARDIS/Modacom, with CDPD, data over cellular, and paging. The two packet radio services are quite similar in structure and services provided. They are presently installing networks throughout the world to achieve coverage that is satisfactory for their initial customers. CDPD leverages the investment in current cellular services by deriving a packet service from the same frequency spectrum and much of the same equipment. The CDPD standard is complete, and the consortium members are busy installing networks to span the US. The status of CDPD relative to RAM/Mobitex and ARDIS/Modacom appears in Figure 9.7.

Whether a CDPD service emerges in other parts of the world depends on how quickly GSM can provide a packet service like CDPD. If it is slow in providing the service, CDPD may indeed emerge in countries that have implemented GSM.

The majority of Mobile Data traffic today is carried over analog cellular. Analog cellular modems provide over 14.4 Kbps uncompressed with slightly more expense than a wired modem. Ironically, data over digital cellular is lagging behind data over analog cellular because it is provided on the basis of an equivalent voice channel. It is typically limited to about 9.6 Kbps. This can be increased in the future by combining equivalent voice channels. This possibility is being considered in GSM and other digital cellular standards and could yield from 30 Kbps to over 100 Kbps.

Paging is flourishing in the US and in Asia. Its low cost, excellent coverage, and long battery life make it attractive for a significant market segment. It is not very popular in Europe because its cost has been kept by the service providers and because GSM had the SMS feature from the start.

| | RAM | ARDIS | CDPD | Data over cellular |
|---|---|---|---|---|
| Metropolitan areas | 100+ | 400+ | 700+ | 700+ |
| Base stations | 800+ | 1300+ | 9000+ | 9000+ |
| In building penetration | yes | more | some | some |
| Power (watts) | 2 | 3 | 0.6–1.2 | 0.6–3 |
| Performance (Kbps) | 8 >>19.2 | 4.8 >> 19.2 | 19.2 | 14.4 |

**Figure 9.7**   Comparison of Mobile Data services.

Two-way paging networks use the Unlicensed PCS bands that come in 50 KHz allocations. This allocation can provide a service on par with packet radio networks.

Asymmetrical two-way paging networks are similar to simple one-way paging, with a higher-density incoming network that allows the two-way pagers to remain simple. Their structure is illustrated in Figure 9.8.

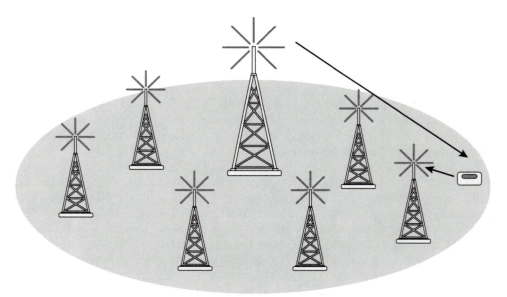

**Figure 9.8**   Asymmetrical two-way paging network.

Symmetrical two-way paging networks also exist that look very much like packet radio networks. Finally, some providers are using the narrow band PCS allocations to build voice messaging paging networks that deliver the voice messages themselves to the pager.

# Wireless Networking Technology Primer

In the fourth chapter, we presented a series of topics that are the basis for Wireless Networking technologies discussed in later chapters. We started with spread spectrum techniques. We described FHSS and DSSS and compared them in detail. They are depicted in Figures 9.9 and 9.10.

Apparently, FHSS is superior given today's processing speeds.

We discussed MAC alternatives, including slotted ALOHA, CSMA/CA, and possible combinations with TDMA. The MAC alternatives are organized in the four categories in Figure 9.11.

Slotted ALOHA is most often found in Mobile Data networks. The performance of ALOHA protocols are compared with CSMA/CA in Figure 9.12.

CSMA/CA is usually found in Wireless LANs, and some of the newer products are using combined CSMA/TDMA to improve the throughput under heavy load and to have the opportunity of providing asynchronous service as well as isochronous service. We discussed the problem of hidden nodes in Wireless Networks you see in Figure 9.13, and ways of dealing with them by use of the RTS/CTS/ACK protocol.

We discussed security alternatives for Wireless Networks, including public keys and symmetric keys, and showed how the combination key scheme in Figure 9.14 satisfies most requirements.

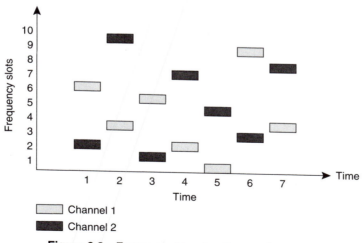

**Figure 9.9** Frequency Hopping Spread Spectrum.

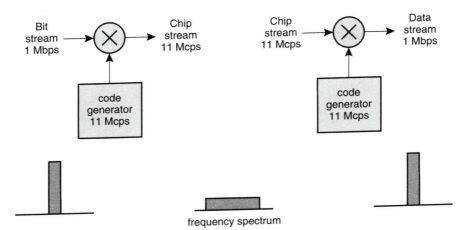

**Figure 9.10** Direct Sequence Spread Spectrum.

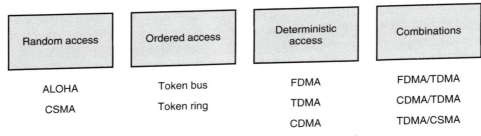

**Figure 9.11** Medium Access Control alternatives.

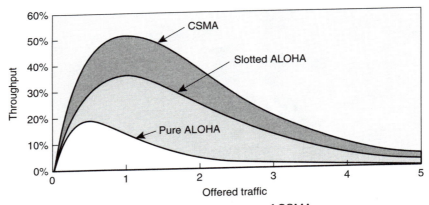

**Figure 9.12** Performance of CSMA.

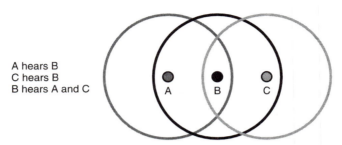

A hears B
C hears B
B hears A and C

**Figure 9.13**    Hidden nodes in Wireless Networks.

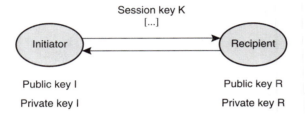

Session key K
[...]

Initiator

Recipient

Public key I

Public key R

Private key I

Private key R

Session key encrypted using public/private keys
Messages encrypted in session key

**Figure 9.14**    Combination keys.

Finally, we reviewed infrared technology, both the sources of IR and the most popular baseband modulation schemes, namely OOK (On-Off Keying) and PPM (Pulse Position Modulation).

## Mobile Data Technologies

In the fifth chapter, we focused on the technologies behind Mobile Data networks. We presented the structure of the RAM/Mobitex network and the Motorola ARDIS/Modacom network; the two are very similar in structure. They both have a central hub where most of the network intelligence is located. The base stations are connected to the hub via a network of wired circuits that may be leased from a private line provider. The protocols used on both packet radio networks are similar, both using slotted ALOHA at the MAC layer. They both use fairly robust error detection and correction codes over the air channel as well. The data rates are comparable. The network structure and protocol layers of the RAM/Mobitex network appear in Figure 9.15.

CDPD has an innovative approach. It derives a packet service from the gaps between circuit switched cellular calls, which exist because of the statistics of voice and other circuit switched

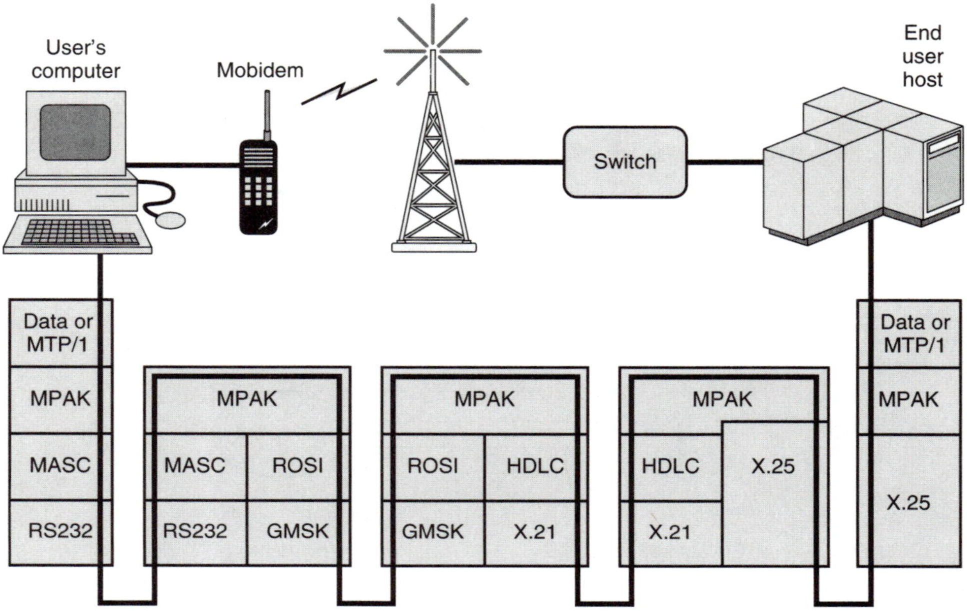

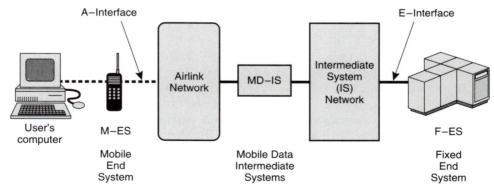

**Figure 9.15** Mobitex protocol layers.

calls. The gaps are small relative to the length of voice call, but are quite sizable relative to an average data message. By providing equipment that can utilize these gaps without affecting the service quality experienced by the voice calls, CDPD can provide a packet service using much of the same cellular equipment of existing cellular networks. Figure 9.16 shows the CDPD network architecture.

**Figure 9.16** CDPD network architecture.

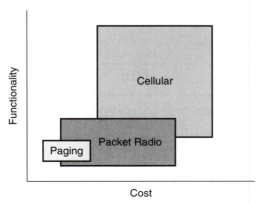

**Figure 9.17**    Cost/performance comparison of Mobile Data options.

The CDPD providers are themselves cellular providers, so in essence they are deriving additional service revenues from the same licenses and the same cellular network infrastructure. GSM Phase 2+ will also have a packet service that is designed after the fact to add this feature to already implemented circuit switched cellular networks. Tetra, a Public Access Mobile Radio standard that is developed by ETSI, actually provides both a circuit switched and a packet switched service definition from the start.

Metricom uses Wireless LAN technology, namely FHSS, to provide what might be called a Wireless Metropolitan Area Network. The data rates are about one-tenth as high as for typical Wireless LANs, and the range is about 10 times as large.

Data over cellular can provide about 10 Kbps initially, rising to 100 Kbps or more as faster speed circuit switched data services are defined in the standards. The majority of data traffic today is carried by analog cellular, because many people have cellular phones. A cellular modem is relatively inexpensive and the air time is not prohibitively expensive, even for short messages. The cost and functionality of data over cellular, packet radio, and paging are compared in Figure 9.17.

Many service providers are providing combined circuit switched and packet switched services by combining a cellular modem with a CDPD modem. This setup provides the user with both options so that he can optimize his performance cost relative to the kind of data he needs to transmit.

# Wireless LAN Technologies

In the sixth chapter, we explore various aspects of Wireless LAN technologies. We begin the chapter with a summary of technology trends, particularly in the radio field, as they relate to the cellular market and contrast it to the Wireless LAN market. Many of the developments in the cellular and PCS markets can be useful in the Wireless LAN market. We develop a wish list that a user may desire for a Wireless LAN.

Next, we analyze FHSS systems. First, we provide a list of systems design goals, followed by a system engineering discussion that deals with details of the radio. The next section shows how multipath can cause Inter Symbol Interference and that in contrast to cellular systems, Wireless LANs avoid the problem of multipath by keeping the data rate below about 2 Mbps. Cellular systems do deal with multipath through equalization or rake filtering. Wireless LANs avoid the cost of these sophisticated techniques.

Various modulation techniques are analyzed, including CPFSK, 0.39 GMSK, and others. Next, the philosophy behind frequency hopping pattern selection is presented. For the approximately 80 frequencies available in the 2.4 GHz ISM bands, about 15 to 20 channels, or frequency hopping patterns, are possible. The channels cellularize an office building or office campus, as suggested in Figure 9.18.

Finally, the preamble required to achieve and maintain synchronization in an FHSS system is studied. The result is that a preamble of about 96 bits is sufficient for the job.

Moving up the protocol stack, the next topic is Wireless LAN MAC protocols. Three protocols are studied. The Listen Before you Talk protocol is essentially nonpersistent CSMA and is the one used by the majority of Wireless LAN products. All the products do use different variations of it since they were developed before the standard was finalized. The final standard is also based on this basic LBT MAC. The other two protocols are an integrated CSMA/TDMA protocol and a

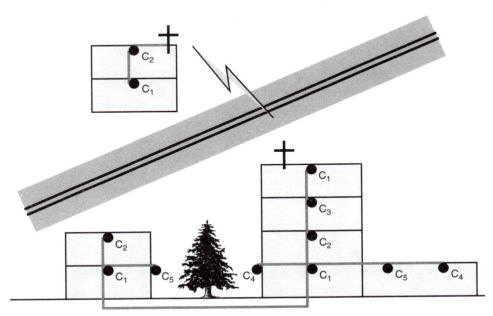

**Figure 9.18** An example of an office campus layout.

Reservation/Polling protocol. These two protocols are used by two Wireless LAN products and, interestingly, are the ones favored by the stock trading applications since they are very fair algorithms, even though they do not have the fastest response time.

The next topic is power management. Two design points are studied, the notebook computer model, and the palm-top computer model. One has a battery with average lifetime ranging from two to four hours moving towards four to eight hours, the other using AA or AAA batteries that are expected to last for weeks. We present ways of saving battery life that include sleeping almost all the time except when the computer has something to transmit or receive. The MAC support needed to implement these power saving features are outlined.

Interconnection to backbone networks is discussed for both mobility within the same network and mobility among different networks. For mobility within the same network illustrated in Figure 9.19, spanning tree MAC level bridges are favored.

These bridges are very similar to their wired LAN cousins, with the exception that the age-out timers are much shorter, being on the order of minutes instead of hours in length. Mobility among different networks is presented in light of Mobile IP. The protocol is essentially a tunneling or encapsulation scheme. It relies on some of the routers in the Internet, implementing Home Agents and Foreign Agents to take care of Mobile Hosts. The Home Agents reenvelope packets destined for a Mobile Host that is away from home. This operation is depicted in Figure 9.20.

Finally, Chapter 6 deals with naming and directory services such as DNS, which are hierarchical, distributed name spaces that provide a scalable structure that can handle the growth of the Internet, including Mobile Hosts, in a way similar to the cellular and PCS networks. Its operation is shown in Figure 9.21, contrasted to the operation of cellular and PCS networks in Figure 9.22.

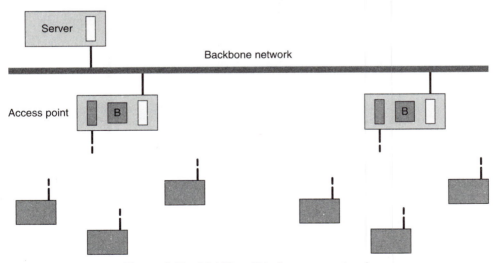

**Figure 9.19** Mobility within the same network.

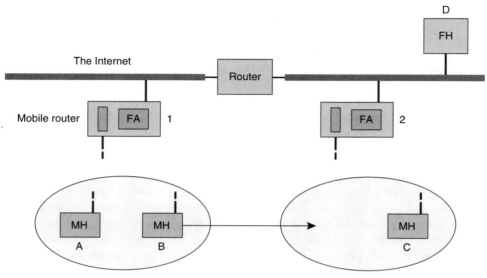

**Figure 9.20**  Mobile IP operation.

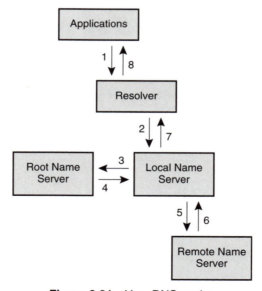

**Figure 9.21**  How DNS works.

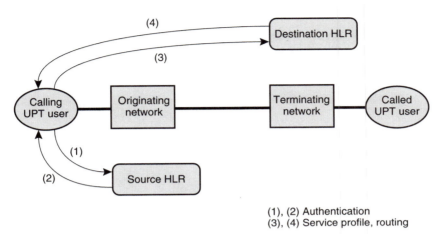

(1), (2) Authentication
(3), (4) Service profile, routing

**Figure 9.22**   PCS call flow.

# Wireless LAN Products

In the seventh chapter, we discussed Wireless LAN products. The products are classified according to whether they are for the mobile market or for the wire replacement market, and whether they use radio or infrared. The ability to support the PCMCIA product qualifies a product for being mobile. The mobile Wireless LAN products usually have a network topology that Figure 9.23 shows.

The wire replacement Wireless LAN products have a topology similar to the one depicted in Figure 9.24.

Figure 9.25 compares the mobile Wireless LAN products.

The comparison shows that most of the products provide between 1 and 2 Mbps with the exception of Spectrix, which provides 4 Mbps. The difference between 1 and 2 Mbps is probably not perceptible at the end-user level. With that small difference, looking at the specific implementation of the MAC is more important to see what the ultimate performance would be.

The frequency of operation is in the 2.4 GHz band, which is internationally available. The AT&T product is available at both 900 MHz and 2.4 GHz. The technology used is all FHSS except for the AT&T product, which was one of the first introduced and has remained with DSSS. The range of the products is nominally close to the 50 meter number, with slight variations. The variations may point to the AT&T product as having a slightly larger range and the Xircom product as having a slightly shorter range. All the products support ad hoc networking and do not require an Access Point, with the exception of the IBM product and the Spectrix product. Interestingly, those two products are the first to be tried by the stock market trading floor applications.

The range of the infrared products is on the order of 10 meters, instead of 50 meters for the radio products. The number of Access Points required by infrared is much larger than for radio, and

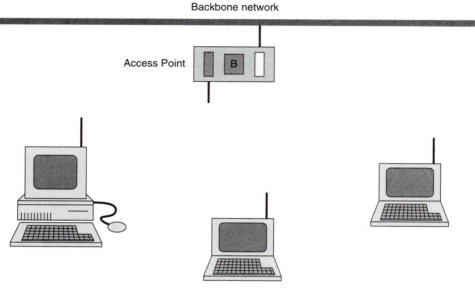

**Figure 9.23** Wireless LAN network topology.

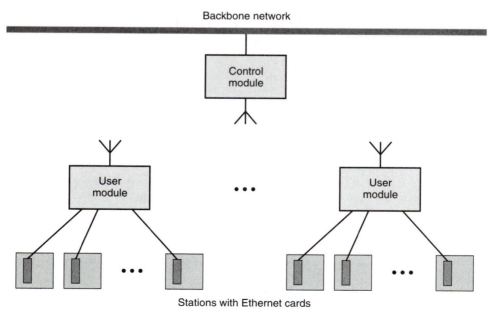

**Figure 9.24** Wire replacement LAN network topology.

| Product | Data rate | Frequency | Technology | Range | Access Point |
|---------|-----------|-----------|------------|-------|--------------|
| Lucent GIS | 2 Mpbs | 900 MHz | DSSS | 50 m | Optional |
| IBM | 1 Mpbs | 2.4 GHz | FHSS | 50 m | Required |
| Proxim | 1.6 Mpbs | 2.4 GHz | FHSS | 50 m | Optional |
| Xircom | 1 Mpbs | 2.4 GHz | FHSS | 50 m | Optional |
| Photonics | 1 Mpbs | IR | PPM | 10 m | Optional |
| Spectrix | 4 Mpbs | IR | OOK | 10 m | Required |

**Figure 9.25** Comparison of Wireless LAN products—mobile.

an Access Point is needed in every room where coverage is required. The two infrared products in Figure 9.25 use OOK and PPM modulation techniques that are discussed in detail in Chapter 7.

Figure 9.26 is a comparison of the wire replacement products.

These products have a form factor that does not allow them to fit inside a mobile computer. But the network topology of all these three products is similar. A number of stations share one user module and are connected to it via a cable. The user module communicates with a control module that is connected to the backbone network. Thus, these products avoid having to run a separate cable down from the ceiling to each station, but still require a cable from the station to a user module that may be situated in the middle of the stations sharing it. The user module can be located on a desk, a table, or in another convenient place in the middle of the users sharing it.

The Motorola system uses the 18 GHz band. Motorola has obtained licenses in over 20 countries for this product. The maximum range between the control module and the user module is about 15 meters. The radio uses fairly low power. The Windata network is another product that has continued to use DSSS. Windata also uses both the 2.4 GHz band and the 5.7 GHz band. It uses one of the bands for the up link, and the other for the down link.

| Product | Data rate | Frequency | Technology | Range | Access Point |
|---------|-----------|-----------|------------|-------|--------------|
| Motorola | 10 Mpbs | 18 GHz | Narrowband | 15 m | Required |
| Windata | 10 Mbps | 2.4, 5.7 GHz | DSSS | 50 m | Required |
| InfraLAN | 4, 16, 10 Mbps | IR | OOK | 25 m | Required |

**Figure 9.26** Comparison of Wireless LAN products—Wire replacement.

All three products require an Access Point, so they do not support ad hoc networking. Ad hoc networking is not a strong requirement for desktop wire replacement configurations.

## Wireless Spectra and Standards

In the eighth chapter, we dealt with Wireless Networking spectra and standards. We started with the ISM bands that are available in the US, Europe, and most other parts of the world now. They appear in Figures 9.27 and 9.28.

At this time, the most available band is the 2.4 GHz band. About 80 MHz are available in the US, Europe, and other parts of the world. In Japan only 26 MHz are available. Also, other ISM bands are available at higher frequencies, and some manufacturers are beginning to use them for commercial products. At the very high bands that range all the way up to 60 GHz, some experimental radios point the way to future very high-performance systems.

To use the ISM bands, we must use complex spread spectrum technology that complicates the products. The Unlicensed PCS bands provide primary usage for Wireless LANs and for Wireless PBXs. These bands are shown in Figure 9.29.

The bands for Wireless PBXs are beginning to be cleared. The bands for Wireless LANs are not moving ahead very rapidly due to difficult startup issues such as obtaining initial revenues to relocate the incumbents in the band. To preserve the UPCS band from becoming unusable, an etiquette is specified. The etiquette provides limits on the transmission in the band along four dimensions: power, bandwidth, duration of transmission, and method of access. The etiquette is enforced through type approval.

The IEEE 802.11 standard contains a MAC standard and three PHY standards for FHSS, DSSS, and IR. The architecture of the standard appears in Figure 9.30.

The specifics of the four standards are summarized. They are focused on the 2.4 GHz band at this time and in the first release provide asynchronous service but not isochronous service. They

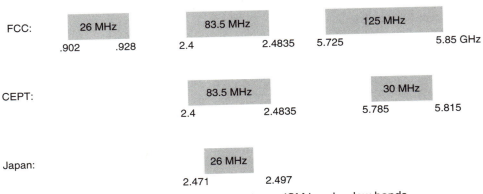

**Figure 9.27**   FCC, CEPT, and Japan ISM bands—low bands.

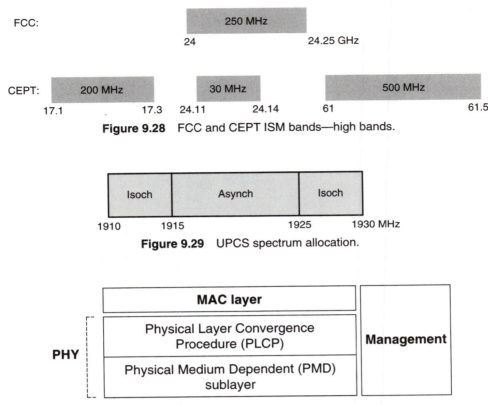

FCC:

250 MHz

24                    24.25 GHz

CEPT:    200 MHz          30 MHz                500 MHz

17.1          17.3    24.11        24.14    61                61.5

**Figure 9.28**   FCC and CEPT ISM bands—high bands.

| Isoch | Asynch | Isoch |

1910        1915            1925    1930 MHz

**Figure 9.29**   UPCS spectrum allocation.

| MAC layer |
| Physical Layer Convergence Procedure (PLCP) | Management |
PHY
| Physical Medium Dependent (PMD) sublayer |

**Figure 9.30**   Architecture of the 802.11 standard.

provide ad hoc networking capability that requires a distributed control function. The data rates provided by the PHYs are either 1 Mbps or 2 Mbps if the channel supports them. The higher data rate is achieved through higher order modulation. The frame format of the common MAC layer is depicted in Figure 9.31.

The Hiperlan standard type 1 provides data rates on the order of 20 Mbps. It operates at the 5 GHz band and the 17 GHz band. The new effort by Apple to obtain spectrum at 5 GHz in the US is probably aimed at this kind of high-performance Wireless LAN. The next version of Hiperlan uses a Wireless ATM protocol. Wireless ATM is in the research stage at this time. It is facing some challenges but is proceeding well. We expect to see standards in this area in the near future.

The Mobile Data field relies mostly on de facto standards such as the Mobitex protocol from Ericsson and the packet standards from Motorola. Of course the cellular modem standards are available for carrying data over circuit switched analog cellular. And we have the data over digital cellular standards such as IS 136, IS 95, and GSM. Also, data over other cellular services such as PCS and DECT can range all the way up to almost 1 Mbps, in the case of DECT.

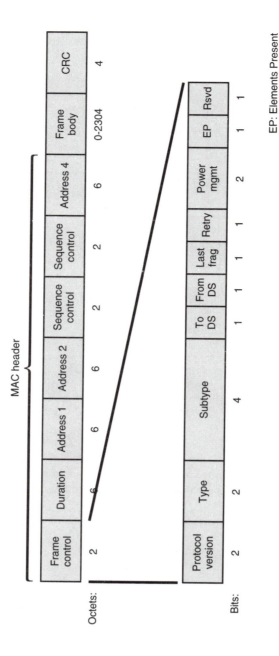

**Figure 9.31**    802.11 General MAC frame format.

# A Look at the Future

In this final section, we explore some of the work that is taking place at Xerox Park in the area of computing in the next century. They developed a model that has the three components in Figure 9.32.

The tab is a wearable device that is very light and unobtrusive. It is attractive enough that we would wear it even if it did nothing! The Star Trek communicator is a good example. Smart badges and watch-sized devices are good examples as well. A tab is illustrated in Figure 9.33.

It is a small microprocessor. Among other possible functions, it broadcasts the identity of its wearer. Of course it is wireless. When a person is wearing a tab that is broadcasting her identity,

- The "right" doors automatically open
- Rooms greet people by name
- Telephones are forwarded automatically
- Needed files are downloaded to board computers in conference rooms

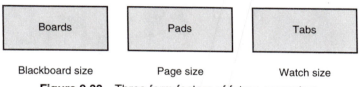

**Figure 9.32**   Three form factors of future computers.

**Figure 9.33**   A tab.

**Figure 9.34**    A pad.

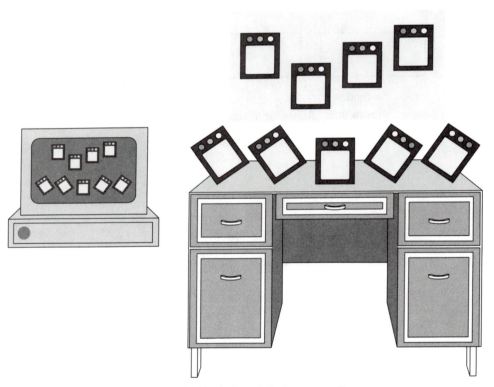

**Figure 9.35**    Evolution of desktop paradigm.

Objects can be animated with tabs as well as people. For example, luggage in busy airports can have a tab to help them find their way through the maze of luggage transportation belts.

A pad is a cross between a sheet of paper, a notebook computer, and a palm-top computer. Depicted in Figure 9.34, a pad can be called intelligent paper.

Current computers use the desktop metaphor. On the monitor screen, we have objects, files, folders, and so on as you see in the left part of Figure 9.35.

Different people work in different ways. For some, during the creative part of a project, they need to see many different items at the same time. With this wide angle view, their brains are able to integrate what they see before them and create new ideas. For those people, one computer screen is confining. They tend not to use the computer during the creative part of a project. They go back to pencil and paper until they have created the new ideas, and then they are able to work within the confines of the screen.

What if they had access to several pads, as shown in the left part of Figure 9.35. Each pad would be performing a different function. Each is a computer; each is intelligent paper. And they are all wireless, of course.

A board computer is the size of a blackboard. Conference rooms would each have one. They allow people in the room to work on them with electronic chalk, as illustrated in Figure 9.36.

Boards can also be located in common areas, similar to bulletin boards. Combined with a tab, the board can anticipate a person coming and customize itself to that person's specific interest profile, as depicted in Figure 9.37.

**Figure 9.36**  A board.

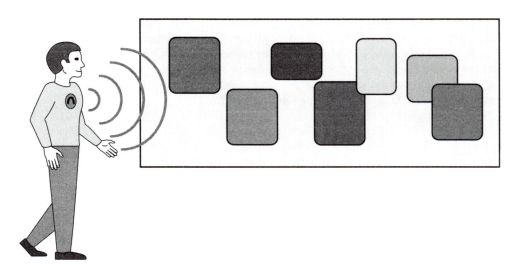

**Figure 9.37** Personalized bulletin board.

**Figure 9.38** Friendly office.

Going back to his office, our wireless person's tab precedes his arrival with its broadcasts. When the person arrives at his office, his tab greets him by name, as imagined in Figure 9.38.

As he enters the office, the tab briefs him of his voice, fax, and electronic mail messages, as well as events in his calendar that need his attention, in the order of priority it has learned he prefers.

The future is Wireless. Don't you agree?

# *Bibliography*

"Special Issue on RACE Mobile Communications," *IEE Electronic and Communications Engineering Journal,* No. 3, June 1993.

Kipereos, T., "Satellites and PCS: The Hybrid Approach," *Proc. Second International Conference on Universal Personal Communications,* ICUPC, Ottawa, Canada, Oct. 12-15, 1993.

Freeburg, T.B., "Enabling Technologies for Wireless In Building Network," *IEEE Communications Magazine,* Vol. 29, No. 4, April 1991.

IEEE 802.11, "Wireless LAN Requirements," Document IEEE 802.11/91-108.

Rappaport, T.S., "Indoor Radio Communications for Factories of the Future," *IEEE Communications Magazine,* May 1989.

Hayes, V., "Standardization Efforts for Wireless LANs," *IEEE Network Magazine,* Vol. 5, No. 6, November 1991.

Tolly, K., and D. Newman, "Wireless Inter Networking," *Data Communications Magazine,* 1993.

Leonard, M., "PCMCIA Sized Radio Links Portable Wireless LAN Terminals," *Electronic Design,* Aug. 5, 1993.

Special Issue on "Personal Communications Systems," *IEEE Network Magazine,* Vol. 30, No. 12, December 1992.

"Radio Data Link Access Procedure (RD LAP)," Motorola Data Systems, Schaumburg, IL, March 1991.

McCaw Cellular et al, CDPD System Specification, July 1993.

Davie, M.C., and J.B. Smith, "A Cellular Packet Radio Network," *Electronics and Communications Engineering Journal* (IEE), Vol., 3 No. 3, June 1991.

Saleh, B.M., and R. Valenzuela, "Statistical Model for Indoor Multipath Propagation," *IEEE J. of Selected Areas in Communications,* Vol. SAC 5, Feb. 1987.

Ganesh, R., and K. Pahlavan, "On the Arrival of the Paths in Multipath Fading Indoor Radio Channels," *IEEE Electronics Letters,* June 1989.

Alexander, S.E., "Radio Propagation Within Buildings at 900 MHz," *IEEE Electronics Letters,* Oct. 1982.

Zhang, K., and K. Pahlavan, "Relation Between Transmission and Throughput of the Slotted ALOHA Local Packet Radio Networks," *IEEE Trans. on Communications,* Vol. 40, No. 3, 1992.

"Mobile Communications Towards the Year 2000," *Proc. of IEEE Professional Group E8* (radio communications systems), London, October 17, 1994.

Lee, W.Y.C., *Mobile Cellular Telecommunications Systems,* New York: McGraw-Hill International, 1989.

Calhoun, G., *Digital Cellular Radio,* Norwood, MA: Artech House, 1988.

Macario, R., *Personal & Mobile Radio Systems,* Peter Peregrimus Ltd., 1991.

Hodges, M.L., "The GSM Radio Interface," *Br. Telecom Technol. Journal,* Vol. 8, No. 1, Jan. 1990.

Steele, R., *Mobile Radio Communications,* London: Pentech Press, 1992.

ETSI, *European Telecommunication Standard,* DECT, ETS 300 175, Parts 1-9, and *ETS 300 176.*

Mulder, R.J., "DECT, A Universal Cordless Access System," *Phillips Telecommunication Review,* Vol. 49, No. 3, Sept. 1991.

ETSI, European Telecommunications Standards Institution, "Recommendations for GSM 900/DCS 1800," Published by ETSI, 06921 Sophia Antipolis, Cedex, France.

Ramsdale, P.B., and W.B. Harrold, "Techniques for Cellular Networks Incorporating Micro Cells," *IEEE Conf. PIMR 92 Boston,* Oct. 1992.

Gilhousen, K.S., et al, "On the Capacity of a Cellular DCMA System," *IEEE Trans. on Vehicular Technology,* Vol. VT-40, No. 2, May 1991.

Gudmundson, B., et al, "A Comparison of CDMA and TDMA Systems," *Proc. 42nd IEEE Vehicular Technology Conf.,* Denver, May 1992.

Selected proceedings of the IEEE 802.11 Standards Committee and its subcommittees.

Selected proceedings of the T1 Standards Committee and its subcommittees.

Selected proceedings of the TR45 Standards Committee and its subcommittees.

# Mobile Computing Devices and Operating Systems

**APPENDIX**

In this Appendix, we focus on the device level and the operating system level of the Mobile Computing chart shown in Figure A.1.

In particular, we cover:

- Mobile computing devices
- Pocketable computing devices
- Underlying technologies
- Mobile operating systems
- Market forecasts

## Mobile Computing Devices

We can think of mobile devices as falling in the categories in Figure A.2.

Fixed devices are included in Figure A.2 to emphasize that they are very much a part of the picture as they provide connectivity to the backbone networks and to the servers that hold much of the information we need. The largest mobile computing devices are what can be referred to as *carriables*. They include notebook computers and pen computers. They are of a size that would fit in a briefcase. They are easily carried around in an office or on business trips, but most people would not carry them much of the time.

The next category includes PDAs, Information Appliances, Personal Communicators, cellular phones, PCS phones, and future navigators of various kinds. They could provide several media, starting with voice and data and eventually evolving to provide video. Their size is small enough so that they can be put in a pocket or a pocketbook without unduly weighing down the user. A person may take a *pocketable* with them to dinner; some people may carry a pocketable with them

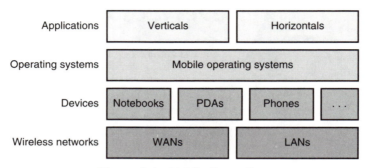

**Figure A.1**   Mobile Computing.

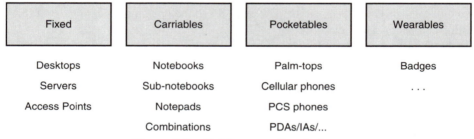

**Figure A.2**   Mobile computing devices.

often or most of the time. A pocketable could include a person's directories and calendar, among other items of frequent use.

The next category is *wearables*. This category includes smart badges, watch-sized pagers, watch-sized phones, and other extremely light devices that are smaller than today's pagers. Some envision ring-sized devices performing very simple functions. The Star Trek communicator falls in this category! In Chapter 9 we discuss future technologies, and this category of mobile computing devices is referred to as *tabs*.

Another way of looking at mobile computing devices is in perspective relative to fixed devices of different sizes, as shown in Figure A.3.

At the bottom of Figure A.3 are mainframes. Their number is the smallest and their cost is the highest. Next we have minicomputers, workstations, and desktop PCs, followed by notebook computers and pen-based computers. Finally, at the top we have pocketables and wearables of different kinds. The potential volume of the devices increases as we move upwards in the diagram. The device cost generally drops as we move upwards in the diagram. The devices that benefit from mobility are the ones in the top three layers, including carriables, pocketables, and wearables.

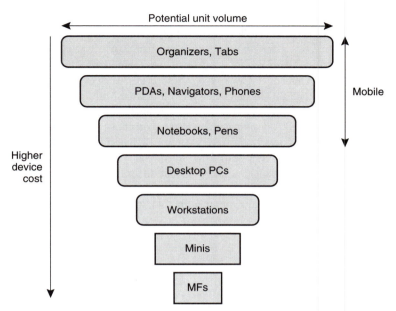

**Figure A.3**    Computing device cost, potential volume, and mobility.

## Pocketable Computing Devices

Let us focus for a moment on the pocketable category. The most common names for these devices are:

- Personal Digital Assistants
- Information Appliances
- Personal Communicators

At first the names may seem whimsical. When considered at a deeper level, they reflect the culture of the part of the industry that coined the term. For example, the term PDA was coined by Apple Computer, and was given to the Newton device that some say launched the PDA market, albeit too early and with little initial acceptance. What is a PDA? It is a computer that is very simple to use. One can write on it with a pen, after much practice. Its user interface is very simple for a computer, but it is still a computer.

What is a Personal Communicator? This term was coined by AT&T and others who have a culture in the telephony industry. A Personal Communicator is a phone that does a lot more, for example calendaring, directories, and notetaking. Its user interface begins as that of a phone that a five-year-old can operate and goes from there. It is likely to have a wholly different paradigm from a PDA.

What is an Information Appliance? That term was coined by Hewlett Packard. The first pocketable products that HP introduced were the LX series of devices. They look like calculators. They have buttons like a calculator. In fact, they have the same buttons as the very first calculator that HP produced over 30 years ago, the HP 45. The buttons felt good then and they still feel good now! Interestingly, when the HP 45 first came out, it cost about $400 and was basically a four function calculator that we can now obtain for less than $10. The LX series of devices are full MS-DOS machines with 1 Megabyte or more of RAM, starting at $400.

What is an Information Appliance and how does it differ from a Personal Digital Assistant or a Personal Communicator? An Information Appliance comes with the HP heritage. That heritage is changing, but starts out as a computing device. In fact, the LX series typically comes with a spreadsheet in ROM.

What can pocketable devices do? They:

- Capture information
- Organize information
- Communicate information

They are built for:

- In-the-field mobile workers
- On-the-go managers
- Mass market consumers

What do they cost? They vary over a large range, all the way from under $100 to over $2000. Who will be able to buy each kind? Vertical application users can typically afford the most expensive devices; they can justify the cost of the device more easily. The benefit can be quantified into added functionality in their jobs or functions. For example, a package delivery service can justify a pocketable device because it provides added competitive features that are important to the end user. An example is notifying the sender of a parcel that the parcel has just been delivered and signed for by the recipient.

The next category of user is the on-the-go managers. To be attractive to the on-the-go manager, the cost needs to be below $1000. On-the-go managers are all the people who spend much of their time away from their desks. They benefit from having critical information with them at their fingertips. Their applications are more horizontal, like electronic mail, and have more difficulty justifying a large expense.

Next we have the general consumer, and at least two or three subcategories of consumers exist. To attract them, the cost needs to be in the $100 range. Below $100, the market expands significantly to include younger consumers.

# Underlying Technologies

To understand the structure of mobile computing devices and how their power will grow with time, we need to look inside one of them (see Figure A.4).

The basic components are: Processors, different kinds of memory, and a battery power system. These components are tied together by buses. In addition, with multimedia we are seeing more and more Digital Signal Processing chips. Add-on devices are conforming to the Personal Computer Memory Card Industry Association form factor and are called PCMCIA cards or simply PC cards. Let us now address each of these areas in turn.

Faster processors provide better mobile applications. Mobile devices need the fast processing capability of the newest processors, but they also require small size, cool running, and low cost. The newest fast processors tend to run at high temperature, and they consume a lot of power. These factors are being addressed and will be solved in the near future. The fast processors are also too expensive for most mobile devices, which are not large expensive workstations where the cost of the processor is a small percentage of the total cost of the machine. This problem too is being addressed with simpler streamlined versions of the processors that are still fast but provide a specific set of functions that are aimed at Mobile Computing. The result is processors with the following characteristics:

- Ultra low-power consumption
- Small size
- Cool running
- Low cost

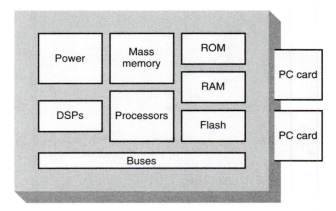

**Figure A.4**    The components of a mobile computing device.

Faster bus architectures are needed to handle the data generated by faster processors. To speed the data among the components of the device, we need higher and higher performance buses. Without faster buses to match the faster processors, moving the data within the computer becomes a bottleneck, and the overall performance is reduced.

In this area, the winners are moving towards a distributed bus architecture, with local buses carrying the "local" traffic and sharing a backbone bus. The backbone bus of choice is tending toward the ISA architecture. The trend is towards higher bandwidth and greater flexibility. Emerging distributed architecture, such as the ISA bus combined with local buses, is being chosen rather than 32-bit buses such as EISA.

DSPs are the cornerstone for multimedia. These hardware units are like engines that perform analog and digital processes with speed and efficiency. They process all the signals that start out as analog signals, including speech, video, modem signals, and fax signals. In the area of recognition of speech and handwriting, DSPs are indispensable.

Longer running time and smaller, lighter batteries are another key area of development for mobile devices. In the last decade, the biggest hero had the most MHz, which translates into speed. These processors run at high temperatures and require lots of battery power. In this decade, the heroes combine speed with ultra low-power consumption, as well as cool running. The trend is to move from 5 volts all the way down to 1.5 volts by the end of the decade. Coupled with the drop in voltage, more and more sophisticated power management features will develop. At this time, power management techniques turn off different chips of the computer if they are not needed. In the future, power management systems will turn off *parts* of the chip if they are not needed. In other words, power management will become more and more granular.

One of the keys to lower power and smaller size is small feature size, which is the size of the components on the chips. We expect to achieve 0.25 micron by the end of the decade (see Figure A.5).

More storage space for audio and video provides another dimension of growth for mobile computing devices. Disk drive performance has increased even more quickly than anticipated, due to two new technologies: Magneto sensitive (MR) heads and Partial Response Maximum Likelihood (PRML) technology. In addition, the rotational speeds of the platters where the data is stored

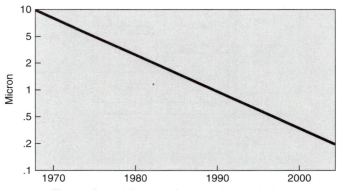

**Figure A.5** Minimum feature size evolution.

is increasing from 3600 revolutions per minute to 5400 revolutions per minute and higher. In this area of storage, we expect 1 Gbyte to be generally available on PCMCIA cards for Mobile Computing by the end of the decade.

RAM is one of the cornerstones of sophisticated applications. It allows the computer to keep larger and larger amounts of data "in mind" as it processes it. Not having enough RAM would require the processor to "page" data in and out of mass memory. The growth of RAM appears in Figure A.6.

This means that parts of a large application or file are actually "paged" into the hard disk when they are not immediately needed. The computer needs to do so in order to free up limited RAM space for it to perform its functions. When that part of the application or file is needed, the processor must take time to bring it back to RAM, and page another part of the application or file into the hard disk. This process greatly slows down the operation of the overall computer. 16 Mbit chips of RAM are common now. 64 Mbit chips are beginning to appear on the market in volume. 256 Mbit chips have been built in the lab and are functioning well at this time.

ROM holds the core functions of the computer. ROM maintains its memory when the power is turned off. In smaller computers such as PDAs, the ROM can hold not only the basic functions of the computer, including its operating system, but also some core applications such as telephone directory, appointment calendar, a small spreadsheet program, and a word processor. We expect ROM to reach a density of 256 Mbit per chip by the end of the decade.

Flash memory is the cousin of ROM. Usually housed in a PCMCIA card, it contains specific applications. Flash cards are experiencing the largest growth in the memory market. Because they can be plugged in and out by the user with ease, flash cards provide great flexibility. By holding different applications, they provide flexibility so that the same computer can address many different scenarios or even different vertical markets.

PCMCIA cards started out being for memory only, as their name reflects. Now they provide all sorts of add-on functions. As we discussed above, ROM PCMCIA cards are what are called "flash cards." Mass memory on a PCMCIA card is a low-profile rotating hard disk. Fax modems and Wireless LAN cards are now available in the PCMCIA form factor. These LAN cards provide

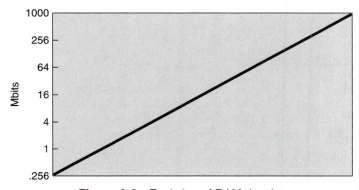

**Figure A.6**  Evolution of RAM density.

over 1 Mbit per second data rate. They provide access from a portable computer or a PDA to a backbone LAN network such as Ethernet. Since a LAN is a private network, the user does not pay usage charges as she would have to if she were using a public network such as a cellular network.

PCMCIA positioning systems are available. These cards have a Global Positioning System (GPS) receiver on them. The receiver receives signals from GPS satellites that allow the user to know where he is with great accuracy. Using this information, he can obtain information on how to get to another location. Finally, service providers can use PCMCIA cards to provide vertical applications for specific market segments such as public safety and real estate professionals. In summary, PCMCIA cards are providing:

- Memory cards
  - ROM
  - RAM
  - Mass memory
- Communications
  - Data/fax modems
  - LAN cards
- Vertical applications, for example
  - Positioning systems
  - Public safety
  - Emergency disaster response
  - Real estate appraisals
  - Consumer guides

How can a supplier achieve good economies of scale and at the same time serve the vertical market? The key is a customizable mobile computer that accepts PCMCIA cards with specific applications to give it the character of the vertical market segment it is serving.

## Mobile Operating Systems

This area, highlighted in Figure A.7, enables applications writers to develop applications with ease and without the undue burden of having to write complicated networking drivers.

Some examples of current mobile operating systems are:

- General Magic's Magic Cap
- Apple Newton operating system
- Penpoint

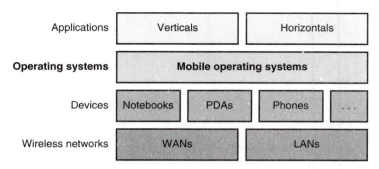

**Figure A.7**   Mobile operating systems level.

- PenDOS
- Geos

With a good mobile operating system, the applications writers can focus on the vertical market or horizontal market they are serving. They do not have to hire and train networking experts to develop interface software to the different kinds of networks. Mobile operating systems simplify and speed the writing of applications.

We hear a lot about software agents, which are software entities that act as macros. They take a simple user command, such as find the nearest Chinese restaurant, and translate it into data retrieval queries, network access commands, and so forth. Agents are especially important in large complex networks such as the Internet. They are indispensable for tasks such as finding files of interest and other resources that may be on any one of thousands of hosts all over the world. We will see agents of all kinds being used in Mobile Computing to ease the user interface.

## Market Forecasts

In this section, we present some relative market forecasts, not so much for their absolute value, but rather so that we understand the relative trends among different parts of the Mobile Computing, Mobile Data, and Wireless LAN markets. The mobile professional market appears in Figure A.8.

The first striking feature of Figure A.8 is that although the market for Mobile Data, mobile computers, and PDAs is quite large, it is small compared to the market for paging and cellular phones. However, Figure A.8 shows the number of *users*. If it showed *total revenues* instead, the difference would not be as dramatic.

Next, we see that cellular has overtaken paging in terms of number of users. In terms of revenues, the acceleration of the cellular market is even more dramatic. The Mobile Data curve re-

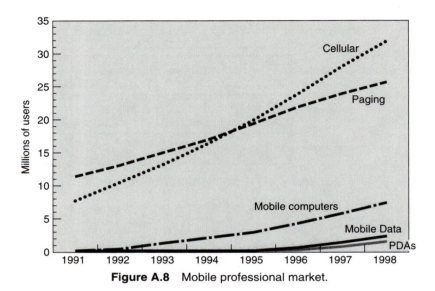

**Figure A.8**  Mobile professional market.

flects all Mobile Data adapters in all kinds of devices, including mobile computers, PDAs, cellular phones, and so on. The next curve above that is for mobile computers, and we all know how well that industry has been performing. Finally, the PDA market is shown.

Figure A.9 shows the number of mobile computers with no networking, the number having Wireless WAN connectivity, and the ones having Wireless LAN connectivity.

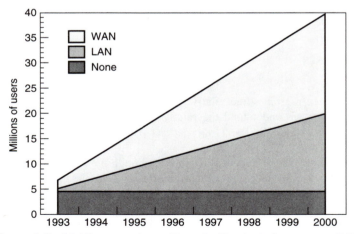

**Figure A.9**  Mobile computers with and without wireless connectivity.

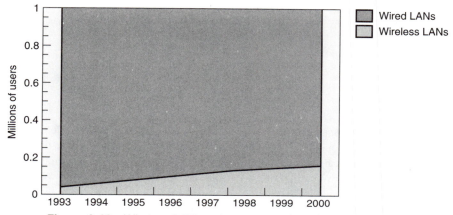

**Figure A.10**   Wireless LAN market compared to wired LAN market.

Originally the Wireless LAN market was considered part of the wired LAN market. Now we know that the Wireless LAN market is a complement to the wired LAN market. Growth rates are greater than originally anticipated and the unit prices are lower. Figure A.10 shows the percent of the LAN market that is wireless.

Wireless LANs by no means replace wired LANs. Instead, they rise to about 20% of the market by the end of the decade. This prediction is sensitive to the price of the devices. The price of the devices can drop dramatically if we have a viable standard according to which manufacturers can build chip sets.

Finally, Figure A.11 shows the Wireless LAN market as a portion of all wireless data that includes both Wireless LANs and Mobile Data.

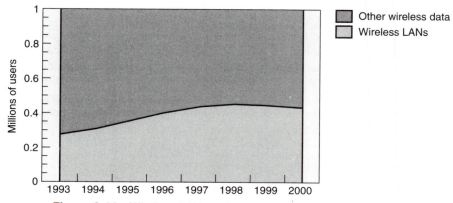

**Figure A.11**   Wireless LAN market compared to all wireless data.

The Wireless LAN market eventually garners about a 40% share of the market. The other 60% of mobile devices have Wireless WAN or Mobile Data connectivity.

## Summary

In this appendix we discussed two layers of Mobile Computing: the Mobile Computing devices layer and the mobile operating system layer. In Appendix B we discuss the applications layer. The rest of the book deals with the networking layer in detail. In this first appendix, we discussed Mobile Computing devices that are carryable, pocketable, and wearable. We showed that the potential volume for the smaller size devices can be much larger than for the bigger, more expensive devices, and showed that the smaller devices benefit most from mobility functions.

Focusing on pocketable devices, we discussed the heritages of the different factions of the industry that are introducing mobile devices, including the computer companies and the telephony companies. The character of the devices and their names are different. Watching the evolution of these devices is exciting, as more and more functionality is added to them. We discussed the cost of the devices and their appeal to the vertical markets, the horizontal professional market, and the horizontal consumer market.

Next, we explored the evolution of the technologies underlying Mobile Computing devices, including: processors, buses, power subsystems, DSPs, and memory systems including ROM, RAM, flash, and PC cards. We showed the evolution in the technology for each of these components. We saw that the emphasis for mobile devices is around ultra low-power consumption, small size, cool running, low cost, and ability to handle speech, handwriting, pen strokes, and perhaps eventually video. DSPs play an especially important role here.

We discussed the importance of a good mobile operating system. Operating system providers including Microsoft are providing these mobile capabilities as part of the core operating system. Having a good mobile operating system speeds the emergence of good applications that are key to the growth of the industry.

Finally, we presented some relative market forecasts. The key points that emerged are that the Mobile Computing, Mobile Data, and Wireless LAN markets are very significant, but they are small when compared with the market for cellular and paging, in terms of number of users. Next, we noted that the majority of Mobile Computing devices will have either a Mobile Data connection, a Wireless LAN connection, or both. We showed that the Wireless LAN market grows to about 20% of the total LAN market, and that the Wireless LAN market peaks at about 40% of the total Wireless Data market that includes both Mobile Data and Wireless LANs.

# B

**APPENDIX**

# *Encapsulation versus Source Routing*

In this Appendix, we discuss encapsulation versus source routing for Mobile IP. The comparison is based on early work done at Columbia University and elsewhere on the Mobile IP protocol. First, we start with a description of Mobile IP that includes:

- Design objectives
- How it works
- Addressing architecture
- Route dissemination

The design objectives are:

- Mobility is handled at the network layer
- Transport and higher layers are unaffected
- Applications do not need to change
- The infrastructure of non-mobile routers is unaffected
- Non mobile hosts are unaffected

The basic premises are:

- A Mobile Host (MH) always keeps its IP address
- The IP of an MH comes from a reserved set of IP addresses
- A special class of routers called Mobile Support Routers (MSRs) routes packets between MHs and the rest of the network
- Routing to mobile hosts is decoupled from routing to the rest of the network
- Optimization is done for local mobility

The situation is depicted in Figure B.1.

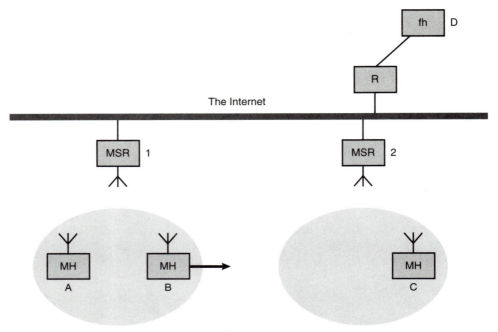

**Figure B.1**

Mobile IP works as follows:

- MSRs broadcast a periodic beacon
- MHs entering a cell receive the beacon
- MH sends a greeting
- MSR ACKs a greeting
- The new MSR sends a Forwarding Pointer (FWDPTR) to the old MSR
- The old MSR sends a Forward ACK (FWDACK)
- MH sets its new default router to the world as the new MSR
- The new MSR marks the MH as local

The traffic paths are:

- MH to MH within the same cell (A to B): Processed locally
- MH to fh (A to D): Routed normally
- fh to MH (D to A): Goes to nearest MSR

- MSR routes it by encapsulation to the remote MSR; the receiving MSR decapsulates it and delivers it to the destination MH
- MH to MH in another cell (A to C): Originating MSR encapsulates datagram to destination MSR

Figure B.2 depicts the "Mobile subnet."

The mobile subnet is an embedded network approach. MHs belong to this subnet. An MH is found in this way: MSRs advertise routes to the mobile subnet using ordinary internal routing protocols such as RIP. MSRs have cache. If not in cache, an MH can query other MSRs. The one handling the MH responds, and the response is cached. When away from home:

- MHs away from home acquire a temporary address
- They use it to handshake with their home MSR
- The home MSR tunnels packets to their temporary location
- Traffic from other MHs checks local MSR cache first
- If most traffic is local, back hauling is avoided

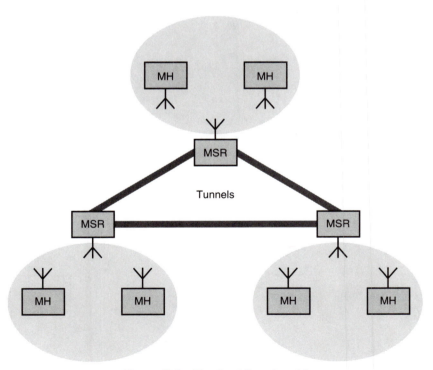

**Figure B.2**   The "mobile sub net."

New protocols for Internet mobility include:

- IPIP: IP inside IP encapsulation protocol
- M!CP: Mobile Internetworking Control Protocol
- New protocols are needed instead of using UDP (User Datagram Protocol)

The design goals of the Mobile IP that is based on the Loose Source Route (LSR) options within IP are:

- No changes required to non-mobile hosts
- No changes required to non-mobile routers
- No changes required to mobile hosts at layers above the network layer

The topology is depicted in Figure B.3.
The addressing plan is as follows:

- A mobile host (MH) retains its IP address while moving
- That address may not be related to its location

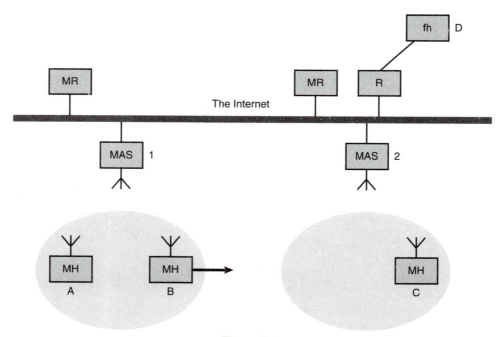

**Figure B.3**

- Each MR is assigned a set of Mobile IP prefixes
- Each MH is associated with a specific MR as long as the MH retains the same IP address
- Packets to an MH go to the appropriate MR

It operates as follows:

- MH to MH in the same cell
  - May involve at most one MAS (Mobile Application Subsystem)
  - No MR involvement is needed
- MH to fh
  - Involves exactly one MAS, unless MH is moving
  - Involves at most one MR, but only sporadically
- MH to MH in a different cell
  - Involves exactly two MASs, unless MHs are moving
  - Involves at most 2 MRs, but only sporadically

It allows the source to supply routing information to Internet routers. The Loose Source and Record Route (LSRR) option allows routers to record route information, as shown in Figure B.4.

The route data includes a series of Internet addresses, if the pointer is greater than the length of the source route, the source route is empty and the recorded route is full, then routing is based on the destination address field.

The source routing options based on FRC 1122 state that if a host receives a datagram with a completed source route (the pointer points beyond the last field), the datagram has reached its final destination. The recorded routed is passed up to the transport layer and is reversed and used for a return source route for reply datagrams. An IP header cannot contain more than one source route.

Details of operation are specified for:

- MH to MH in the same cell
- MH to fh
- fh to MH
- MH to MH in another cell

type 131

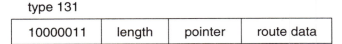

| 10000011 | length | pointer | route data |
|----------|--------|---------|------------|

**Figure B.4**   LSRR packet header.

For MH to MH in the same cell, we have:

- Depends on level 2 technology in that cell
- LSR = IP address of destination MH
- Destination Address of the IP header = IP address of the MAS
- Can it support "MAS-less" communications?

Let us consider Figure B.5.
For "MAS-less" communications, we have:

- MAS sends a redirect message to the source MH
- Source MH ARPs for destination MH address
- When it receives an ARP reply, it sends subsequent packets directly (no LSR option)
- ARP time-out timer needs to be short due to possible frequent mobility

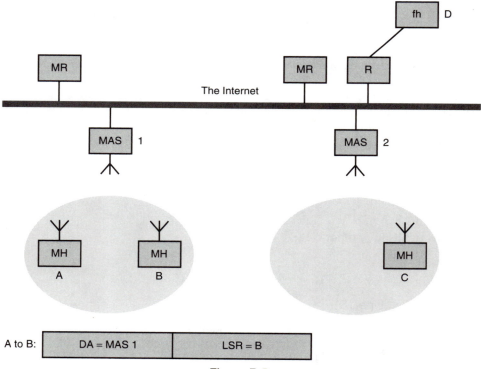

Figure B.5

- Or MH can send a message when it is about to change cells; then other MHs will purge ARP entry

In the case of MH to fh, we have:

- Destination Address of the IP header = IP address of the MAS
- LSR = IP address of fh
- No MR is involved

The reply message has:

- Destination address = IP address of MAS
- LSR = IP address of MH

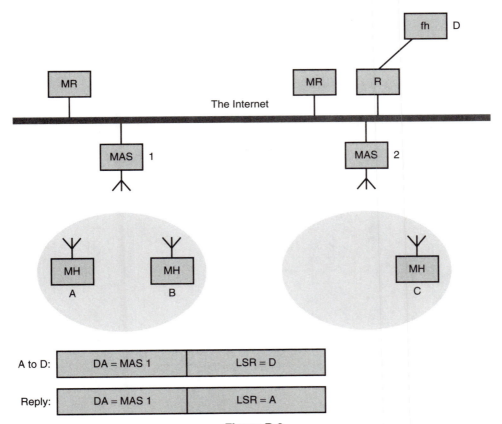

**Figure B.6**

- Normal Internet route first delivers packet to MAS, then to fh
- No MR is involved

In the fh-to-MH case, we have:

- Normal Internet routing delivers packet to associated MR
- MR sets LSR = destination address of the received header = Address of MH
- Destination address = IP address of appropriate MAS
- Proceed with Internet routing

The packet delivery involves:

- Packets are delivered to serving MAS and then to MH
- Return packets from MH to fh go as above for MH to fh

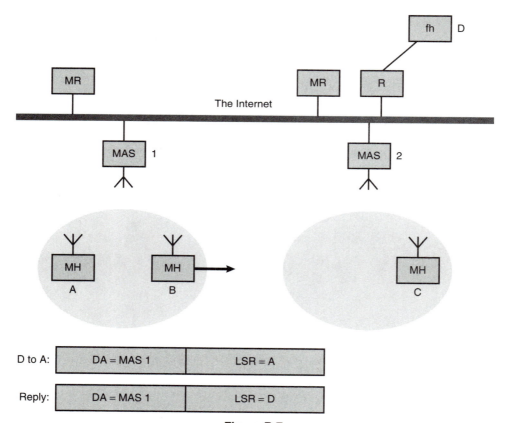

**Figure B.7**

- They bypass the MR
- No MR needed in steady state

As the MH moves, it modifies its outbound packets to reflect the IP address of the new MAS with which it is becoming associated. For MH to MH in another cell, we have:

- Destination address = IP address of source MAS
- LSR = IP address of destination MH
- Packet is sent to the source MAS
- MAS sends it to MR associated with destination MH

The MR actions are:

- MR appends the IP address in destination address (address of source MAS) to end of LSR
- Destination address = IP address of destination MAS
- The packet is delivered to the destination MAS and then to the destination MH

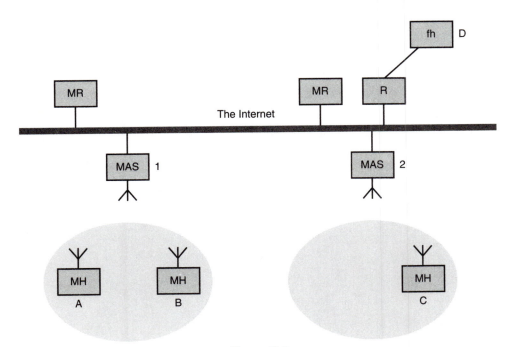

**Figure B.8**

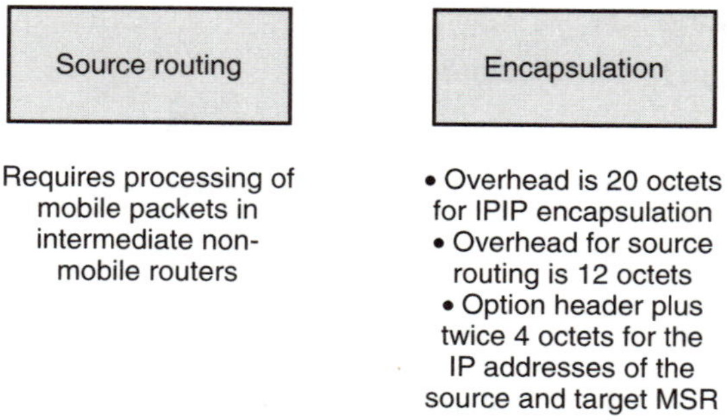

| Source routing | Encapsulation |
|---|---|
| Requires processing of mobile packets in intermediate non-mobile routers | • Overhead is 20 octets for IPIP encapsulation<br>• Overhead for source routing is 12 octets<br>• Option header plus twice 4 octets for the IP addresses of the source and target MSR |

**Figure B.9**    Comparison of source routing and encapsulation.

The reply involves:

- The destination MH reverses the addresses in the LSR
- After the initial exchange of packets, both MRs will not be involved
- If either MH moves to another MAS, it modifies the destination address of its outgoing packets to the IP address of the new MAS
- No modification of the LSR is needed

In summary, for source routing and encapsulation, we can say:

- In source routing the datagram is first routed to the destination MR
- Source routing is an IP option
- Encapsulation delivers data to remote Mobile Hosts by tunneling through normal Internet routers that do not know how to route to Mobile Hosts

This summary is depicted in Figure B.9.

Source routing requires processing of mobile packets in intermediate non-mobile routers. Encapsulation has an overhead is 20 octets for IPIP encapsulation, an overhead for source routing of 12 octets, and option header plus twice 4 octets for the IP addresses of the source and target MSR.

# C

## APPENDIX

# Random Medium Access Control Techniques

The random access Medium Access Control techniques have variations as follows:

- ALOHA
  - Asynchronous ALOHA
  - Slotted ALOHA
- CSMA
  - CSMA/CA: Collision Avoidance
  - CSMA/CD: Collision Detection
  - Nonpersistent
  - P-persistent

Asynchronous ALOHA, or pure ALOHA, is the simplest form of random MAC. The way it works is as follows:

- If you have data to transmit, transmit
- If no ACK is received before a timer runs out
  - Wait a random time
  - Transmit the same packet again

The maximum efficiency of pure ALOHA is about 18% of the data rate of the channel, as shown in Figure C.1.

The performance curves are drawn in terms of the ratio of offered traffic to data rate, meaning that if the ratio is one, the offered traffic is equal to the data rate—for example, for Ethernet that would be 10 Mbps. As you can see, the maximum possible throughput of ALOHA is about 18%, not very good. Such is the price of extreme simplicity.

Now suppose that we synchronize the system so users can transmit at specified instants instead of at any time. This concept is slotted ALOHA. Several packet radio networks, most notably

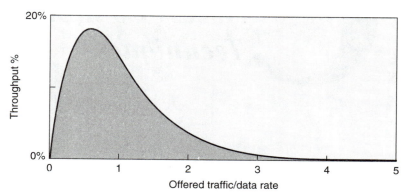

**Figure C.1**   Performance of Pure ALOHA.

ARDIS, or Modacom as it is called in other parts of the world besides the US, and Mobitex use slotted ALOHA.

Figure C.2 shows that the performance of slotted ALOHA is double that of pure ALOHA.

The delay performance of slotted ALOHA, as well as of random access MACs, has the disturbing shape you see in Figure C.3.

As the offered traffic approaches the maximum data rate of the network, the delay increases rapidly. In other words, most of the users are colliding and no one is getting through. This drawback of random access schemes is well-known. It is the price to pay for quick and simple access. The way to deal with this drawback is to plan the network such that the traffic does not approach this steep knee. More about that possibility later in relation to Wireless Networks.

The next most sophisticated random access scheme is CSMA, and that is the one that is used in most LANs, as well as in most Wireless LANs with some modifications, as we will discuss shortly.

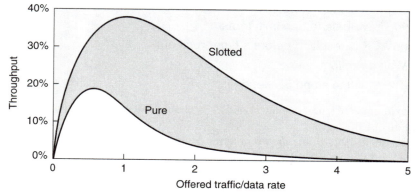

**Figure C.2**   Performance of pure and slotted ALOHA.

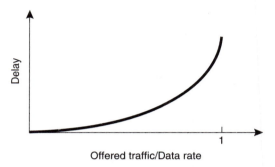

**Figure C.3**    Delay performance of random access MACs.

CSMA works as follows:

- Check if a carrier is present before transmitting
- If the channel is free
  - Transmit
- If the channel is busy
  - Wait a random time and try again
- Back off a random time

The most common distribution for a back-off distribution is the binary exponential back-off, which is described by:

- After the first collision
  - Wait 0 or 1 slots before trying again
- After the second collision
  - Wait 0, 1, 2, or 3 slots before trying again
- After the $i^{th}$ collision
  - Wait 0, 1, ..., $2^{i-1}$ slots before trying again
- The maximum wait time is set at 1023 slots

This exponential back-off algorithm provides good average response time, and improves the performance of CSMA. The performance curve of CSMA, as compared with pure ALOHA, and slotted ALOHA is depicted in Figure C.4.

CSMA peaks at about 65%. Still, when the traffic becomes heavy, it degrades badly. Ways of dealing with that problem exist, including using p-persistence. The way p-persistence works is as follows:

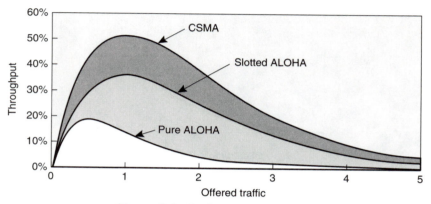

**Figure C.4** Performance of CSMA.

- Check if a carrier is present before transmitting
- If a channel is free
  - Transmit with probability p
  - Wait till next slot with probability 1-p
- If that slot is also free
  - Transmit with probability p
  - Wait till next slot with probability 1-p
- Repeat until either the frame is sent or the channel is busy
- If the channel is busy

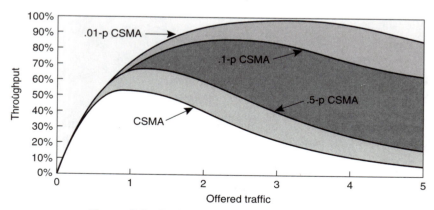

**Figure C.5** Performance of p-persistent CSMA.

- Wait till the next slot
- Start again

P-persistence in essence is like a metering light to get onto the network. Even though the network is free, the traffic is not allowed on the network all the time. This approach has the effect of removing some of the contention. It does improve the performance under heavy load, as you can see in Figure C.5.

The improvement is obtained at the expense of increased average delay, as would be the case with metering lights. Note that only a very low p can achieve significant improvement.

# APPENDIX D

# List of Wireless Networking Companies

## A

Advanced Wireless Communications, Inc.
435 Indio Way
Sunnyvale, CA 94086
408 736 8833

Alcatel Network Systems
12245 N. Alma Rd.
Richardson, TX 75081
214 996 5000

Advantis
3401 W. Dr. Martin Luther King Jr. Blvd.
Tampa, FL 33607
813 878 4207

Air Communications, Inc.
274 San Geronimo Way
Sunnyvale, CA 94086
408 749 9883

AirTouch Teletrac
7391 Lincoln Way
Garden Grove, CA 92641
714 890 7626

ALPS Electric, Inc.
3553 North First St.
San Jose, CA 95134
408 432 6544

American Mobile Satellite Corp.
10802 Parkridge Blvd.
Reston, VA 22091
703 758 6000

American Personal Communication
1025 Connecticut Ave.
Washington, DC 20036
202 296 0005

Ameritech Mobile Communications
2000 West Ameritech Center Dr.
Hoffman Estates, IL 60195
708 234 9700

Apple Computer
2025 Mariani Ave.
Cupertino, CA 95014
408 974 6790

ARDIS
300 Knightsbridge Parkway
Lincolnshire, IL 60069
708 013 1215

Arther D. Little, Inc.
Acorn Park
Cambridge, MA 02140
617 864 5770

AT&T
67 Whippany Rd.
Whippany, NJ 07981
201 386 7765

AT&T Network Systems
111 Madison Ave.
Morristown, NJ 07962
201 606 4060

AT&T Paradyne
8545 126th Ave.
Largo, FL 34649
813 530 8167

# B

Bell Atlantic Mobile Systems
180 Washington Valley Rd
Bedminster, NJ 07921
908 306 7583

Bellcore
290 West Mt. Pleasant Ave.
Livingston, NJ 07038
800 523 2673

Bell South Cellular
1100 Peachtree St.
Atlanta, GA 30309
404 249 5000

BIS Strategic Decisions
One Longwater Circle
Norwalk, MA 02061
617 982 9500

BT Ltd.
Annandale House 1 Hanworth Rd.
Surrey 44
932 765 766

BT North America
2560 North First St.
San Jose, CA 95161
800 872 7654

# C

California Microwave, Inc.
985 Almandor Ave.
Sunnyvale, CA 94086
408 732 4000

Casio, Inc.
570 Mt. Pleasant Ave.
Dover, NJ 07801
201 361 5400

Cellular One
5001 LBJ Freeway
Dallas, TX 75244
214 443 9901

CTIA
1250 Connecticut Ave.
Washington, DC 20036
202 785 0081

Cincinnati Microwave, Inc.
One Microwave Plaza
Cincinnati, OH 45249
513 489 5400

C. Itoh & Co.
251 Kita Aoyama
Tokyo 107, Japan
03 3497 3186

Claris Corp.
201 Patrick Henry Dr.
Santa Clara, CA 95052
408 987 4000

Communications Industry Association of Japan
92 Ohtemachi, 1 chome
Chiyoda ku, Tokyo, Japan
03 3231 3156

Cylink
310 North Mary Ave.
Sunnyvale, CA 94087
408 735 5817

# D

Dauphin Technology, Inc.
377 East Butterfield St.
Lombard, IL 60148
708 971 3400

Digital Microwave Corp.
170 Rose Orchard Way
San Jose, CA 95134
408 973 0777

Digital Ocean, Inc.
11206 Thompson Ave.
Lenexa, LS 66219
913 888 3380

# E

Electronic Industries Assoc.
2500 Wilson Blvd.
Arlington, VA 22209
703 524 5550

EMI Communications Corp.
PO Box 4872
Syracuse, NY 13221
315 433 0022

E-Plus Mobilfunk
Hans Guenther Sohl Strasse 1
4000 Duseldorf 1, Germany
49 211 967 7590

Ericsson Business Communications, Inc.
5757 Plaza Dr.
Cypress, CA 90630
714 236 6500

Ericsson Radio Systems, Inc.
740 East Campbell Rd.
Richardson, TX 75081
214 238 3222

Ex Mahnica, Inc.
45 East 89th St.
New York, NY 10128
718 965 0309

# F

Federal Communications Commission
1919 M. St., NW
Washington, DC 20055
202 632 7557

Office of Engineering and Technology
202 653 8117

Spectrum Allocations
202 652 8108

Common Carrier Bureau
202 634 7058

Frost & Sullivan International
4 Grosvenor Gardens
London, UK
071 730 3438

Fujitsu Personal Systems, Inc.
5200 Patrick Henry Dr.
Santa Clara, CA 95054
408 982 9500

# G

Gandlaf Mobile Systems, Inc.
2 Gurdwara Rd.
Nepean, Ontario, Canada
613 723 6500

GeoWorks
2150 Shattuck Ave.
Berkeley, CA 94704
510 644 0883

GEO Systems
227 Granite Run Dr.
Lancaster, PA 17601
717 293 7500

GPS International Assoc.
206 East College St.
Grapevine, TX 76051
800 269 1073

Granite Communications, Inc.
9 Townsend West
Nashua, NH 03063
603 881 8666

GTE PCS Group
600 N. West Shore Blvd.
Tampa, FL 33609
813 282 6154

GTE Mobile Communications
245 Perimeter Center Pkwy.
Atlanta, GA 30348
404 391 8386

# H

Hewlett-Packard Co.
5301 Stevens Creek Blvd
Santa Clara, CA 95052

Hong Kong Telecom, Ltd.
City Plaza Three
Hong Kong
852 803 8231

Hutchison Paging, Ltd.
Manlong House
911 615 Nathan Rd
Kowloon
Hong Kong
852 710 6828

# I

IBM Personal Computer Co.
1000 NW 51st St.
Boca Raton, FL 33432
407 443 2000

InfraLAN Technologies, Inc.
12 Craig Rd.
Acton, MA 01720
508 266 1500

IEEE
445 Hoes Lane
Piscataway, NJ 08855
908 981 0060

Iridium, Inc.
1350 I St.
Washington, DC 20005
202 371 6889

# J

Japan Ministry of Posts and Telecommunications
132 Kasumigaseki, Chiyoda ku
Tokyo 10090, Japan
03 3504 4086

Japan R&D Center for Radio Systems
1516 Toranoman
Minato ku Tokyo 105, Japan
03 3592 1101

# K

Kenwood USA Corp.
2201 E. Dominiquez St.
Long Beach, CA 90810
310 639 9000

# L

Loral Aeorospace Corp.
7375 Executive Place
Seabrook, MD 20706
301 805 0591

Link Resources Corp.
79 Fifth Ave.
New York, NY 10003
212 627 1500

# M

Matra Marconi Space
7 Rue Hermes
31520 Ramonvill St Agne, France
33 61 750565

McCaw Cellular Communications, Inc.
PO Box 97060
Kirkland, WA 98083
206 827 4500

Megahertz Corp.
4505 South Wasatch Blvd.
Salt Lake City, UT 84124

Mercury Communications Ltd.
90 Long Acre
London 2C239N UK
44 71 836 2449

Metricom, Inc.
980 University Ave.
Los Gatos, CA 95030
408 299 8200

Motorola Cellular Infrastructure Group
1501 West Shure Dr.
Arlington Hts., IL 60004
708 632 5000

Motorola, Inc.
Cellular Subscriber Group
600 North US Highway 45
Libertyville, IL 60648
708 523 5000

Motorola/EMBARC
1500 NW 22nd Ave.
Boyton Beach, FL 33426
407 364 2000

# N

NTIA
US Department of Commerce
Washington, DC 20230
202 377 1866

WaveLAN Products
1700 South Patterson Blvd.
Dayton OH 45479
800 255 5627

NEC America
Mobile Radio Division
383 Omni Dr.
Richardson, TX 75080
800 421 2141

NEXTEL Communications
201 Route 17 North
Rutherford, NJ 06707
201 438 1400

Nokia Mobile Phones
2300 Tall Pines Dr.
Largo, FL 34741
813 536 4443

Northern Telecom
2221 Lakeside Blvd.
Richardson, TX 75208
214 684 8821

NovAtel Communications Ltd.
6732 8th St
Calgary, Alberta
Canada T2E8M4
403 295 4949

NYNEX Mobile Communications Co.
2000 Corporate Dr.
Orangeberg, NY 10962
914 365 7712

# O

Oki Telecom
437 Old Peachtree Rd.
Suwanee, GA 30174
404 995 9800

Omnipoint Corp.
7150 Campus Dr.
Colorado Springs, CO 80920
719 591 0823

# P

Pacific Communications Sciences, Inc.
10075 Barnes Canyon Rd.
San Diego, CA 92121
619 535 9500

PCTel Corp.
2999 Oak Rd.
Walnut Creek, CA 94596
510 210 3645

PCMCIA
1030 East Duane Ave.
Sunnyvale, CA 94086
408 720 0107

Photonics Corp.
2940 N. First St.
San Jose, CA 95134
408 955 7930

Pinpoint Communications, Inc.
12750 Merit Cir.
Dallas, TX 75251
214 789 8900

Proxim, Inc.
295 North Bernardo Ave.
Mountain View, CA 94043
415 960 1630

# Q

Qualcomm, Inc.
6455 Lus Blvd.
San Diego, CA 92121
619 587 1121

# R

Racoteck, Inc.
7401 Metro Blvd.
Minneapolis, MN 55439
612 832 9800

Radiance Communications, Inc.
2338 A Walsh Ave.
Santa Clara, CA 95051
408 980 5380

RadioMail Corp
2600 Campus Dr.
San Mateo, CA 94403
415 286 7800

RAM Mobile Data
10 Woodbridge Ctr.
Woodbridge NJ 07095
908 602 5603

# S

SkyTel Corp.
1350 I St, NW
Washington, DC 20005
202 408 7444

Southwestern Bell Mobile Systems
18111 Preston Rd.
Dallas, TX 75252
214 613 0000

SpectraLink Corp.
1650 38th St.
Boulder, CO 80301
303 440 5330

Sprint Cellular
8725 W. Higgins Rd.
Chicago, IL 60631
312 399 2828

Stanford Telecommunications, Inc.
2421 Mission College Blvd.
Santa Clara, CA 95056
408 746 1010

Symbol Technologies, Inc.
46 Wilbur Place
Bohemia, NY 11716
800 SCAN-234

# T

Technologic Partners
419 Park Ave.
New York, NY 10016
212 696 9330

Telecom Denmark
Telegrade 2
DK 2630 Hoje Taastrup
AS reg. nr. 193312
45 42 52 9111

Telecommunications Industry Association
2001 Pennsylvania Ave.
Washington, DC 20006
202 457 8737

Teledesic Corp.
16161 Ventura Blvd.
Encino CA 91436
818 907 1302

Traveling Software
19802 North Creek Parkway
Bethel, WA 98011

# U

United States Telephone Association
1401 H St., NW
Washington, DC 20005
202 326 7300

US West
3350 161st Ave.
Bellevue, WA 98008
206 747 4900

# W

Windata
10 Bearfoot Rd.
Northboro, MA 01532
508 393 3330

# X

Xircom
26025 Murearu Rd.
Calabasas, CA 91360
818 878 6409

# Y

Yankee Group
200 Portland St.
Cambridge, MA 02114

# Z

Zenith Data Systems
2150 East Lake Cook Rd.
Buffalo Grove, IL 60089
800 553 0331

# *Glossary*

## A

**ACK:** ACKnowledgment
A short packet sent to confirm the reception of an information packet.

**ADPCM:** Adaptive Delta Pulse Code Modulation
A voice coding technique that results in a bit stream with a rate of 32 Kbps.

**ALOHA:** (Hello and Good-bye in Hawaiian!) Not an acronym
A simple random access technique for Medium Access Control that is used in data networks.

**AM:** Amplitude Modulation
A modulation technique that places the information of the signal in the amplitude of the carrier.

**AMPS:** Advanced Mobile Phone Service
An analog cellular standard that is used in North America as well as many other parts of the world.

## B

**BTA:** Basic Trading Area
A term used to signify a small metropolitan area in the United States. It is used to allocate frequencies for communications purposes.

# C

**CAI:**   Common Air Interface
The interface between the mobile unit and the base station.

**CDM:**   Code Division Multiplexing
A coding technique that digitized analog voice. The resulting data rate is 64 Kbps.

**CDPD:**   Cellular Digital Packet Data

**CEPT:**   Conference of European PTs
A government agency in Europe that allocated spectrum. It is analogous to the FCC in the US.

**CSMA:**   Code Division Multiple Access
A Medium Access Technique that is used in data networks.

**CT:**   Cordless Telephone
A short range wireless phone that communicates to a nearby base station. There are many varieties of cordless phones ranging from simple ones found in many homes to more complex public systems for use in high density areas such shopping malls and densely populated urban areas.

# D

**DCS:**   Digital Communications Services
A part of the GSM digital cellular standard that operates in the higher bands around 1800 GHz.

**DECT:**   Digital European Cordless Telephone
A cordless telephone standard that was developed in Europe but is likely to receive wide acceptance throughout the world for applications in wireless PBXs, residential cordless, and public cordless.

**Demux:**   Demultiplexer
A component responsible for separating signals that have been multiplexed together for transmission.

**DES:**   Data Encryption Standard
An encryption standard that was developed for making data transmission private. It relies on a symmetric that is used for both directions of transmission.

**DQPSK:** Differential Quadrature Phase Shift Keying
A modulation technique that transmits two bits for each sample using the phase of the carrier to convey the information.

**DSSS:** Direct Sequence Spread Spectrum
A kind of spread spectrum modulation that relies on a direct sequence pseudo noise code that the information bit stream modulates.

**DSP:** Digital Signal Processor
A kind of circuit that is used in many mobile devices to perform functions such as analog to digital conversion, hand writing recognition, voice recognition, and other functions.

**DSRR:** Digital Short Range Radio
An ETSI standard that was aimed at standardizing Private Mobile Radio.

# E

**ECMA:** European Computer Manufacturers Association
An association of computer manufacturers in Europe.

**EDC:** Error Detection and Correction
A method for adding redundant bits to the information stream that allow the detection and correction of errors that may occur during transmission.

**EEC:** European Economic Community
The community of European countries that is negotiating various ways for the members countries to cooperate.

**EIA:** Electronics Industry Association
A standards association in the US that supports several member committees including the committees that produce cellular standards in the US.

**ERMES:** European Radio Message Service
An ETSI standard that is aimed at paging systems.

**ETSI:** European Telecommunications Standards Institute
A major standards body in Europe that is responsible for many important standards including GSM and DECT.

# F

**FCC:** Federal Communications Commission
The regulatory agency in the US that is responsible for allocating frequency spectrum.

**FDD:** Frequency Division Duplexing
A way of providing full duplex channels that relies on frequency division. Each direction of transmission uses a channel of a different frequency.

**FDM:** Frequency Division Multiplexing
A multiplexing method in which each channel uses a different frequency.

**FDMA:** Frequency Division Multiple Access
A multiple access technique where each channel uses a different frequency.

**FHSS:** Frequency Hopping Spread Spectrum
A spread spectrum technique that spreads the information signal by hopping the information from one frequency slot to another over a pre specified band.

**FSK:** Frequency Shift Keying
A modulation scheme that relays the information by shifting the frequency of the carrier.

# G

**GFSK:** Gaussian Frequency Shift Keying
A type of Frequency Shift Keying that has a Gaussian shape in the frequency domain.

**GMSK:** Gaussian Minimum Shift Keying
A type of Minimum Shift Keying that has a Gaussian shape in the frequency domain.

**GPS:** Global Positioning System
A system that uses satellites to provide positioning information. This is used for locating airplanes and ships and many other devices for new applications.

**GSM:** Global System for Mobility.
An ETSI standard for digital cellular communications that is being implemented in Europe and many other parts of the world.

# H

**HH:** Hand Held
A device that is held in the hand such as a palm top computer or a cellular phone.

**HLR:** Home Locations Register
A data base that is used to store information about subscribers of a cellular system.

# I

**IA:** Information Appliance
A hand held device that is also known as a Personal Digital Assistant.

**IEEE:** Institute of Electrical and Electronics Engineers
A standards body in the US that develops standards for many applications such Local Area Networks.

**IEIE:** Institute of Electronic and Information Engineers
A standards body in Japan that is analogous to IEEE in the US.

**ISDN:** Integrated Services Digital Network
The future world wide digital network that provides digital voice as well digital data of various rates.

**ISI:** Inter Symbol Interference
The type of degradation that involves the interference between subsequent symbols in an information data stream. This kind of impairment is most commonly caused by multipath.

**ISM:** Industrial Scientific and Medical
A set of bands that are earmarked for equipment in the industrial and scientific and medical areas. These bands are also designated for use with spread spectrum equipment such as DSSS and FHSS systems.

# J

**JDC:** Japanese Digital Cellular
Digital cellular standards in Japan.

**JTC:** Joint Technical Committee
A committee composed of members of the T1 committee and the TIA committee that was formed to produce air interfaces for PCS in the US.

# L

**LAN:** Local Area Network
A network serving a local area such a building or an office campus.

**LEO:** Low Earth Orbit
A kind of satellite system that uses relatively low orbits compared to Geostationary satellites.

**LLC:** Logical Link Control (layer)
The higher sub layer of the second layer, or the Data Link Layer of the ISO protocol stack.

# M

**MAC:** Medium Access Control (layer)
The lower sub layer of the second, or the Data Link Layer of the ISO protocol stack.

**MPT:** Ministry of Public Telecommunications
The regulatory agency in Japan that is similar to the FCC in the US and CEPT in Europe.

**Mux:** Multiplexer
A circuit that combines different signals together for efficient transmission over the medium.

# N

**NMT:** Nordic Mobile Telecommunications
An analog cellular standard that is used predominantly in Europe, particularly the Nordic countries.

**NoR:** Notice of Rule making
A step in the FCCUs process of allocating spectrum.

**NPRM:** Notice of Proposed Rule Making
A step in the FCCUs process of allocating spectrum that comes before the NoR.

# P

**PAMR:** Public Access Mobile Radio
A term that is used in Europe and other parts of the world to signify a cellular system that is used by a number of users for specialized services.

**PBX:** Private Branch eXchange
A telephony switch that is privately owned by a company to serve a building or office campus.

**PCMCIA:** Personal Computer Memory Card Industry Association
A kind of computer interface card that is the size of a credit card and widely used in portable computers.

**PCN:** Personal Communications Network
A term that used mainly in Europe and other parts of the world to refer to small cell size cellular systems that are intended to serve high density areas.

**PCS:** Personal Communications Services
A term that is used mainly in America and in other parts of the world to signify a small cell size cellular systems that are intended to serve high density areas.

**PDA:** Personal Digital Assistant
A hand held computer that is about the size of an average humanUs hand.

**PHY:** PHYsical (layer)
The lowest layer of the ISO protocol stack that is responsible for transmission of bits over the medium.

**PM:** Phase Modulation
A kind of modulation that puts the information onto the phase of the carrier.

**PMR:** Private Mobile Radio
A term used mainly in Europe and other parts of the world to signify a private cellular system that is used by a closed user community such as a police department or a taxi cab company.

**POCSAG:** Post Office Code Standardization Advisory Group
A paging standard that is used in Europe as well as other parts of the world.

**POS:** Point of Sale
A device such as a cash register that is used at the point of sale in the retail environment.

**PSK:** Phase Shift Keying
A kind of digital modulation that puts the bits onto the phase of the carrier.

**PSTN:** Public Switched Telephone Network
The telephone network that connects most of the world today.

# Q

**QAM:** Quadrature Amplitude Modulation
A kind of amplitude modulation that has two bits per sample.

**QPSK:** Quadrature Phase Shift Keying
A kind of phase shift keying that has two bits per sample.

# R

**RELP:** Residually Excited Linear Predictive
A kind of linear predictive coding technique that is used to reduce the data rate of voice down in the range of 10 Kbps.

**RES:** Radio Equipment and Systems
A part of the ETSI standards committee in Europe that is concerned with radio systems.

**RSA:** Rivest/Shamir/Adelman
A public key encryption system that is commonly used in communications systems. The names in the acronym are the names of the people who invented the algorithm.

**RX:** Receiver
Common shorthand for receiver.

# S

**SIM:** Subscriber Identity Module
A module that is the size of a credit card or in some instances the size of a postage stamp that identifies the user and other pertinent information.

**SMR:** Specialized Mobile Radio
The term used in North America and other parts of the world for private mobile radio systems such as taxi camp companies and police departments.

**SMS:** Short Message Service
A service that is found in GSM and other cellular standards that short in length like a two paging signal.

**SS:** Spread Spectrum
A technique for spreading the spectrum of the information signal for the purpose of using Code Division Multiple Access, or for using spectrum bands on a secondary basis.

# T

**Tab:** Not an acronym
A term used to signify a wearable device the size of a credit card or smaller such as a smart badge.

**TACS:** Total Access Communications System
An analog cellular standard that is used in Europe and other parts of the world.

**TCP/IP:** Transmission Control Protocol/Internet Protocol
The network layer and transport layer protocol that has become a defacto standard throughout the world, particularly for the internet community.

**TDD:** Time Division Duplexing
A way of providing full duplex transmission by splitting the two directions of the transmission by time division.

**TDM:**  Time Division Multiplexing
A way of combining channels in the time domain.

**TDMA:**  Time Division Multiple Access
A way of access channels of the communications systems that relies on division of the available time.

**TX:**  Transmitter
A common shorthand for transmitter.

# U

**UPT:**  Universal Personal Telecommunications
A term used to signify future communications systems that will be person based, in particular they will involve each person having a personal telephone number such as we have in cellular systems.

**USDC:**  US Digital Cellular
Digital cellular standards in the US.

# V

**VAN:**  Value Added Network
A network providerUs network that leases the basic lines from a common carrier and then adds value to them and resells the result to end users.

# W

**WAN:**  Wide Area Network
A network that serves the wide area as opposed to a Local Area Network that serves a building or office campus.

**WARC:**  World Administrative Radio Conference.
A worldwide conference that meets to harmonize frequency allocations throughout the world. It does not have the power to allocate frequency spectrum. It makes suggestions to regulatory agencies throughout the world so that worldwide operation can be possible.

# *About the Author*

Dr. Dayem is Principal and Founder of Altamont Research, a market and technology analysis firm focusing on Wireless Networking in Cupertino, CA, USA. He is a pioneer in the field of Wireless Networking. He received degrees in physics and engineering from Cornell and Stanford. At Bell Labs he was instrumental in designing private network services. At Apple, he spearheaded the Wireless Networking effort.

Dr. Dayem has presented seminars and chaired sessions on Wireless Networking in the US, Europe, and Asia, most recently at NetWorld+Interop, Frost & Sullivan, Institute for International Research, Wireless Datacom, and Mobile Solutions. His consulting clients include computer manufacturers, chip manufacturers, Mobile Data companies, Wireless LAN companies, retail chains including Sears, and other end users such as Walt Disney. He is the author of two books: *Mobile Data and Wireless LANs,* and *PCS and Digital Cellular Technology,* published by Prentice Hall.

At Apple, Dr. Dayem was a key member of a team addressing the user needs, technology options, and the standards and regulatory issues leading to a Wireless Networking strategy for the company. He led the software development of local area network connectivity products for the Macintosh. He led the Campus Network Development Department in developing and implementing a voice and local area network for the Apple campus. The network serves as the foundation for critical applications such as electronic mail, directory, and growing multimedia applications.

At Northern Telecom, he was director of product marketing, Integrated Office Systems. He established a major accounts technical marketing program. His responsibilities included numerous discussions with customers as well as applications studies. The product line included network services, PBXs, packet switches, and transmission systems.

He worked ten years at Bell Telephone Labs, where he made key contributions in areas of private networks, microwave radio, and satellite communication. In particular, his contributions included: combined circuit and packet switching for multimedia applications, and equalization in the presence of deep fading, which was instrumental in tripling the capacity of microwave radio channels in the Bell System.

Dr. Dayem obtained a BS with distinction in Physics from Cornell University, an MS in Physics/EE from Stanford University, and a PhD in Physics/EE from the University of Pennsylvania. He also obtained an MBA as a member of the charter class of the San Jose State MBA program at Apple Computer. He is a member of Tau Beta Pi, and was president of Phi Sigma Kappa.

# *INDEX*